S0-AFS-374

W.W. Wilson Eng.r & Print.r Boston.

BOSTON,
DAYTON & WENTWORTH,
1854.

[Frontispiece to the original edition]

THE MODERN ARCHITECT

A CLASSIC VICTORIAN STYLEBOOK AND CARPENTER'S MANUAL

EDWARD SHAW

With a New Introduction by

EARLE G. SHETTLEWORTH, JR.
Director, Maine Historic Preservation Commission

DOVER PUBLICATIONS, INC.
NEW YORK

Copyright

Copyright © 1995 by Earle G. Shettleworth, Jr.
All rights reserved under Pan American and International Copyright Conventions.

Published in Canada by General Publishing Company, Ltd., 30 Lesmill Road, Don Mills, Toronto, Ontario.
Published in the United Kingdom by Constable and Company, Ltd., 3 The Lanchesters, 162–164 Fulham Palace Road, London W6 9ER.

Bibliographical Note

This Dover edition, first published in 1995, is an unabridged republication of the work originally published by Dayton and Wentworth, Boston, in 1854, under the title *The Modern Architect; or, Every Carpenter His Own Master.* A new introduction has been written specially for the Dover edition by Earle G. Shettleworth, Jr.

Library of Congress Cataloging-in-Publication Data

Shaw, Edward, b. 1784.
The modern architect : a classic Victorian stylebook and carpenter's manual / Edward Shaw.
p. cm.
Originally published: Boston : Dayton and Wentworth, 1854.
ISBN 0-486-28921-4 (pbk.)
1. Architecture, Victorian—United States—Handbooks, manuals, etc. I. Title.
NA710.5.V5S52 1996
720—dc20 95-47173
CIP

Manufactured in the United States of America
Dover Publications, Inc., 31 East 2nd Street, Mineola, N.Y. 11501

EDWARD SHAW, ARCHITECT AND AUTHOR

ASHER BENJAMIN, MINARD LAFEVER AND EDWARD SHAW rank as the three major authors of American builders' handbooks during the second quarter of the nineteenth century. While Benjamin and Lafever have been the objects of considerable study and their books have been reprinted in recent years, Shaw and his works have remained in obscurity. This may result in part from the conservative nature of the plates in his most popular volume, *Civil Architecture*, when contrasted with the more appealing decorative designs of his two contemporaries. Nonetheless, Shaw produced publications that went through multiple printings, demonstrating their widespread use during the formative years of the architectural profession in America.

Like Benjamin and Lafever, Edward Shaw began his career in modest circumstances as a rural carpenter. His parents, John and Molly Dustin Shaw, were married on October 29, 1783, and resided in North Hampton, New Hampshire. Edward, the first of their eight children, was born in North Hampton on August 2, 1784. In 1790 the family moved to Sanbornton, New Hampshire, where Edward spent the balance of his childhood and presumably began his apprenticeship as a carpenter, reaching his majority in 1805. Three years later he married Mary Abrams, and the couple settled in Chester (now Hill), New Hampshire. There Shaw pursued his trade as a builder until moving to Boston in about 1822.[1]

During his first years in Boston, Edward Shaw was listed as a housewright in the city directories. One of Boston's leading architects, Peter Banner, was the primary source of Shaw's architectural training. Architect Alexander Parris may also have provided Shaw with instruction. That they knew each other is confirmed by Shaw's having lived with Parris or rented his Poplar Street residence in the late 1820s.[2] This association coincides with Shaw's first directory entry as an architect in 1828, the title being attached to his name in the listings through 1855. Shaw himself traced his transition from tradesman to professional in the note appended to the Publishers' Preface to *The Modern Architect*:

> In answer to many inquiries respecting my practical knowledge as a Carpenter and Joiner, I would say, that I served in that capacity twenty years—fourteen of which, as a contractor and builder, drawing all of my own plans and designs for private and public dwellings costing from five hundred to forty thousand dollars each. Since which time I have spent fifteen years in the theoretical practice and science of Architectural Drawings and Plans, both ancient and modern.

While the time periods cited by Shaw do not reconcile precisely with actual records concerning him, his development from a carpenter and joiner to a contractor and builder who drew his own plans, and finally to a full-time designer, was a route traveled by most architects of his generation.

During his 27-year practice in Boston, Edward Shaw must have received many commissions. Yet, characteristic of the obscurity that has surrounded him, only nine projects have been identified. The first three are major design competitions for the Albany City Hall (1829), Philadelphia's Girard College (1832) and the Boston Custom House (1837). While Shaw failed to win any of them, his participation indicates a professional confidence to compete in the same arena with the foremost architectural talent of his day.

The Albany City Hall competition was announced through newspaper advertisements in June 1829. The design program called for a building "to consist of a high basement and two stories of proportionate height."[3] In order for a chance to win the $100 premium, architects were required to submit floor plans, elevations and at least one cross section. By July 27, 14 sets of drawings had been received by the building committee. Boston was represented by Edward Shaw, Isaiah Rogers, Peter Banner and John Kutts, while the New York entrants were Minard Lafever and the firm of Town & Davis. The committee awarded a joint commission to the local architect Philip Hooker for the building itself and to John Kutts for his cupola design. Although Kutts received half the premium, Hooker became responsible for overseeing the construction of Albany's marble Greek Revival City Hall between 1829 and 1832.

While Edward Shaw's Albany City Hall drawings have not survived, his seven plans for Girard College in Philadelphia and their accompanying description are part of the extensive documentation of the first competition for an American academic complex.[4] When merchant Stephen Girard died in 1831, he left much of his $7.5 million fortune to his adopted city to found a school for orphans. In his will, Girard gave explicit instructions that the institution be housed in a three-story main building to measure 110 by 160 feet with at least four adjacent support buildings. These structures were to be built in "the most durable materials, and in the most permanent manner, avoiding needless ornament, and attending chiefly to the strength, convenience, and neatness of the whole."[5]

On June 14, 1832, the Select and Common Councils of Philadelphia agreed to conduct a nationwide competition for the design of Girard College. Like their Albany counterparts, they solicited submissions through newspaper advertisements, offering cash premiums to the three winning entries. At least 21 architects from the northeastern United States responded, including John Haviland, William Strickland and Thomas U. Walter of Philadelphia; Town & Davis of New York; and Edward Shaw, Isaiah Rogers and John Kutts of Boston. Early in 1833 the drawings were shown in Independence Hall, and that February the winning entries were chosen, with Walter placing first, Strickland second and Rogers third. Walter's selection marked the beginning of a 15-year, $2 million project that would result in one of the nation's most ambitious examples of the Greek Revival.

Edward Shaw's failure to place in the Girard College competition may have been due in part to his paying "the strictest attention" to "the letter of the Will" in presenting a design characterized by its simplicity and restraint.[6] Shaw proposed a three-story granite classroom structure flanked at each corner by a four-story brick dormitory. The severe granite walls of the main building are relieved at the corners by monumental Ionic pilasters that support an entablature surmounted by a low parapet and decorative acroteria. In addition, recessed panels appear below the second- and third-story windows. Apparently concerned that this design would prove too austere, the architect provided an alternative scheme in which the corner pilasters are continued across each elevation, a treatment reminiscent of Charles Bulfinch's University Hall of 1813 at Harvard. Also New England in origin are Shaw's four adjacent brick dormitories, three reserved for student use and one for the faculty. These simple rectangular hipped-roof buildings are based directly on Federal-style dormitories at Harvard, Amherst, Bowdoin and other colleges in the region. The only difference is found in the larger scale of Shaw's proposed Girard College dormitories, which allowed for interior courtyards.

The competition for the U. S. Custom House in Boston held none of the constraints of Stephen Girard's will. The goal was to make an architectural statement befitting the commercial success of a great American port city. In 1835 Congress authorized the construction of a new Custom House on the Boston waterfront. To implement the project, the Secretary of the Treasury appointed a Board of Commissioners, which conducted a competition in 1837. Among those architects answering the board's call were Richard Upjohn, Ammi B. Young and Edward Shaw. Young was awarded the commission for a building that took a decade to complete and cost more than a million dollars.[7]

The Custom House designs submitted by Upjohn, Young and Shaw provide insights into the transitional nature of New England architectural design in the 1830s. Reflecting his English background, Upjohn's building is conservative in character. Classical corner pavilions enframing arcades and Ionic colonnades give a Regency, if not Georgian, appearance. In contrast, fresh from the success of his Vermont State House of 1833, Young boldly employed a simple cross plan with one long and one short axis. The building is faced with monumental Doric columns and is covered by a gabled roof with four pediments. At the intersection of the cross arms was a large rotunda, surmounted by a Roman saucer dome.

Shaw's design *(Figs. 1 & 2)* is similar in concept to Young's, but its exterior fenestration is much more refined in comparison. Where Young places sweeping entrance staircases, Shaw carefully delineates a series of small doorways and windows on the basement level. The attenuated Corinthian columns of Shaw's four large porticos recall the facade of Charles Bulfinch's Massachusetts State House of 1795. Only in the saucer dome and the grand rotunda beneath it does Shaw capture Young's sense of Greek Revival monumentality.[8]

The same year in which Edward Shaw competed for the Boston Custom House, he was employed by the Middlesex County Commissioners to design a House of Correction at Third and Spring Streets in East Cambridge. In 1813 Charles Bulfinch had designed a courthouse and a jail for the county. Erected between 1814 and 1816, Bulfinch's jail was a three-story, hipped-roof granite structure that measured 95 by 45 feet. By 1837 the building was overcrowded, and the county commissioners were faced with the choice of replacing it or constructing an addition. On April 7, 1837, Shaw presented the commissioners with a folio of 12 drawings for a new prison. Shaw's design called for a handsomely proportioned four-story granite building featuring a monitor roof. Each of the four floors contained a 24-unit cell block. The needs of both body and soul were provided for in a kitchen, a bathing room and a chapel.

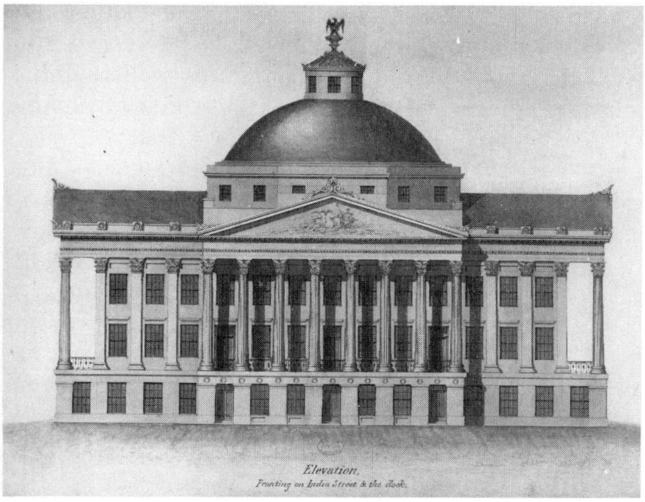

FIGURE 1. Edward Shaw's elevation drawing of his competition design for the U.S. Custom House in Boston, 1837. *(Courtesy of the Trustees of the Boston Public Library)*

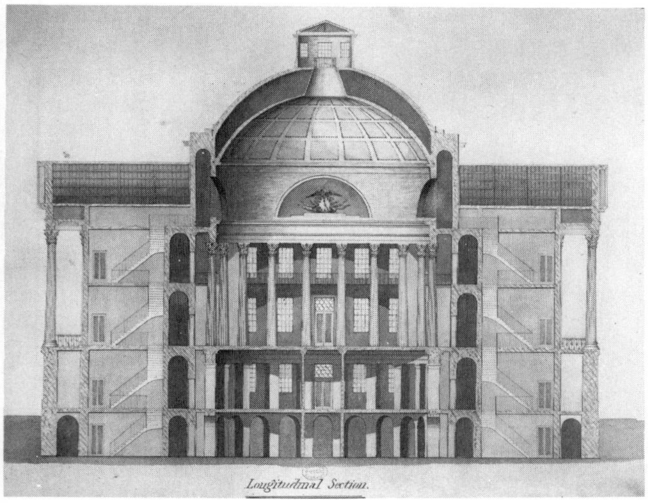

FIGURE 2. Edward Shaw's cross-section drawing of his competition design for the U. S. Custom House in Boston, 1837. *(Courtesy of the Trustees of the Boston Public Library)*

Edward Shaw's proposal was rejected as too costly, and on June 27, 1837, he offered a second set of nine drawings for a House of Correction to be added to the Bulfinch jail. Shaw recommended a building of essentially the same design as his April submission, but reduced in size from six bays to four and lacking the kitchen and chapel. The commissioners accepted Shaw's revised scheme, paying him $190 for his two sets of drawings and $12 for the two and a half days he spent on the building site laying out the foundation lines. Completed in 1839, the House of Correction survived the 1872 demolition of the Bulfinch jail and was incorporated into a new jail complex designed by Alexander R. Esty, which stood until 1965.[9]

Considering Boston's rapid growth as an urban center in the second quarter of the nineteenth century, residential design must have played an important part in Edward Shaw's architectural practice. Yet only three of his domestic commissions have been identified: town houses for George I. Galvin and A. W. Thaxter, Jr., and a country house for David Sears.

No longer standing, the two houses that Shaw designed in 1827 for lumber merchant George Galvin on Essex Street are known only through a ten-page building contract between the client and his carpenters, Edward Hatch and Abraham Green.[10] In this minutely detailed document, presumably written by the architect, the Galvin houses emerge as typical transitional Federal–Greek Revival brick row houses. Their narrow 24-foot-wide facades rose four stories with a dormered attic. Following traditional practice, the dining room and kitchen were located on the street level, the front and rear parlors on the second story, and the bedrooms on the remaining floors. The contract authorized Edward Shaw to examine the work at any time during the construction period of September 1827 through May 1828. This stipulation that Shaw provide supervision indicates that he had assumed the role of architect by 1827, a year before he is identified as such in the city directory.

The lack of a visual record of the Galvin houses is more than compensated by Edward Shaw's residence for Adam Wallace Thaxter, Jr., at 59 Mount Vernon Street *(Figs. 3 & 4)*. Long admired as the finest Greek Revival town house on prestigious Beacon Hill, Thaxter's home was designed by Shaw in 1836 and built the following year. The architect furnished his client with an elaborate folio of drawings that delineated elevations, floor plans, cross sections and framing as well as architectural and construction details. Accompanying this comprehensive set of plans were printed contracts for the masonry and carpentry work. On March 6, 1837, Thaxter executed the masonry agreement with Thomas Moulton for $9,770 and the carpentry contract with Luther Farwell, Jr., and Elisha Magoun, Jr., for $7,000. The house was to be completed by October 1, 1837.[11]

Edward Shaw's plans called for a Mount Vernon Street facade four bays in width with three principal stories, an attic story lighted by four dormers, and an octagonal cupola atop the roof. Constructed of brick with brownstone trim, this elegant exterior featured a bowed front at one side, a classical marble doorway with Ionic columns in antis, marble panels between the second and third story windows and Grecian cornice wreaths spaced between the third story windows and the dormers. Subsequently, a fourth story was added.

As early as 1905, *The Brickbuilder* magazine singled out the Thaxter entrance as an exceptional example of the Greek Revival, and Howard Major illustrated it in his pioneer study of Greek Revival architecture in 1926.[12] Behind that celebrated doorway lies an equally fine interior. Gracing the entrance hall is a grand circular staircase that extends to the upper floors. The curvature of the stair is echoed in the front and rear walls of the first-floor reception room, which displays elaborate Greek Revival door and window surrounds as well as Ionic pilasters. Here the traditional Boston town-house

FIGURE 3. Edward Shaw's elevation drawing for the Adam W. Thaxter, Jr., House, 59 Mount Vernon Street, Boston, 1836. *(Courtesy of Fogg Art Museum, Harvard University)*

FIGURE 4. Doorway of the Adam W. Thaxter, Jr., House, 59 Mount Vernon Street, Boston, 1837, as pictured in Plate 13 of *The Domestic Architecture of the Early American Republic* by Howard Major, 1926.

plan takes over, with the balance of the first floor devoted to the dining room and kitchen, the second reserved for parlors and the third and fourth containing bedrooms.

Edward Shaw's tour de force for Thaxter's Mount Vernon Street house must have attracted the attention of Boston society. In 1842 the city's wealthiest citizen, David Sears, turned to Shaw for the design of a country house in Brookline.[13] Sears had resided since 1819 on Beacon Street in an imposing granite residence designed for him by Alexander Parris. At the time he was building this house, Sears acquired 200 acres in nearby Brookline and spent the next half century gradually developing it from farmland into a garden suburb called Longwood. In 1840 one of Sears's sons wrote, "We went all over [Longwood] and examined different sites, which were delightful spots to build cottages upon."[14] By 1842 David Sears had decided to establish his own country house there and chose the newly popular Gothic Revival as the appropriate style for a rural residence. As Sears had given Bostonians a significant preview of the coming use of granite in his town house, once again he assumed a fashion-setting role in his choice of a romantic revival style for his country house.

While the construction of the Sears house may have begun in 1842, apparently most of the work was accomplished in 1843, according to a four-page account of construction costs.[15] The result was a picturesque two-story dwelling constructed of brick made to look like stone through the use of sanded paint and actual brownstone trim. Asymmetrical in both exterior appearance and interior plan, the house exhibited such decorative features as a pointed arched portico, hooded moldings over the windows and carved bargeboards on the eaves.

Edward Shaw was quick to publish his design of the Sears house by including two elevations and two floor plans in *Rural Architecture*, which appeared in 1843. His description of the plates omits any mention of architectural style, but stresses instead the modern conveniences: "cooking range in kitchen; bathing room, water-closet, &c., in the second story; and a Bryant and Herman's furnace set in the cellar; also a well and cistern."[16] Shaw cited the overall cost of Sears's country house at $8,000, but the four-page estimate made in June 1843 outlined a budget of more than $15,000. Did Sears dramatically scale back expenses or did the architect choose not to disclose the full extent of his client's expenditures?

David Sears's country house in Brookline was only one of several Gothic Revival designs to appear in Edward Shaw's *Rural Architecture*. Plate 51 pictures the facade elevations of two churches, figure one of which directly relates to the most distinctive building of Shaw's career, the Manchester, New Hampshire, City Hall of 1844–45 *(Fig. 5)*.

FIGURE 5. City Hall, Manchester, New Hampshire, built in 1844–45 from designs by Edward Shaw. *(Courtesy of Manchester Historic Association)*

In the decade following 1831, the Amoskeag Manufacturing Company established a series of mills on the Merrimack River, resulting in the removal of Manchester's local government to the new industrial center along the river. In 1841 the community built a brick Greek Revival town hall at Market and Elm Streets, which was destroyed by fire in 1844. A town meeting held on August 30, 1844, resulted in a vote to build a new hall on the site of the previous one. The task was assigned to a building committee to work in conjunction with the selectmen. A call for plans and specifications produced several proposals, of which Edward Shaw's Gothic Revival scheme was selected for "the beauty of its architecture, convenience of the plan, and durability of the structure."[17] The architect was paid $75 for his drawings and contracted to provide $1,427 worth of supervision. Construction began in the fall of 1844 and was completed in October 1845 at a cost of $35,000.[18]

A complex blend of architectural influences came together in Edward Shaw's Manchester City Hall. Following the New England market-house tradition, Shaw's building provided for five stores on the ground floor with a public assembly hall and municipal offices above. To dramatize the City Hall's Gothic style, Shaw arranged its secular functions within the exterior form of a religious structure complete with a central tower and belfry similar to figure one of Plate 51 in his book *Rural Architecture*. How understandable that the local historian Charles E. Potter commented in 1856, "It is a very peculiar style of architecture, nothing of the classical or pure about it, but still a fine looking structure."[19] Potter went on to disclose a major modification of Shaw's intentions for the hall:

> The design of the architect was that the building should have been entirely of stone, the columns hammered and the wall of ashlar work; but the committee deviated from his plan, and the building is of stone and brick, the columns and caps being of hammered stone, while the walls are of brick, painted and sanded to imitate stone. The building is one hundred feet in length by sixty feet in width . . .[20]

Despite this alteration in materials, no expense was spared in carrying out Shaw's extraordinary range of Gothic Revival features, including a two-story pointed-arch window over the Market Street entrance, a series of five two-story Gothic window bays on the Elm Street elevation, a crenelated tower balustrade and an octagonal belfry capped by a pinnacle at each corner. In describing the Manchester City Hall in *Mill and Mansion*, John Coolidge wrote admiringly:

> The whole is spiced with delightful Gothic detail, octagonal buttresses, bands of quatrefoils, battlements, tracery, all those favorite forms culled from Pugin's *Specimens*. But while their application is anything but Gothic, it is nowise haphazard but is carefully considered and effectively executed. One realizes that for years American architects had been starved of variety in detail, and that it was this which the Gothic revival provided them. But here, as in the best early romantic buildings, the new discovery does not run away with the designer. At bottom there remains a splendid sense of proportions and of the relationship of masses, while the detail merely gives a needed touch of fantasy to the severe regularity of the scheme.[21]

During the construction of Manchester City Hall, Edward Shaw entered the 1845 competition for the Boston Athenaeum. This distinguished cultural institution sought plans for a building that required two principal facades, one on Tremont Street and the other facing Court Square. In order to address this site requirement and a grade change, Shaw submitted a proposal for two freestanding but connected rectangular structures, each with a front elevation based directly upon the Elm Street facade of the Manchester City Hall. The only significant variation was the substitution of a pair of Gothic roof pavilions for the tower and belfry. Shaw's Athenaeum drawings call for the granite-wall construction that he had been forced to abandon in Manchester.

Edward Shaw and other entrants lost the Athenaeum competition to their fellow local architect George M. Dexter in June 1845. Within the next year the trustees decided upon the present Beacon Street location and held a second competition, which resulted in the selection of the Renaissance Revival design of Edward C. Cabot.[22]

Intriguing as his building projects may be, Edward Shaw's reputation rests more on his contributions to the architectural literature of his time. Of the titles which he produced, the most popular was *Civil Architecture*, a Greek Revival treatise that first appeared in Boston in 1830. While the books of Minard Lafever and Asher Benjamin went out of print before the Civil War, an eleventh edition of *Civil Architecture* was released in 1870, and was reprinted as late as 1900. Talbot Hamlin ascribed the book's durability to its being "more of a complete builder's and architect's handbook than are the Benjamin items; it has fewer designs and details, though more material on geometry, mensuration, and construction."[23]

Shaw aimed *Civil Architecture* at two groups: the local builder and the architectural student. In his "Advertisement to the First Edition," Shaw stated that his purpose was:

> principally to assist the practical mechanic as well as the student. . . . pains have been taken to lay down the fundamental principles of architecture in a clear, distinct and intelligible manner, and to apply the whole to practice by plain and obvious examples and illustrations. I have endeavored to arrange the contents so as to be useful to the students as well as to all classes of operative builders.

At the time Shaw wrote *Civil Architecture*, there were at least five architectural schools in Boston conducted by architects such as Solomon Willard and John Kutts. That *Civil Architecture* was used in this context is affirmed by the copy owned by the Kittery, Maine, builder Charles G. Bellamy, which bears the inscription, "Bought at Boston, Mass., in October, 1834. Price $7.50. While he was a student with Professor John Kurtz (Kutts) the celebrated Architect and a Dane . . ."[24]

Civil Architecture provided architect and builder alike with a comprehensive compendium of text and plates derived from the Roman Vitruvius and the more recent English authorities, Stuart, Chambers and Nicholson, all tempered by Shaw's own practical New England perspective. Following a 26-page introductory essay, Shaw presented sections covering geometry, drawing, the orders, moldings, woodwork, stairs, carpentry, building, bridge construction, architectural terms and rules of work. In contrast to Benjamin and Lafever, Shaw included only a few of his own designs for mantels and doors, preferring to devote most of his plates to an explanation of technical matters and the orders. Those decorative features which Shaw did choose to illustrate are generally more restrained in their Greek Revival detailing than those of his contemporary authors.

Edward Shaw produced an updated sixth edition of *Civil Architecture* in 1852 with the help of two young Boston architects, Thomas W. Silloway and George M. Harding, who were in partnership from 1850 to 1852.[25] In a prefatory note, Shaw explained the changes made to the fifth edition:

> I have been induced by the advice of my friends to secure the valuable services of Messrs. Silloway and Harding, architects of Boston, gentlemen well versed in the science they profess, to assist in revising the fifth edition, and prepare additional drawings for a sixth, which has resulted in the exclusion of several old plates, and the substitution of twenty new ones of a character in keeping with the improvements of the day, and of great practical use to the carpenter and builder, among which are four plates of Gothic details selected from Pugin, one of the best English authors on the subject.

While much of Shaw's Greek Revival handbook remained intact in this revision, Silloway and Harding's additions of Gothic Revival and Italianate plates are a clear statement by the authors of the growing importance of the romantic revival styles. Gothic is addressed in a six-page essay accompanied by the four Pugin plates. The Italianate is illustrated in eight plates of original designs by Silloway and Harding, six for architectural features such as doors and windows and the other two showing actual buildings, the A. C. Mayhew House and the Pearl Street Universalist Church, both located in Milford, Massachusetts.

Edward Shaw's sixth edition of *Civil Architecture* gave the volume a renewed value that carried it beyond its author's lifetime to the beginning of a new century. By 1856 the book was in its tenth edition. The Philadelphia technical publisher Henry Carey Baird issued an eleventh edition in 1870, which was reprinted in 1876, 1887 and 1900.[26]

Edward Shaw's second book, *Operative Masonry* (1832), responded to the increasing demand for brick and stone construction in Boston and other urban centers by providing both builders and clients with practical guidance on the subject. Considered the first comprehensive American treatment of masonry construction, this volume is a fund of period technical information. However, because of its narrower focus, the book never equaled the popularity of *Civil Architecture*. An expanded version did appear in 1846 under the title of *Practical Masonry*. Included in this edition is an important discussion of the emerging technologies of central heating and cooking ranges, illustrated with ten plates.

Having dispensed a wealth of practical knowledge in *Civil Architecture* and *Operative Masonry*, Edward Shaw felt free in his third book, *Rural Architecture*, "to lay before the reader, and especially the practical architect, a variety of plans, elevations, &c., of edifices, principally dwelling houses, and places of public worship . . ." Published in 1843, *Rural Architecture* (of which *The Modern Architect* is an expansion) is divided into three parts: a history of architecture; a discussion of the Egyptian, Classical and Gothic styles; and plates of Doric, Ionic, Corinthian and Gothic houses as well as Gothic churches.

After describing the principal architectural styles, Shaw ended the second section of his book with an insightful four-page essay entitled "Architecture of America." Writing from a New England perspective, he noted that the country lacked the monuments of Europe because the Puritan settlers had consciously repudiated the architecture of the Old World. Their philosophy had given birth to a spirit of enterprise that transformed dense forests into new cities of "shingle palaces, erected to endure but for a generation."[27] This spirit had brought America to a locomotive age of railways and canals that had produced "a transient people, flitting from place to place; and each builds a hut for *himself*, not for his successors."[28]

While Shaw despaired that "the architecture of our country is at present . . . undefined," he was encouraged by the improvements he had witnessed in his own lifetime, particularly in the area of public buildings.[29] Speaking from personal observation, he praised the Capitol in Washington; the United States Bank, the Exchange, the Mint and Girard College in Philadelphia; and the Custom House and the New York University in New York. Of Boston he commented, "we have many beautiful buildings, but few of pure architecture."[30] Local examples of the Greek Revival which he admired included the Quincy Market, St. Paul's Church, the Tremont Theatre and the Merchants' Exchange. Apparently not one to bear a grudge at losing a competition, he headed this list with Ammi B. Young's Custom House. As for Gothic Revival, Shaw singled out Charles Bulfinch's Federal Street Church of 1809, an early example of the style from which he derived the belfry and spire of the church in Plate 51 of *Rural Architecture*.

Characterizing American domestic architecture as "yet in its infancy," Edward Shaw stated that the main purpose of his book was to establish "a pure and correct taste" in this branch of design.[31] In asserting this need, he described the ideal home in prophetically modern rationalist terms:

> We would only suggest that in constructing a dwelling-house, the convenience and comfort of the interior should ever receive more attention than the exterior elegance and symmetry; and that the beauty of a private house consists not so much in the nearness of its resemblance to a Grecian temple, a Chinese pagoda, or a Gothic church, as in its fitness for the purpose for which it is designed. It is neces-

sary, above all things, to remember that houses are made to live in, and the convenience of their inmates is the first thing to be considered; after that, ornament may be added.[32]

Part Three of *Rural Architecture* was devoted primarily to house designs which Shaw labeled as Doric, Ionic, Corinthian and Gothic. These designs are presented in both elevation and perspective in conjunction with floor plans, reflecting the influence of the new trend of pattern books such as Andrew Jackson Downing's *Cottage Residences* of 1842. However, Shaw's perspectives are precise line drawings, in contrast to Downing's illustrations, which are more painterly in their manner.

Shaw's Grecian houses represent a broad range of options, which include traditional New England capes and two-and-a-half-story dwellings as well as the more recent gable end and amphiprostyle examples introduced in the Greek Revival. All four of these forms were in wide use in New England during the decade before *Rural Architecture* was published, and Shaw's inclusion of them is an affirmation of current popular taste.

However, Shaw also challenged his audience of architects, builders and clients with newer concepts of double houses, villas and cottages. Plate 30, which depicts freestanding Ionic and Gothic double houses, was copied from the English architect S. H. Brooks's *Designs for Cottage and Villa Architecture* (1839). Plates 25 through 28 represent two designs for Ionic houses which derive their inspiration from English Regency villas. Finally, there are Plates 47 and 48, which reproduce Shaw's drawings for David Sears's Gothic cottage in Brookline.

While the Sears House is the only building in *Rural Architecture* which Edward Shaw identified as having been constructed, the influence of the book's designs was widespread. Benjamin S. Deane, the leading architect of Bangor, Maine, based his George Stetson House of 1847–48 on the two-story Ionic residence shown in Plates 23 and 24 *(Fig. 6)*. These plates were also used by the unknown designer of the Snow House in Rockland, Maine.[33] In Orford, New Hampshire, the local architect Moses Gerrish Wood planned the Congregational Church, line for line, from Plate 51. Designed in 1851, this handsome frame Gothic Revival Church was constructed in 1854.[34]

New England architects and builders of the 1840s and 50s readily accepted architecture according to Shaw because of its comfortable balance between traditional forms and new ideas, all of which were grounded in sound building principles. Observing that *Rural Architecture*'s plates "are thoroughly in the Boston tradition," Talbot Hamlin remarked, "Shaw's Greek Revival design has the same forthright heaviness as Benjamin's, and something of the same robust beauty."[35] Both in style and material, these qualities reflect an architecture in which local builders strove to express historical masonry in wood.

For all its popularity, *Rural Architecture* had its critics as well, indicative of the rapidly changing professional scene of mid-nineteenth-century American architecture. From the new generation of young men trained as architects instead of rising from the ranks of carpenters came Arthur Gilman of Boston. At the age of 23, Gilman wrote what was ostensibly a book review of *Rural Architecture* for the April 1844 issue of the *North American Review*. In reality, Gilman's review was a sweeping essay on the direction of architecture in the United States. In the course of this discussion, Shaw and his generation were branded as "those old fashioned five-order men, who have grown antic in the decline of their favorite system, and have endeavored, by a vigorous push, to accommodate themselves to the surprising achievements of their later and more successful rivals."[36]

Undaunted by such criticism, Edward Shaw continued with his architectural practice as well as with his mission to instruct his fellow architects and builders. At the age of 70, he produced his final book, *The Modern Archictect*, which was published in 1854 and reprinted in 1855, 1856 and 1859. This popular volume was an expansion of *Rural Architecture*. To the text and plates of his earlier publication, he added designs for a Gothic church, a system of stair-building, Italianate stores, an oriel window and an Italian villa. Ever balancing established building practices with new technology, Shaw illustrated two stores, one with a traditional masonry facade and the other of modern cast-iron construction.

FIGURE 6. George Stetson House, Bangor, Maine, 1847–48. Bangor architect Benjamin S. Deane based his design of the Stetson House on Plates 23 and 24 of Edward Shaw's *Rural Architecture*, 1843. *(Courtesy of Bangor Assessor's Office)*

In addition to the store designs, the Italianate style is represented by Plate 63 of an oriel window and Plate 64 of a villa. These plates are similar to the Silloway and Harding designs found in Plates 69 and 96 of the sixth edition of *Civil Architecture* (1852). In both cases, the window and the villa provide a means for Shaw to address the new Italianate style.

In books written over a quarter of a century, Edward Shaw repeatedly stressed the value of architectural instruction. His earnest belief in self-improvement through self-education is expressed in the subtitle of his last work, *The Modern Architect; Or, Every Carpenter His Own Master*. This theme is repeated in the Publishers' Preface, which states that the book is intended "to arrest the attention of every Mechanic deserving the name of Carpenter, and who may have a desire to become his own master."[37]

The vision of this ladder to success is embodied in the engraved frontispiece, which depicts a stylishly dressed architect supervising a carpentry crew on the building site of an Italianate house. This scene ranks as one of the memorable graphic images in nineteenth-century American architecture. As described by James F. O'Gorman in *On The Boards*, "the modern architect in top hat and frock coat, with ruler and compass in hand, is distinguished from the bareheaded, shirtsleeved workers. While they work or watch, he sits at a makeshift desk, directing building operations by interpreting his graphic directions."[38]

Having produced *The Modern Architect* in 1854, Edward Shaw must have felt that his long career was complete. The following year he retired to Chester, New Hampshire. When he died there in April 1859, at the age of 75, the *Boston Transcript* referred to him as "formerly of Boston."[39] Appropriately, this brief death notice identified him as "the author of Shaw's Architecture." As in 1859, Edward Shaw is now remembered not so much for any particular building as for his contributions to an emerging body of American architectural publications and their effect upon the New England landscape.

EARLE G. SHETTLEWORTH, JR.

Augusta, Maine
August 1995

NOTES

1. Rev. M. T. Runnels, *History of Sanbornton, New Hampshire, Genealogies*, volume II, Boston 1881, p. 699; Harriet F. Farwell, *Shaw Records, A Memorial of Roger Shaw*, Bethel, Maine, 1904, pp. 56–57.
2. Thomas W. Silloway, "The Park Street Steeple," *Boston Transcript*, January 5, 1903. Silloway states that "Mr. Shaw was a pupil of Mr. Banner, and later on took up Mr. Banner's practice." Denys Peter Myers brought this article to the author's attention. Edward F. Zimmer, "The Architectural Career of Alexander Parris," volume I, Boston University Doctoral Dissertation, 1984, p. 258.
3. Edward W. Root, *Philip Hooker*, New York, 1929, p. 178; Mary R. Tomlan, *A Neat Plain Modern Style: Philip Hooker and His Contemporaries, 1796–1836*, Amherst, Massachusetts, 1993, pp. 262–279.
4. Agnes Addison Gilchrist, "Girard College: An Example of the Layman's Influence on Architecture," *Journal of the Society of Architectural Historians*, XVI, 2, pp. 22–27; John B. Cutler, "Girard College Architectural Competition, 1832–1848," Yale University Doctoral Dissertation, 1969, pp. 56–60; Bruce Laverty, *Girard College Architectural Collections*, Philadelphia, 1994. The author wishes to thank Stephen Jerome for bringing the Gilchrist article to his attention and Bruce Laverty of the Athenaeum of Philadelphia and Phyllis Abrams of Girard College for access to Shaw's competition drawings in the college collection.
5. Henry W. Arey, *The Girard College and Its Founder*, Philadelphia, 1852, p. 67.
6. Edward Shaw, cover sheet to "Plan and Specification of a College to be built in conformity with the Will of the late Stephen Girard of Philadelphia," Girard College Collection, Philadelphia.
7. Margaret Supplee Smith, "The Custom House Controversy," *Nineteenth Century*, Summer 1977, pp. 99–105.
8. Edward Shaw, "Proposed Plan of a Custom House in

Boston . . . December 30, 1837," portfolio of eight drawings with written description, Rare Book Room, Boston Public Library.

9. Edward Shaw, "Plan of a House of Correction for the County of Middlesex, Massachusetts . . . April 7, 1837," portfolio of 12 drawings with written description, Middlesex County Courthouse, Cambridge; Edward Shaw, "Plan of a House of Correction for the County of Middlesex, Massachusetts . . . June 27, 1837," portfolio of nine drawings with written description, Middlesex County Courthouse, Cambridge; County Commissioners Records, Middlesex County Courthouse, Cambridge; Susan E. Maycock, *East Cambridge*, Cambridge, 1988, pp. 143–144. Susan Maycock brought the original documents relating to the House of Correction to the author's attention.
10. Building contract between Hatch & Green and George Galvin, September 21, 1827, Suffolk County Registry of Deeds, Boston, Book 322, pp. 121–125. Stephen Jerome brought this contract to the author's attention.
11. Edward Shaw, "Plan of a Dwelling House for A. W. Thaxter, Jr., Boston, 1836," portfolio of drawings with printed contracts and specifications, Fine Arts Library, Fogg Art Museum, Harvard University, Cambridge; Building contract between Thomas Moulton and A. W. Thaxter, Jr., March 6, 1837, Suffolk County Registry of Deeds, Boston, Book 417, p. 95.
12. *The Brickbuilder*, February, 1905; Howard Major, *The Domestic Architecture of the Early American Republic, The Greek Revival*, Philadelphia, 1926, Plate 13.
13. Edward Shaw, *Rural Architecture*, Boston, 1843, Plates 47, 48, pp. 92–93.
14. Manuscript journal beginning September 14, 1839, Sears Papers, Massachusetts Historical Society, Boston.
15. "Estimate for House agreeably to Plans; the exterior to be of Brick and Freestone, Boston, June, 1843," four-page manuscript account, Sears Papers, Massachusetts Historical Society, Boston.
16. Shaw, *Rural Architecture*, p. 92
17. S. D. Bell, "A History of Manchester from Its Earliest Settlement to the Present Time," *Manchester American*, July 11, 1845.
18. *Reports of the Selectmen . . . of the Town of Manchester for the Year 1844–45*, Manchester, 1845, p. 18; *Reports of the Selectmen . . . of the Town of Manchester for the Year 1845–46*, Manchester, 1846, pp. 10–12.
19. Charles E. Potter, *The History of Manchester*, Manchester, 1856, p. 617.
20. Ibid.
21. John Coolidge, *Mill and Mansion*, New York, 1942, p. 97.
22. Josiah Quincy, *The History of the Boston Athenaeum*, Cambridge, 1851, pp. 162–165; Margaret S. Smith, "The Italianate Style in Mid-19th-Century Boston," *Journal of the Society of Architectural Historians*, December 1975, pp. 312–313; *Change and Continuity, A Pictorial History of the Boston Athenaeum*, Boston, 1976. The Athenaeum's collection of 1845 competition drawings includes one elevation and three floor plans that can be attributed to Edward Shaw on the basis of the design's close similarity to the Elm Street facade of the Manchester City Hall.
23. Talbot Hamlin, *Greek Revival in America*, New York, 1944, p. 164.
24. Edward Shaw, *Civil Architecture*, Boston, 1832. Inscribed copy in the author's collection.
25. A native of Newburyport, Massachusetts, Thomas W. Silloway (1828–1910) was a prolific Boston church architect and an ordained Universalist minister. Silloway authored eight books in addition to serving as co-editor of the sixth edition of *Civil Architecture*. Born in Chatham, Massachusetts, George M. Harding (1827–1910) practiced architecture in Boston, Manchester and Concord, New Hampshire, and Portland, Maine, before permanently settling in the Boston area in 1873. Harding designed a wide range of domestic, religious, public and commercial buildings in New England, employing the Victorian architectural styles of his day in a highly decorative manner.
26. Henry-Russell Hitchcock, *American Architectural Books*, Minneapolis, 1962, pp. 94–95. The post-1876 editions of *Civil Architecture* were located in an OCLC search instituted by James Miller II, who shared his findings with the author.
27. Edward Shaw, *Rural Architecture*, p. 61.
28. Ibid., p. 61.
29. Ibid., p. 59.
30. Ibid., p. 62.
31. Ibid., p. 63.
32. Ibid., p. 63.
33. Deborah Thompson, *Bangor, Maine 1769–1914, An Architectural History*, Orono, 1988, pp. 88–95; Denys Peter Myers, *Maine Catalogue HABS*, Augusta, 1974, p. 223.
34. Alice Doan Hodgson, "Orford, New Hampshire," *Antiques*, October, 1977, pp. 724–725; Bryant F. Tolles, Jr., *New Hampshire Architecture*, Hanover, New Hampshire, 1979, pp. 298–299. The author wishes to thank Christopher Wigren for bringing the Congregational Church of Orford to his attention.
35. Hamlin, *op. cit.*, p. 165.
36. Arthur Gilman, "Architecture in the United States," *North American Review*, April 1844, p. 476.
37. Edward Shaw, *The Modern Architect*, Boston, 1854, Publisher's Preface.
38. James F. O'Gorman, *On The Boards*, Philadelphia, 1989, p. 3.
39. *Boston Transcript*, April 20, 1859. Stephen Jerome brought this death notice to the author's attention. Shaw's death was also noted in the *Boston Post*, April 21, 1859 and the *Manchester* [New Hampshire] *Daily Mirror*, April 25, 1859.

NOTE. In answer to many inquiries respecting my practical knowledge as a Carpenter and Joiner, I would say, that I served in that capacity twenty years,—fourteen of which, as a contractor and builder, drawing all of my own plans and designs for private and public dwellings costing from five hundred to forty thousand dollars each. Since which time I have spent fifteen years in the theoretical practice and science of Architectural Drawings and Plans, both ancient and modern.

EDWARD SHAW, ARCHITECT.

Boston, May 15, 1854.

THE PUBLISHERS' PREFACE

TO THE

MODERN ARCHITECT.

In presenting this work of Modern Architecture to the American public, the publishers aim exclusively to arrest the attention of every Mechanic deserving the name of Carpenter, and who may have a desire to become his own master. No labor, pains or expense, have been spared in the preparation of this treatise, to have the work fully adapted to meet the wants of those who wish to become acquainted with the science. To such we can say, in the opinion of good judges, the present work has not been excelled for minuteness of detail, and practical application to the wants of the practical man.

We address ourselves and our work to the consideration of the Mechanic, the Master, and the Architect, as all have felt the need of a thorough knowledge of the rules and principles of the art. We have, therefore, introduced the Ancient and Modern foundation principles and systems of the Egyptian, Grecian, Corinthian, Doric, Ionic and Gothic modes of building — showing the different plans, elevations, decorations, specifications, estimates, framing, &c.

We conclude with the observation, that a pure Architectural taste is a great gift, or attainment, for any man to be possessed of; and, if this science were more generally studied throughout the United States, we should be exempt from those architectural abortions which now so often disgrace our cities and villages.

Boston, 1854.

CONTENTS.

PART I.

HISTORY AND PROGRESS OF ARCHITECTURE.

PART II.

THE CHARACTERISTICS OF THE DIFFERENT STYLES OF ARCHITECTURE.

PART III.

THE ARRANGEMENT AND CONSTRUCTION OF DWELLING-HOUSES, AND OF BUILDINGS IN GENERAL.

MODERN ARCHITECT.

PART I.

HISTORY AND PROGRESS OF ARCHITECTURE.

AT a very early period, as might be expected, architecture had made some progress; for we are informed by Holy Writ that Cain "builded a *city*, and called the name of the city after the name of his son, Enoch." * But we are wholly in the dark as to the perfection to which it had attained when that awful visitation of the Almighty, the universal deluge, obliterated almost every mark of previous habitation. The next mention of it is in the account of the building of the tower of Babel, which was stopped by the confusion of tongues. This was soon surrounded by other buildings, and walls of great magnitude; and here, therefore, may we date the origin of postdiluvian architecture. Whatever celebrity, however, the wonders of Babylon attained, among the ancients, no remains of them have come down to us; and it is the massive edifices of Egypt, built, apparently, rather for eternity than time, which now excite our admiration as the most ancient as well as stupendous structures existing upon earth. We must not, while under this epoch, omit to notice the remains, and, alas! the only remains, of Indian and Mexican greatness. But for the splendid ruins of Delhi and Agra, and that most singular specimen in the island of

* Genesis 4 : 17.

Elephanta, we should scarcely have known of the existence of civilization among the ancient Hindoos; and the aborigines of Mexico were regarded as little better than savages, before the late discoveries of Mr. Bullock. The dates of these buildings are wholly unknown; but, from the general similarity they bear to those of Egypt, it is supposed they are of equal antiquity. It may not be improper here to observe that the latter country is commonly considered to have been peopled by a colony from India. About the same general date may also be assigned to the architecture of the Hebrews, or, as more properly characterized, the Phœnician style, the greatest monument of which was the far-famed temple of Solomon. The description of this, in the sacred text, will be found, on an accurate consideration, to bear great resemblance to that of many of the Egyptian temples. From the Egyptians the art, such as it was, was learned by the Greeks; but under the protection of that extraordinary people it reached a perfection unheard of before, and, in its peculiar style, unequalled since. The earliest edifices of Greece, however, were by no means remarkable for beauty; the temples, in the time of Homer, being little better than rude huts, sheltered, if sheltered at all, by branches of laurel and other trees. On the decline of Greece, and its conquest by the Romans, the art appears to have been transferred to the conquerors; but among that hardy and warlike race it made little progress before the age of Augustus. Under the protection of that munificent monarch, it rapidly attained to almost as great perfection as in the favored country of the arts; and the "Eternal City" owes much of its present estimation to the noble structures erected by him and his successors. With Rome, however, the art decayed, and was overwhelmed in the general confusion and oblivion of learning, art, and science.

The attention of the Saxons in Europe, probably about the eighth century, was excited by the remains of edifices raised by the Romans during their residence in England. These, in their newly-erected churches, they aspired to imitate; but their workmen, ignorant of the principles which guided the architects of those splendid ruins, produced only the general outlines of their patterns; and those clumsy forms continued to be practised, with little alteration, till the end of the twelfth century. But now, as the tumult excited by the invasion subsided, and the genius of the nation improved, a taste for the fine arts began to show itself, and architecture assumed a different and novel aspect. Instead of tamely treading in the steps of their predecessors, the architects of those times devised a style as scientific as it was grand, and as beautiful as new.

But we must not, while eulogizing those who have adorned their own country with such admirable structures, forget the merits of their contemporaries on the continent. Of these, it seems to be generally acknowledged that the French preceded them in point of time, and the Germans excelled in the size of their edifices; yet no one, on comparing, with an impartial eye, the several buildings, will hesitate to allow that, in purity of style, variety of design, and delicacy of execution, the English cathedral and other churches are not surpassed by those of any nation in Europe; and it is a remarkable fact that English architects and workmen were employed in many of the finest works on the continent.

We must now turn our attention to Italy. It is worthy of notice that the Gothic style never came to so great perfection in this country as in the neighboring nations. Perhaps this was owing to the number of Roman buildings remaining amongst them, and the liberal use they made of their fragments, which is shown even in the finest specimen they possess. The Milan cathedral is probably the purest Gothic building in all Italy. But this is not built of fragments of ancient Roman buildings. It was built chiefly by Bonaparte, or under his auspices, and is of white marble. It is not, therefore, surprising that the Italians should be the first to reject the style altogether. Indeed, there were instances, in the darkest times, of recurrence to the purest models of antiquity,* but these met not the public taste, and were born only to die. "It

* It should be remembered that we here speak of Italian Gothic.

is not," observes Mr. Bromley, "the casual and solitary effort of individuals in a dark age, which can be considered as renovating the decayed principles of pure science. Some minds are naturally stronger and more intent on improvement than others; and where such happen, in some degree, to break through the general obscurity, they only show that the genuine light of refinement is not quite extinct, though the age will be little or nothing the better for those faint glimpses which become the portion of one or two, and are neither attained nor sought by others."

To return to our subject. The Church of the Apostles, at Florence, which was built by Charlemagne in A. D. 805, appears to have been the first effort to revive the forgotten architecture of ancient times, and possessed so much merit that Bruneleschi, six hundred years afterwards, disdained not to accept it as a lesson in one of his own edifices. Two hundred years passed away, and the Church of St. Miniate, in the same illustrious city, momentarily recalled from its apparent oblivion this elegant style. The same period again elapsed, and the genius of Cimabue arose to dispel the mists which had so long enveloped the arts of his country. His attention, though principally devoted to painting, was, like that of most of the great artists of his time, occasionally turned to the sister arts; and it was partly by his instructions that Arnolphi di Lapo became the wonder of the age. The father of this eminent architect, James, was a German by birth, but resided at Florence, where he built the convent of St. Francis, and received the surname of Lapo, from the citizens, for his skill in architecture. The son, Arnolpho, built the cathedral of St. Maria del Fiore, the largest church in Christendom, next to St. Peter's. Although this was principally in the Tedeschi style (the appellation given by the Italians to the debased Gothic of their country), yet so uncommon was the skill displayed in its erection, that, the dome being left unfinished by the death of the architect, a century and a half elapsed before another could be found to raise it. This was Bruneleschi, who died in the year 1444, and may be considered as the reviver of the classical architecture. His principal work was the Palazzo Pitti, in his native city.

It might have been expected that Rome, which possessed so many fine specimens, would have been the first to show to the world her sense of their value by encouraging the imitation of them ; but it was not till the middle of the fifteenth century that Pope Nicholas V. manifested the first symptoms of reviving taste, by the encouragement of Leone Baptista Alberti (the earliest modern writer on architecture), and Bernardo Rossilini. These, however, were principally employed in repairs, and the erection of fountains ; and to Bramante must we concede the honor of being the first who materially adorned this city by his designs. With the *then pope*, the memorable Julius II., he was much in favor, and it is supposed that it is in a considerable degree owing to this architect that that munificent pontiff formed the resolution of rebuilding the cathedral of St. Peter, in a style suited to the importance and magnificence of the see. In the lifetime of Bramante, however, little was done of this stupendous work ; for such was the conception of the architect's colossal imagination, that, although in its present state its section is about double that of St. Paul's, at London, it was reduced by his successor, Balthazar Peruzzi, and more considerably by the next who took it in hand, Antonio de San Gallo. These architects, however, while they exerted their talents on paper, proceeded little with the work; and it was left for the sublime genius of Michael Angelo permanently to fix the design of this master-piece of art, and prince of Christian churches. The edifice, as we now see it, is principally his, except the front, which is considered inferior to the other parts. This work completed, the example thus set by its principal cities was quickly followed in all parts of Italy, which thus gave employment to the talents of Pirro Sigorio, Vignola, Domenico, Fontana, Michael San Michael, Falconetti, Serlio, Barbaro, Scamozzi, and Palladio.

The pure taste which characterized most of these architects, however, was not of long duration. The celebrated artist, Bernini, was one of the first who violated their precepts. He was educated at Rome as an architect and sculptor, and it is related of him, that, returning to his native city late in life, with a fortune, the product of his talents, he was much struck with some of his early works, of the school of Michael Angelo and Palladio. He could not but contrast their elegance with the affected graces of the style he had given into; "but," exclaimed he, "had I continued in this manner, I should not have been what I am now." Contemporary with Bernini was Borromini, who was yet more depraved, and was so jealous of the former's fame that he stabbed himself. After these, Italy cannot boast of any great architects.

We must now return to England, as more interesting in its inhabitants, and, indeed, of more importance in our history, than France, or the other nations of Europe.

From the time of Edward III., there was a visible decline in the style of English architecture, which lost itself in a profusion of ornaments; more attention being paid to the details than to the general form of the buildings.

By the time of Henry VIII., this increased to a great extent, and the chapel erected by his father at Westminster was one of the last buildings which showed any taste in the style. This depraved manner naturally excited disgust in the minds of those persons who had seen the purer style then prevailing in Italy, which, as might be expected, they endeavored to introduce. The nation, however, had been too long accustomed to the Gothic readily to surrender it, and during the reigns of Elizabeth and James the mixture of, or compromise between, these styles, produced a most barbarous result. But this could not last long; the prejudices of the people, in the course of time, gave way, and Italian architecture, in all its purity, was first executed in this country by Inigo Jones. This father of modern English architecture was born about 1572, and died in 1652. At the expense either of the Earl of Pembroke, or the Earl of Arundel, he travelled into Italy, and from the sight of the elegant buildings in that country, both of ancient and modern erection, he imbibed a taste for architecture, which he put in practice, with great success, on his return to England. His first work, in that country, was the interior of the church of St. Catherine Cree, in London; and his most considerable design, the projected palace of Whitehall, the part of which that is executed, the banqueting-house, being barely one-fiftieth part of that magnificent idea. After the death of Jones, no considerable architect appeared, till the talents of Sir Christopher Wren (before that time devoted to philosophy and general learning) were called to the aid of the languishing art. He was born in the year 1632, and died at the age of ninety-one, in 1723, after being, in his eighty-sixth year, barbarously dismissed from the office of surveyor-general, which he had held with unparalleled ability fifty-one years. When that temporarily disastrous yet permanently useful event, the fire of London, occurred, this great man was almost solely employed in rebuilding the numerous public edifices destroyed by the conflagration, and chiefly the cathedral of St. Paul, his execution of which arduous task, whatever be the objections raised against parts of it, by the taste of some, and the jealousy of others, remains a lasting monument of his genius in decorative and unexampled skill in constructive architecture.

Before the death of Wren, appeared Sir John Vanbrugh, who was employed by the nation to erect that monument of national gratitude, Blenheim House. Both the architect, and this, his greatest work, were alternately neglected and censured, till Sir Joshua Reynolds vindicated his fame in his lectures to the Royal Academy. Next in order were Hawksmoor, the pupil of Wren, Lord Burlington, Kent, and Gibbs, of the last of whom Mr. Mitford observes, that, allowing his talents to be small, how much do we owe to Lord Burlington, that by his precepts such a man was enabled to build one of the finest modern works, St. Martin's Church in the Fields. To Lord Burlington, indeed, it is probable we owe more than is generally acknowledged; for, besides the patronage he afforded to the artists of his time, and the assistance he gave them from his own genius, it is, perhaps, owing to his example that a general feeling of attachment to the arts was conceived by the young men of rank and fortune in England. The Turkish government, which, in its prosperity, ruled with a rod of iron the once fertile plains of Greece, began now, in its decline, to relax a little of its ancient rigor, and these gentlemen were thus enabled to extend their travels (which before were bounded by the Archipelago) into this important country. Some of them formed, at their return, the Dilettanti Society, for the encouragement of researches into those (to modern times) new regions. These proceedings could not but excite great interest and curiosity in the public mind, which were fully gratified, after some years, by Mr. Stuart; who, during a long residence at Athens, made accurate drawings of most of the ancient buildings then existing. These were published in three volumes, folio, to which a fourth was afterwards added by Mr. Revely. The effect of these importations may be seen in every street in London.

The revival of the neglected architecture of the middle ages constitutes a new era in our history. Perhaps the first person who dared to recommend, by writing and example, a style so long in disrepute, was the celebrated Horace Walpole, Earl of Orford, who built the well-known villa of Strawberry Hill to testify his fondness for it. This was succeeded by Lee Priory, by Mr. Wyatt, who quickly outstripped all the professors of his day, both in this style and the Roman. His greatest work, in Gothic architecture, was Fonthill Abbey, the merits of which building, when we consider that the architect had no model to work from (there being not another house of magnitude, in this style, in the whole kingdom), are truly extraordinary; the purest taste reigns throughout the whole of this splendid structure, and the architect has bequeathed to succeeding professors a legacy of incalculable value.

Having now brought our sketch down to the present time, we shall proceed to the second part of our design.

PART II.

THE CHARACTERISTICS OF THE DIFFERENT STYLES OF ARCHITECTURE.

With Assyrian architecture, as was before observed, we are acquainted only by vague and uncertain report; we will, therefore, commence by the description of

The Egyptian Style.

Did we not know it to be a fact, we have every reason to believe, that, in the early ages of the world, stability was the first consideration. That men by nature are in a state of great inequality, is a truth which no rational person would be inclined to controvert. Some are weak, and some strong, and others have great powers of mind; to these, those incapable of defending themselves would naturally apply for protection against their more powerful neighbors, and hence the origin of civilized society. But it is enough for our present purpose that from this combination proceeded the subject of our inquiry. Under these hands, as was before observed, massive strength would be more attended to than form or adornment. But we do not mean to insinuate that the buildings now to be considered are exactly of this class; mighty and ponderous they are, but (excepting the pyramids, which did not admit of it) not destitute of decoration; and some may even be said to possess a degree of elegance.

It may probably be expected that, in delineating the peculiarities of the architecture of Egypt, we should begin with the pyramids, as most readily presenting themselves to the generality of readers. Little description, however, will suffice to give an idea of these stupendous monuments. The largest of them stands not far from the city of Cairo ; it is built on a rock ; its base is square, and its sides are equilateral triangles, except that there is a platform at top of about sixteen feet square, which, comparatively, is so small that it is said not to be discernible from below. The stones of which it is composed are of a prodigious size, the least of them thirty feet in length. These are disposed so as to present a series of steps on the exterior. But, though we have thus thought fit to give a brief description of these mysterious and mighty monuments, it is not the pyramids that characterize the Egyptian style of architecture. Its distinguishing marks are to be found in the numerous temples dispersed through the country.

As we know of no proportions attended to in the construction of these edifices, and have no means whereby to judge of their respective dates but by their richness or simplicity (qualities which, though they may be some general guides, are not alone sufficient data from which to form a chronological classification of edifices), we can have little more to say under this head, than to refer the reader who may wish to make himself acquainted with this style to the work of Denon, where he will find accurate delineations of the principal specimens. We cannot quit the subject, however, without remarking the great variety and beauty of *the capitals*, in the elegant forms of some of which, borrowed from the palm-tree and the lotus, is found a far more probable origin for the Corinthian capital of the Greeks and Romans than in the pleasing yet probably fictitious story of Vitruvius.

Grecian and Roman Architecture.

The architecture of the Romans having been almost entirely borrowed from that of their masters in art, though subjects in dominion, the Greeks, we shall, for greater clearness and brevity, consider them together. The various parts, of which both

Greek and Roman orders are composed (the distinguishing members excepted), being nearly the same in all of them, we shall commence by a description of these. And, first, the greater members, which all possess in common. On referring to plate 33, fig. 3, it will be seen that we have marked letters, answering to dotted lines, proceeding from the order to the right hand.

Of these, the upper division, *a* is the *cornice*, *b* the *frieze*, and *c* the *architrave ;* these form the horizontal part of the order, and are called the ENTABLATURE ; *d* is the *capital*, *e* the *shaft*, and *f* the *base ;* these together form the COLUMN, or upright supporting part. The column is usually placed on a square tile, called the plinth. These, according to the variation of their parts, form what are called the *orders* of Greek and Roman architecture, which will be presently the subject of our consideration.

The prototype of this arrangement is supposed by Vitruvius, and a host of followers, to be the wooden hut, of which we find the following account in Sir William Chambers: "Having marked out the space to be occupied by the hut, they fixed in the ground several upright trunks of trees, &c., to form the sides, filling the intervals between them with branches closely interwoven and spread over with clay. The sides thus completed, four beams were laid on the upright trunks, which, being well fastened together at the angles of their junction, kept the sides firm, and likewise served to support the covering or roof of the building, composed of smaller trees, placed horizontally, like joist, upon which were laid several beds of reeds, leaves, and earth or clay. By degrees other improvements took place, and means were found to make the fabric lasting, neat and handsome, as well as convenient. The bark and other protuberances were taken from the trees that formed the sides; these trees were raised above the dirt and humidity on stones, were covered at the top with other stones, and firmly bound round at both ends with osiers or cords, to secure them from splitting. The spaces between the joists were closed up with clay or wax, and the ends of them either smoothed or covered with boards. The different beds of materials that composed the covering were cut straight at the eaves, and distinguished from each other by different projections. The form of the roof, too, was altered; for, being on account of its flatness unfit to throw off the rains, which sometimes fell in great abundance, it was raised in the middle on trees, disposed like rafters, after the form of a gable roof.

"This construction, simple as it appears, probably gave birth to most of the parts that now adorn our buildings, particularly to the orders which may be considered as the basis of the whole decorative part of architecture; for when structures of wood were set aside, and men began to erect solid stately edifices of stone, having nothing nearer to imitate, they naturally copied the parts which necessity introduced in the primitive hut, insomuch that the upright trees, with the stones and cordage at each end of them, were the origin of columns, bases and capitals; the beams and joists gave rise to architraves and friezes, with their triglyphs and metopes; and the gable roof was the origin of pediments; as the beds of materials forming the covering, and the rafters supporting them, were of cornices with their corona, their mutules, modillions, and their dentils."

Such is the account which has been transmitted to us of the origin of these *orders;* and it has sufficed for and been unhesitatingly received by all, or the greater part, of our forefathers; but the restless scepticism of modern times has not spared even this venerable and harmless notion. It is alleged that it is very improbable that stone should have been the immediate successor of wood as a building material; the working of this substance of itself being no small acquirement, and not consistent with the rudeness of the times; the employment of brick most probably intervened, and this was actually used at the tower of Babel. That the Greeks derived their knowledge of this art from Egypt is generally allowed; but, in the large hollowed crown mouldings and flat roofs of the temples of that country, little resemblance is found to this model. Another objection to this hypothesis will be found in the description of the Doric order, where it will be better introduced and understood than in this place.

The Roman ovolo and cavetto are never found in the Grecian architecture, nor the Greek echinus in that of the Romans; the rest they possess in common. The Greek mouldings are chiefly distinguished from the Roman by being composed of ellipses and other conic sections, while the Roman are formed of segments of circles. The Greek echinus and cyma-reversa are also, for the most part, *quirked;* that is, the contour is returned under the fillet above, as is shown in the Grecian echinus. In some early specimens of the Doric order, a straight line is used instead of the curve for the echinus, as in the capital of the portico of Philip, in the island of Delos.

When the projection of these mouldings is required to be greater or less than usual (which is sometimes the case, from peculiarity of situations), the best method of overcoming the difficulty is to make them of segments of ellipses, by which means it is evident any required projection may be obtained, and the shadows will be such as not readily to discover the defect. In places where the composition is unusually higher or lower than the eye, it is sometimes necessary to deviate from the customary manner of executing the mouldings, to make them appear of their proper forms. It is very rarely, however, that an expedient of this kind is necessary, and it should never be resorted to; but when it is, the forms, when closely examined, are very unpleasing.

All the mouldings, except the fillet, admit of decoration; but, even in the most enriched profile, it is proper to leave some uncarved, to prevent confusion, and give a due repose to the composition. It is a fundamental rule, in the sculpture of mouldings, to cut the ornaments out of the contour, beyond which nothing should project, as this would inevitably alter its figure. The fillet may be used at all heights, and in most situations. The torus, only in bases. The scotia, below the eye and between the fillets attached to the torus. The echinus, only above the eye, and is fit for supports. The inverted cyma is also used as a supporting member. The cyma-recta and cavetto are only fit for crowning mouldings, for which their forms are peculiarly adapted, being incapable of holding water, which must necessarily drop from their extreme points.

Having thus presented the reader with the key to our future language, we proceed to the description of the *orders*.

The orders of architecture are strictly three, the Doric, the Ionic, and the Corinthian; and are found in the greatest perfection in Greece. But the Romans, determined to produce novelty, at the expense of excellence, formed, out of the first of these, two new orders, one of which they denominated the Tuscan, and the other, though very dissimilar to the ancient order of that name, they likewise called the Doric. The Ionic they altered less, but that likewise was decidedly for the worse, considering the orders for the temples of Minerva Polias, and Ilyssus, as the standard of Grecian art. The Corinthian they must be allowed to have improved, but formed a variation of it, frequently seen in the Roman buildings' particularly in the triumphal arches, which has been erected by the moderns into a fifth order, under the name of Roman, or Composite. The difference between this and the Corinthian, however, is much less than between the Greek and Roman Doric.

Before we give the orders in detail, it will be necessary to observe that columns are tapered in their shafts; that is, the circumference of the shaft at the capital is less than it is at the base, thus making a frustum of a cone; but in most, or all of the ancient examples, the line, instead of being perfectly straight, is slightly curved. Sometimes the shaft is continued from the base, cylindrically, to about a quarter or third of its height, and then diminished rectilinearly to the top. This is called *entasis*, and in all the examples of antiquity is so slight as to be scarcely perceptible. Vitruvius having obscurely hinted at the practice, several of the modern Italian artists, intending to conform to his precept, but not perceiving the result in the originals, carried it to an absurd excess, and made the thickness greater at the middle than at the foot of the shaft.

The Tuscan Order.

The Tuscan order, as an antique, exists only in the works of Vitruvius; the description in which being very obscure, has left a wide field for the ingenuity of modern architects. Among these, Palladio composed two profiles, one from the description of the ancient master, and the other according to his own idea of a simplification of the Doric. That of Vignola, however, has been most generally approved and adopted.

The base of this order consists of a simple torus with its fillet; it is, as are in general all the Roman orders, accompanied with a plinth. The proportions, from Sir William Chambers, are as follows: the column, fourteen modules; the entablature, three modules, fifteen minutes. Of the former, the base occupies one module; the shaft, including the astragal, which divides it from the capital, twelve modules, and the capital, one. Of the latter, the architrave, including the fillet, thirty-one minutes and a half; the frieze, the same; and the cornice, forty-two minutes. The intercolumniations, in all the orders except the Doric, are the same, namely: the eustyle, which is most common and beautiful, four modules, twenty minutes; the diastyle, six modules; and aræostyle, seven modules.

The Tuscan order admits of no ornaments, nor flutes in the columns; on the contrary, rustic cinctures are sometimes represented on the shaft of its column. But this practice, though occasionally used by good architects, is seldom compatible with good taste.

This order may be employed in most cases where strength and simplicity are required, rather than magnificence; such as prisons, market-places, arsenals, and the inferior parts of large buildings.

The Doric Order.

This order, of which numerous ancient examples exist, will, in consequence, furnish us with more materials for description than the preceding. We will commence with the story of its origin, as given by Vitruvius. "Dorus, son of Hellen and the nymph Orseis, reigned over Achaia and Peloponnesus. He built a temple of this order, on a spot sacred to Juno, at Argos, an ancient city. Many temples similar to it were afterwards raised in other parts of Achaia, though at that time its proportions were not precisely established." This account, as well as of those of the orders which we shall presently examine, is very incredible, and is now generally rejected.

From theory, however, we must now proceed to fact and description, and will commence with the Doric of the Greeks, referred to by Vitruvius, who, nevertheless, confounds this with what was commonly executed at Rome in his time. The most perfect example of this order is the Parthenon, or Temple of Minerva, on the Acropolis at Athens, erected by Ictinus, under the administration of Pericles, who lived B. C. 450. We shall therefore now give its proportions. The column (including the capital), ten modules, twenty-seven minutes and one-half; the whole entablature, three modules, twenty-seven minutes and three-quarters; the capital, twenty-seven minutes and three-quarters; the architrave (with its fillet), one module, twelve minutes and three-quarters; the frieze, to the square member of the corona, one module, nineteen minutes; and the cornice, twenty-six minutes. Diameter of the column at the top, one module, sixteen minutes. — Through the politeness of the Rev. John Pierpont, I have received the following note, which may be of consequence to the reader in ascertaining the magnitude of this edifice.

Boston, June 10, 1853.

MY DEAR SIR:

In compliance with your request, I here send you the dimensions of the different parts of the columns of that most exquisite of all the specimens of the Doric architecture, — the Parthenon, — from my own careful measurement, in April. I give the dimensions, not in modules and minutes, but in English feet and inches.

Diameter of the column at base,	6 feet,	2 inches.
Width of the flutings at base,		$11\frac{15}{24}$ "
" " " at the top,		$9\frac{1}{2}$ "
Thickness of abacus,	1 "	$1\frac{7}{12}$ "
Projection of the abacus beyond the echinus,		$\frac{5}{8}$ "
From the bottom of the abacus to the upper annulet, measured on the slope of the echinus,	1 "	$1\frac{5}{8}$ "
The four annulets occupy		$2\frac{1}{3}$ "
Each annulet,		$\frac{7}{12}$ "
From bottom of the lower annulet to the bottom of the capital, that is, to the groove into the upper part of the fluting,		$7\frac{1}{3}$ "
Height of whole capital,	2 "	$9\frac{1}{2}$ "
Horizontal distance from the lower annulet, to a perpendicular dropped from the face of abacus,		8 "
Angle formed by a perpendicular, and the upward line of the echinus, considered as a right line,		$37\frac{1}{2}$ degrees.
Angle formed by the pitch of the roof, and a horizontal line, at the eaves,		13 "
This angle, according to Col. Leake, is		$15\frac{1}{2}$ "

I have some confidence, however, in my measurement; for I measured the angle on two different days, once mechanically, and once mathematically, by proportionate numbers.

The height of the columns of the Parthenon, according to Col. Leake, is	34 feet.
Height of the whole temple,	65 "
Length of the same,	228 "
Breadth,	102 "

I am, sir, very respectfully, your obedient servant,

JOHN PIERPONT.

MR. EDWARD SHAW.

I proceed to the order designated by this title by the Romans. Very few ancient examples of this variation exist. The most perfect is that of the Theatre of Marcellus, if, perhaps, we except that elaborate pile, Trajan's column, which is generally pronounced to be Tuscan. It is, therefore, principally indebted for its existence to the modern Italian architects, who, having little of antiquity before their eyes, appear to have bestowed more attention upon this order than the others; and it must be confessed that they have made of it a very elegant design, though, as before observed, essentially different from the original and true Doric. The measures, from Sir William Chambers, are as follows: the base, thirty minutes; the shaft, thirteen modules, twenty-eight minutes; and the capital, thirty-two minutes; the architrave, thirty minutes; the frieze, to capital of triglyph, forty-two minutes; and cornice, forty-five minutes. Upper diameter of column, fifty minutes.

In no example of antiquity is the Doric column provided with a base. I am inclined to think, either the architects had not yet thought of employing bases to their columns, or that they omitted them, in order to leave the pavement clear, as the architects of those times frequently placed their columns very near each other; so, had they been made with bases, the passage between them would have been extremely narrow and inconvenient; however, the Romans have introduced the attic base, which is common to all of the orders except the Tuscan, though it more properly belongs to the Ionic. This base has two tori, a scotia and two fillets between them; above the upper torus is an inverted cavetto and fillet properly belonging to the shaft of the column, as is also that under the capital; for which reason they are commonly considered as belonging to the shaft. The plinth or square member beneath the base is usually considered indispensable in Roman architecture, although Palladio has omitted it in his Corinthian order; but it is scarcely found in the Greek specimens. The intercolumniation takes from this style, in no small degree, the imposing grandeur which is so characteristic of the Grecian style. The most striking peculiarity of the Doric order is the triglyph, which admits of the idea of the beams being placed transversely on the architrave, which more conforms to Grecian examples; hence, the angles are supplied with a beam forming the flanks; but this will not hold good in the Roman examples, where the beams at the angles are placed over the centre of the column, which leaves the wall destitute of a beam to support the roof. The triglyph is surmounted by the mutule, in the Greek, and, in some Roman examples, inclined, but in most modern profiles, horizontal; on its soffit are represented guttæ, or drops. The spaces between the triglyphs on the frieze are called metopes, which, in the modern Doric, are invariably perfectly square, and generally enriched with sculptures. A part of the ornamented metopes of the Parthenon were brought to England by Lord Elgin, and now form the principal attraction in the collection which is known by his name in the British Museum. In the modern order, these sculptures are most commonly an alternate bull's skull and patera. The extreme projection of all these ornaments should be less than that of the triglyph itself, thus keeping a due subordination between mere decorations and essential parts. All the Grecian Doric columns are fluted,* and in both Greek and Roman this is performed without fillets between, as in the other orders.

The intercolumniations in this order differ from those of the others, on account of the triglyph, the metopes being required to be exactly square. They are as follows: The coupled columns, of course, must stand under adjoining triglyphs; this makes their distance, at the foot of the shaft, twenty-one minutes. The next intercolumniation is the monotriglyph, which has one between the columns; the distance is three modules. The diastyle, — two triglyphs, five modules and a half. The aræostyle, which has three between, eight modules. This last is a size which should never be resorted to but in cases of great necessity; and, indeed, is seldom practicable.

* Though some examples are so only a little way up from the base, and again just at the top of the column.

TABLE OF PROPORTIONS.

FROM AIKIN'S ESSAY.

NAMES OF EXAMPLES.	Bottom Diameter.	Top Diameter.	Height of Column.		Archi-trave.	Frieze.	Cornice.	Intercolum-niation.	
	Minutes.	Minutes.	Diam.	Min.	Minutes.	Minutes.	Minutes.	Diam.	Min.
Portico of the Agora, at Athens, . . .	60	47	6	2½	40	42	21	–	—
Temple of Minerva, at Sunium, . . .	60	45¾	5	54	48½	48½	—	1	28
Temple of Jupiter Nemæus, ...	60	49	6	31	38⅔	43½	—	–	—
Temple of Jupiter Panhellenius, . . .	60	44½	5	24	51⅓	51½	—	1	41
Temple of Theseus, ...	60	46⅔	5	42⅓	50	49½	—	1	37½
Temple of Minerva, at Athens, . . .	60	47	5	33½	43	43	32	1	17⅔
Temple of Corinth, ...	60	44⅔	4	4	48⅔	—	—	1	14
Portico of Philip, ...	60	49½	6	32½	38½	43¾	25½	2	42⅔
Temple of Apollo, ...	60	42½	6	3¾	49⅔	42½	—	–	—
Temple of Minerva, at Syracuse, . . .	60	46	4	24½	44½	4	—	1	5⅔
Temple of Juno Lucina, ...	60	45⅓	4	42	55	45	—	1	15
Temple of Concord, ...	60	46	4	45¼	46⅘	46⅓	25	1	10⅔
Pseudodipteral Temple, at Pæstum, . .	60	40⅓	4	27	50	—	—		{ 59½ { 67⅔
Hexastyle Temple, at Pæstum, . . .	60	43	4	47¾	45¾	44¾	24⅔	1	1⅓
Hypaethral Temple, at Pæstum, . . .	60	41¼	4	8	42⅓	40½	21½	1	4¾
Inner peristyle of ditto, ...	60	43	4	13⅓	39	—	—	1	22¾
Upper columns of ditto, ditto, . . .	60	44	3	50	68	—	—	2	49
Temple of Selinus, ...	60	46⅓	4	21¾	46⅓	44⅔	—	–	—
Temple of Jupiter, at Selinus, ...	60	35½	4	34⅓	52	44⅔	26	–	—
Temple of Egesta, ...	60	44¾	–	—	49⅘	52⅔	40¾	1	11
Theatre of Marcellus, ...	60	48	7	51⅔	30	45$\frac{5}{9}$	37$\frac{2}{9}$	–	—

The Ionic Order.

Vitruvius informs us that in a general assembly of the Grecian states thirteen colonies were sent over into Asia, by the Athenians; the expedition was led on by Ion, whom the Delphic oracle, which directed the emigration, had acknowledged for the offspring of Apollo. They settled on the borders of Caria, and built several cities of great fame, of which were Ephesus, Miletus, Samos, and Colophon, to which Smyrna was afterwards added; and, after the expulsion of the original inhabitants, these colonies were denominated Ionian, from the name of their chief. "In this country," continues he, "allotting different sites to sacred purposes, they erected temples, the first of which was dedicated to Apollo Panionius. It resembled that which they had seen in Achaia, and from the species having been first used in the cities of the Dorians, they gave it the name of Doric. As they wished to erect this temple with columns, and were not acquainted with their proportions, nor the mode in which they should be adjusted, so as to be both adapted to the reception of the superincumbent weight, and to have a beautiful effect, they measured a man's height by the length of the foot, which they found to be a sixth part thereof, and thence deduced the proportions of their columns. Thus the Doric order borrowed its proportion, strength and beauty, from the human figure. On similar principles they afterwards built the temple of Diana; but in this, from a desire of varying the proportions, they used the female figure as a standard, making the height of the column eight times its thickness, for the purpose of giving it a more lofty effect. Under this new order they placed a base, as a shoe to the foot. They also added volutes to the capital, resembling the graceful curls of the hair, hanging therefrom to the right and left. On the shaft channels were sunk, bearing a resemblance to the folds of a matronal garment. Thus were two orders invented, one of a masculine character, without ornament, the other approaching the delicacy, decorations, and proportion of a female. The successors of these people, improving in taste, and preferring a more slender proportion, assigned seven diameters to the height of the Doric column, and eight and a half to the Ionic. The species of which the Ionians were the inventors received the appellation of Ionic."

The volute is a distinguishing feature of the Ionic. I now give the proportional figures from Nicholson's Architectural Dictionary, from the Erectheus at Athens. First find the lesser projection of the echinus; let drop a plumb-line 40 minutes of the order, the depth of the volute. Divide this line into 34 parts, give 20 to the upper division, take 2.4 for the radius of the eye, divide the radius into eight parts, then counting from the plumb-line at top, measuring from the centre of the eye; second, 18.3; third, 16.7; fourth, 15.3; fifth, 14; sixth, 12.8; seventh, 11.7; eighth, 10.7. Second revolution—first, 9.8; second, 9; third, 8.2; fourth, 7.5;

fifth, 6.9 ; sixth, 6.3 ; seventh, 5.7 ; eighth, 5.2. Third revolution — first, 4.8 ; second, 4.4 ; third, 4 ; fourth, 3.7 ; fifth, 3.4 ; sixth, 3.1 ; seventh, 2.8 ; eighth, 2.6 ; the diameter of the eye, 4.8.

Another method of forming the spiral lines of a volute with a more regular curve than is practicable in the former method of forming the spiral lines I will now describe.

For the depth of the volute, take 40 minutes of the order. Drop a plumb-line from the lesser projection of the echinus, taking 22.5 minutes from the echinus to the centre of the eye, leaving 17.5 minutes from the centre of the eye to the bottom of the volute; find a right angle from the centre of the eye, take one-half minute in your dividers and space of 3 on each of the angles, from the centre parallel * to each of those angles extending the four lines from the intersection, so that the curve of the first revolution will cut each; then extend the second audinets to the second revolution, the third to the third; take three minutes in your dividers, placing one point of the dividers at the centre, and describe the eye; six minutes being the diameter of the eye, now we form the spiral lines from each quadrant *A*, *B*, *C*. The first extends points of the dividers from *B* to *A;* draw the curve from *A* to *E;* then from *D* to *C* draw to *E;* from *F* to *E* draw *G;* from *H G* to first revolution. Then 11 to 2; from 3.2 to 4; from 5.4 to 6; from 9.6 to 8 — second revolution. Take the inner square and perform the third revolution in the same manner as the first and second, and for four revolutions make the sides of the squares into eight half-minutes, four on each of the angles from the centre, and proceed as in the three revolutions.

The most beautiful Grecian specimens of this order are the temple on the Ilyssus,† and the temples of Neptune Erectheus, and Minerva Polias, on the Acropolis at

* It should be observed that this operation must be repeated for every line in the volute, no two being struck from the same centre.

† This beautiful little temple is now no longer standing.

Athens; the two latter of which are so similar that we shall not here discriminate between them. We are thus reduced to two Greek examples, and they are so exquisitely beautiful that it is difficult to give the preference to either. We will, therefore, describe both. The temple on the Ilyssus is the plainer of the two; its volute consists of a single spiral, with a deep channel between, and is separated from the shaft by the sculptured echinus. The architrave is not broken into fasciæ, as in most other specimens. The cornice consists simply of a square member, with one echinus and fillet, surmounted by the cymatium; the bed-mouldings in the elevations are completely concealed. The base is composed of two tori, the upper of which is channelled horizontally and surmounted by a bead enclosing a very flat scotia, the upper fillet of which projects as far as the extremity of the torus. The fillets are semi-elliptical.

The following are the measures of this order: the column, including base and capital, sixteen modules, fourteen minutes and one-fifth; the base, twenty-nine minutes and four-fifths; the capital, to the bottom of the volute, forty minutes; the architrave, fifty-five minutes and two-fifths; the frieze, forty-nine minutes; the cornice, thirty minutes and one-fifth. Width of the capital, three modules, three minutes; upper diameter of column, fifty-one minutes; intercolumniation, from centre to centre of column, six modules, five minutes and two-fifths.

The order of the temple of Minerva Polias is next to be considered. This example is much richer, yet no less elegant, than the other; the volute, instead of a single spiral, is formed by three; the sculptured echinus beneath is surmounted by a guil-loched moulding, and separated from the shaft by a neck adorned with honeysuckles. The base is very similar to that of the temple on the Ilyssus, except that its beauty is increased by the diminution of its height, the scotia is deeper, and the upper torus is guilloched. The architrave consists of three fasciæ, and the cornice is similar to that of the Ilyssus temple, except that the echinus and bed-mouldings are sculptured, and the astragal of the latter is seen in the elevation beneath the corona. The column, including base and capital, is eighteen modules, seven minutes and one-tenth in height; the base, twenty-four minutes; and the capital, forty-two; the architrave, forty-five minutes and one-fourth; the frieze, forty-seven minutes and four-fifths; and the cornice, to the fillet of the echinus, which is the greatest actual height of the entablature, the cymatium being a restoration, twenty minutes and two-fifths. The width of the capital, three modules, three minutes. Upper diameter of column, forty-nine minutes and a half. Intercolumniation, from centre to centre, nine modules. Both of these examples are destitute of insulated plinths.

Having thus given our readers an idea of the finest Greek specimens of this order, we must now proceed to the Roman and Italian examples of it. It is the peculiarity of this order that its front and side faces are dissimilar. To obviate this inconvenience, the Greeks twisted the extreme volutes of a portico so as to make the two faces alike. But Scamozzi, a famous Italian architect, designed a capital in which the volutes proceeded angularly from the shaft, thus presenting the same front every way; and the capital, so executed, has been generally attributed to the supposed inventor. Sir William Chambers, however, is of opinion that Michael Angelo was the author of one of this description in the Vatican at Rome. This capital is commonly known as modern Ionic, but it has not been executed on large works. The frieze of this order has been by many architects, and Palladio among the number, rounded in its architrave, as though it were pressed down and bent by the superincumbent weight; but the ill effect of this has been so generally perceived, that it is rarely to be seen in late works. The cornice is distinguished from the Greek by its variety of mouldings, among which the most remarkable is a square member in the bed-mouldings, cut into small divisions, somewhat resembling teeth, whence they are called *dentils*. In other points of variation between the Grecian and Roman architecture, there may be a difference of opinion; but with respect to the Ionic capital, we conceive this to be impossible. Whoever compares the meagre, petty form of the temple of Concord with that of the Erectheion, must instantly, whatever be his former prejudices, perceive the amazing difference, and unhesitatingly acknowledge the vast superiority of the latter. The poverty of the solitary revolving fillet, the flat, insipid lines, and the enormous projection of the clumsy echinus, combine to render this the very worst feature in all the Italian orders. The base commonly used is the attic, though Vitruvius has appropriated one to this order resembling the Corinthian without its lower torus. The following are the measures of the order, from Sir William Chambers: the base, one module; the shaft, sixteen modules, nine minutes; and the capital, twenty-one minutes. The architrave, forty minutes and a half; the frieze, the same; and the cornice, fifty-four minutes. Width of capital, two modules, twenty-six minutes. Upper diameter of column, fifty minutes.

"As the Doric order," says Sir William Chambers, "is particularly affected in churches or temples dedicated to male saints, so the Ionic is principally used in such as are consecrated to females of the matronal state." It is likewise employed in courts of justice, in libraries, colleges, seminaries and other structures having relation to arts or letters; in private houses and in palaces; to adorn the women's apartments; and, says Le Clerc, in all places dedicated to peace and tranquillity. The ancients employed it in temples sacred to Juno, to Bacchus, to Diana, and other deities whose characters held a medium between the severe and the effeminate.

The Roman, or Composite Order.

This order, though not considered by them as a distinct one, was employed by the Romans principally in triumphal arches; the column and entablature being the same as, or little different from, the Corinthian. This difference was, however, sufficient for the Italians to ground a new order upon. The capital, as being *composed* of the

Ionic and Corinthian, they termed *composite;* and, to justify the application of the name to the order in general, they combined in the entablature the dentils of the Ionic with the mutules of the Doric, and enrichments of the Corinthian, and gave to the architrave but two fasciæ, thus rendering it in some respects more simple, but more enriched than the latter, while the former had little but the name left in the composition. The whole order may be safely pronounced heavy without possessing grandeur, and rich though destitute of beauty. It has been frequently adopted, and it is to be lamented that Sir Christopher Wren has made so much use of it about St. Paul's. The base commonly appropriated to this order is extremely beautiful; it consists of two tori, the lower of which is considerably the larger, with two scotiæ, enclosing an astragal. This is called the *proper* base of the order, but the attic is usually employed, being more simple, and consequently less expensive, than the other.

The measures of this order, from Sir William Chambers, are as follows: the base, thirty minutes; the shaft, sixteen modules, twenty minutes; and the capital, two modules, ten minutes; the architrave, forty-five minutes; and the cornice, two modules.

The Corinthian Order.

The story of this order, given by Vitruvius, is as follows: "The third species of columns, which is called the Corinthian, resembles, in its character, the graceful, elegant appearance of a virgin, whose limbs are of a more delicate form, and whose ornaments should be unobtrusive. The invention of the capital of this order arose from the following circumstance: A Corinthian virgin, who was of marriageable age, fell a victim to a violent disorder; after her interment, her nurse, collecting in a basket those articles to which she had shown a partiality when alive, carried them to her tomb, and placed a tile on the basket for the longer preservation of its contents. The basket was accidentally placed on the root of an acanthus-plant, which, pressed by the weight, shot forth, towards spring, in stems of large foliage, and, in the course of its growth, reached the angles of the tile, and thus formed volutes at the extremities. Callimachus, who, for his great ingenuity and taste in sculpture, was called by the Athenians κατατεχνος, happening to pass by the tomb, observed the basket and the delicacy of the foliage which surrounded it. Pleased with the form and the novelty of the combination, he took the hint for inventing these columns, and used them in the country about Corinth, regulating by this model the style and proportion of the Corinthian order."

It has been before observed, in our notice of Egyptian architecture, that the capitals to be found in the country are much more likely to have given the hint for the Corinthian than the circumstance here mentioned. The only pure example of this order in Greece is the monument of Lysicrates. The capital of this specimen is exquisitely beautiful, but the same praise cannot, in the opinion of the writer, be justly awarded to the entablature ; the architrave is disproportionately large, and the frieze extremely small ; the bed-mouldings of the cornice, which completely overpower the corona, consist of large dentils, supported by the echinus and surmounted by a cyma-recta under a cyma-reversa, which supports the corona. The base is extremely beautiful, resembling that of the temple of Minerva Polias, except that an inverted echinus is substituted for the upper torus ; the base stands upon a large inverted cavetto, connected with the continued plinth by another inverted echinus. The flutes terminate upwards in the form of leaves, instead of being divided from the capital, as usual, by an astragal. The building is circular, and its centre is the summit of an equilateral triangle, of which the base is in a line bounded by the centres of any two of the columns ; the intercolumniation is six modules, thirteen minutes and two-fifths, of which the base occupies twenty-one minutes ; and the capital, two modules, twenty-seven minutes. The architrave, fifty-three minutes and two-fifths ; the frieze, forty-one minutes and two-fifths ; and the cornice, forty-eight minutes and four-fifths. The finest Roman example of this order is that of three columns in the Campo Vaccino, at Rome, which are commonly regarded as the remains of the temple of Jupiter Stator. This example has received the commendations of all modern artists, yet has seldom been executed in its original form. This is probably owing to the excessive richness and delicacy of it, which renders its adoption very expensive; and perhaps the modifications of it by Vignola is preferable to the original, possessing a sufficient enrichment, without the excessive refinement of the other. In this order, which has been adopted by Sir William Chambers, the base is one module in height; the shaft, sixteen modules, twenty minutes; and the capital, two modules, ten minutes; thus giving ten diameters to the whole column. The architrave and frieze are each one module, fifteen minutes in height; and the cornice, two modules. The cornice is distinguished by modillions interposing between the bed-mouldings and the corona; the latter is formed by a square member, surmounted by a cymatium supported by a small ogee; the former is composed by dentils, supported by a cyma-reversa, and covered by an ovolo. When the order is enriched, which is usually the case, these mouldings, excepting the cymatium and square of the corona, are all sculptured; the column is also fluted, and the channels are sometimes filled to about a third of their height with cablings, which are cylindrical pieces let into the channels. When the column is large and near the eye, these are recommended as strengthening them, and rendering the fillets less liable to fracture; but when they are not approached, it is better to leave the flutes plain. They are sometimes sculptured, but this should be only in highly-enriched orders. The flutes are twenty-four in number, and commonly semi-circular in their plan. The Corinthian base is similar to that of the composite order, excepting that astragals are employed between the scotiæ, instead of one; but the attic is usually employed for the reasons before assigned.

"The Corinthian order," says Sir William Chambers, "is proper for all buildings where elegance, gayety and magnificence, are required. The ancients employed it in building temples dedicated to Venus, to Flora, Proserpine and the nymphs of fountains, because the flowers, foliage and volutes, with which it is adorned, seemed well adapted to the delicacy and elegance of such deities. Being the most splendid of all the orders, it is extremely proper for the decoration of palaces, public squares or galleries, and arcades surrounding them; for churches dedicated to the Virgin Mary, or to other virgin saints; and, on account of its rich, gay and graceful appearance, it may, with propriety, be used in theatres, in ball or banqueting rooms, and in all places consecrated to festive mirth, or convivial recreation."

Persians and Caryatides.

Having now described what are called the regular orders, it is necessary to notice, in the next place, the employment of human figures, instead of columns, for the support of an entablature. We will first give, as in former cases, the account of Vitruvius. "Carya, a city of Peloponnesus, took part with the Persians against the Grecian states. When the country was freed from its invaders, the Greeks turned their arms against the Caryans, and, upon the capture of the city, put the males to the sword and led the females into captivity. The architects of that time, for the purpose of perpetuating the ignominy of the people, instead of columns in the porticos of their buildings, substituted statues of these women, faithfully copying their ornaments, and the drapery with which they were attired, the mode of which they were not permitted to change." There are two great objections to the truth of this story: first, that the circumstance is not mentioned by any of the Grecian historians; and, secondly, that it is certain that animal figures were employed for this purpose long previous to the time assigned by Vitruvius.

Having thus shown our readers what is *not* the origin of these figures, it must next be our business to inform them what *is*, or rather what most probably is; and for this purpose we must trespass on the kindness of Mr. Gwilt, the only writer, we believe, who has given a satisfactory account of them. He conjectures the name to have arisen from the employment of them in temples to Diana, who is supposed to have made the Lacedemonians acquainted with the story of Carya (turned into a nut by Bacchus, who also transformed her sisters into stones), and thence worshipped by them, under the name of *Caryatis.* Thus being first employed in temples to this goddess, they afterwards came into use in other buildings as representations of the nymphs who assisted at the mysteries of the patron goddess. They may be seen at St. Pancras Church, correctly copied from the Pandroseum, the only Greek building remaining where they are employed.

The entablature of this example is extremely heavy, consisting only of an architrave and enormous cornice with dentils, which, however disproportionate in its situation, is, of itself, very beautiful. There are no remains of these figures in ancient Rome. The moderns have assigned the Ionic entablature to Caryatides, and the Doric when the figures of men are employed, which are called Persians.

Caryatides are, when appropriately designed, well adapted for buildings devoted to pleasure, such as theatres, ball-rooms, &c., but are decidedly improper for sacred edifices. They should not be represented much above the natural size, "lest they should appear hideous in the eyes of the fair." For male figures, on the contrary, a large size is desirable ; they are said to be proper for military buildings.

The contradictions of some of the French architects on this subject are very curious. Le Clerc tells us that it is very wrong to represent Caryatides in servile attitudes, such characters being very injurious to the sex. On the contrary, they should be considered the greatest ornaments to buildings, as their prototypes are of creation, and represented in respectful characters. But M. de Chambrai disagrees with his learned friend, and considers this practice as an error, observing that if the text of Vitruvius be attended to, it will be perceived that it is very improper to represent saints and angels loaded like slaves with cornices and other heavy burdens. He likewise considers them as improper for churches, in which, as houses of God, and asylums of mercy, vengeance and slavery ought never to appear. M. Blondel again observes, "that though this remark be just, if the origin of these ornaments be rigorously attended to, yet to serve in the house of God, and particularly at the altar, has always appeared, in the minds of the prophets and saints, so glorious and great, that not only men, but angels, ought to esteem it a happiness; and that, consequently, it can be no indication of disrespect to employ their representations in offices which they would themselves execute with pleasure." Such are the frivolous questions and debates into which blind reverence for antiquity has involved men of considerable talents. Leaving them, however, to such as are inclined to pay them attention, it is now requisite to describe a species of figures, which, on account of its simplicity, has sometimes been substituted for Caryatides. They are called termini, or terms, and derive their name and origin from the boundary-stones of the Romans, to render which inviolate, Numa Pompilius erected the terminus into a deity, and he was first worshipped in the similitude of a stone. This was afterwards improved into a human head upon a pedestal, smaller at the bottom than the top; and they are thus, with numerous variations, represented in buildings.

Pilasters.

Pilasters, when they are attached to walls, are square, projecting from one-fifth to one-half the breadth of the face, and when erected on the angles of buildings show two equal faces. When attached to columns, the width should be nearly equal to the neck of the column to which it may be attached; in this case, the Grecians introduced small projections in the walls, with bases and capitals, termed antæ. These were sometimes erected on the angles of porticos, and in the rear columns, where the walls cause the flanks, uniting with the wall of the building, to give the front that solidity required in large works, in which the width requires more space than a single pilaster. Divide the face into two equal parts, and leave the space between them equal to one-fourth of the anta, or pilaster; these antæ were seldom accompanied with volutes, as were columns of the Ionic.

Pedestals.

Columns are most frequently placed on the ground, but are sometimes raised on insulated basements, called pedestals. A pedestal is, like a column, composed of three parts,—the base, the body, or die, and the cornice,—the decorations of which vary according to the order in which it is employed. The best method of arranging them is that employed by Vignola, who makes them, in all the orders, one-third the height of the column, thus preserving the character of the order. The die is always the same size as the plinth of the column, and the base and cornice are regulated by the delicacy of the order.

Pedestals should never be employed with detached columns, forming porticos; but they are frequently applied to columns which divide arches, and are necessary in churches, where the pews would otherwise conceal the base, and a great part of the column. The same reason will justify their use in all edifices built for the reception of crowded assemblies.

Pediments.

Where columns are employed to decorate the gable of a building, in which situation they usually form what is called a portico, the triangle formed by the roof projecting upwards from the entablatures is called a pediment. The entablature in this case is covered by two straight inclined cornices, the mouldings of which are similar to the horizontal one; the space enclosed is called the tympanum. This was the original pediment, and the only form found in Greece; but the Romans, to vary the form, employed in smaller works a segment, or a circle, instead of the triangle. The former, however, is heavy, and is only used as a covering to gates, doors, windows, and such smaller architectural works, where, by reason of their diminutiveness, they may produce variety, without being disagreeable to the eye. The cymatium, when the horizontal cornice with a pediment, is omitted, and only used in the inclined cornice ; otherwise this moulding would occur twice together in the same profile. The mutules, dentils and modillions, in the inclined or segmental cornice, must always answer perpendicularly to those in the horizontal one, and their sides must be perpendicular to the latter.

The proportion of a pediment depends upon the length of the base line, the cornice being of the same size ; and in a portico with many columns the tympanum will not be of the same proportion to the rest of the composition, as when it is composed by a few. The method of determining the height of the pediment has lately been given in a French pamphlet, more correctly than before. It is this : first, from the summit of an equilateral triangle, the base of which is the upper fillet of the horizontal cornice, with one side of the triangle as radius, describe an arc ; with the point of intersection between this arc and the centre line of the composition as a centre, and with the depth of the horizontal cornice as a radius, describe part of a circle. A line, drawn from the extreme boundary of the upper moulding of the horizontal cornice, passing as a tangent to the circle, gives the inclination of the pediment. In more modern practice, the height of a pediment is more commonly ascertained by dividing the base line into three, four, or five equal parts ; give one to a perpendicular raised from the centre and upper fillet of the horizontal cornice ; draw a line from the extreme point of the fillet to the top of the perpendicular ; draw the crown moulding and the remainder of the cornice below the line of inclination ; either of those angles is sufficient to be made tight by shingles or slating, and a lesser inclination will answer a good purpose for covering with galvanized iron, tin, or copper.

Gothic Architecture.

It has been before observed, that the rude buildings of the Saxons and Normans in Europe, which are evidently copied from those of the Romans, may, by gradual improvement, have given rise to Gothic architecture ; and that this was the case in England, at least, there is no doubt. But there are certain peculiarities, even in these crude and imperfect attempts, though afterwards more fully developed, which require to be noticed before we proceed further ; plainly indicating that the works in question were raised under the influence of a less ardent sun, and more obscure sky. In the happy climate of Greece, where little was to be feared from change of weather, the temples, the only buildings distinguished for architectural excellence, were frequently destitute of covering. Windows, in this case, being entirely superfluous, the walls were, in many instances, pierced only by a single door, which served at once for ingress and egress to both priests and worshippers. Science here, therefore, was not needed, and, indeed, is not to be found. With the practical application of the principle of the arch the Greeks do not appear to have been acquainted; the large stones which, in those early ages, were to be procured in abundance, being sufficient to cover the columns and the opening of the doors. As architecture improved, however, roofs were added to these edifices; and, to throw off the rain, they were inclined downwards from the centre to the extremities. This inclination, in a climate where so little rain or snow fell, required to be but small ; but in Rome, which is more northern, it was found convenient to increase it to meet the exigencies of the situation. In countries far more exposed to vicissitudes of weather than either of those, it is evident that a very different pitch will be requisite ; and this theory is verified by the buildings of northern climates, the architects of which, though totally unacquainted with the works of their southern predecessors, by a singular coincidence adapted their roofs to their latitude in a regular scale of gradation from them. The Saxon and Norman architects, though they did not comprehend this principle in the perfection to which it was afterwards carried, were sensible of the wants of the climate, and made their roofs much higher than those of their Roman prototypes.

This circumstance presenting itself to minds so quick to perceive, and so able to adopt, any novelty which came recommended by utility and beauty, as were those of the architects of the middle ages, could not fail of meeting with the highest attention. It was soon seen that unbroken vertical lines and lofty buildings were necessary, to harmonize with the high pitched roof; and the pointed arch is but a natural and easy deduction from these *data*.

But there is another and an important peculiarity in buildings designed for northern climates, to which we must next call the attention of our readers. This arises from the numerous circumstances which, in these regions, conspire to obscure the rays of the sun. The great darkness which prevails in them, compared with Greece and Italy, evidently requires a very different arrangement in the public buildings, and this circumstance has received no small share of the attention of the architects whose works we are considering. The variety and beauty of its windows is not the least striking peculiarity of Gothic architecture; and, indeed, they form the readiest criterion for distinguishing the several styles, as we shall see hereafter.

A third essential point of distinction, between this style and all others, consists in the different *purposes* for which the edifices were constructed, in which it is most apparent, and the different *ceremonies* for which they were adapted. Although the rites of Greek and Roman Paganism were numerous and splendid, they required little aid from architecture; the ceremonies with which they were connected were principally performed in the open air, and the temple was only used as a receptacle for the statue of the deity before which sacrifices were offered, and to which prayers were preferred.

But Christian worship under papal guidance, and in a country so cold as to render shelter necessary for the performance of its ceremonies, required other arrangements in the edifices dedicated to it. For its numerous and splendid processions, was provided a long, narrow and lofty gallery, called *the naive ;* for the reception of the multitude to witness these, adjacent wings were added, called *aisles.* A *choir* was added for the actual performance of the sacred rites ; and numerous *chapels*, to commemorate the bounty of individuals, were dispersed about the edifice.

All these essential appendages necessarily occupied a space of great magnitude, and the figure of the *cross*, held by the Romish Church in the most profound veneration, was pitched upon to regulate the general form of the building thus constituted. One reason for mentioning these particulars is to show the absolute necessity which thus arose for a degree of science and mathematical knowledge not dreamt of by the architects, whose works are received as the sole standards of excellence, by most of the professors of modern times. The narrow intercolumniations of the Grecian buildings would have been ill adapted for the display of feudal magnificence, and the stones within the reach of the builders were far too small to cover even these. Thus the arch became, unavoidably, a prominent feature in the style. To give greater magnificence to the nave, it was made a story higher than the aisles. The wall of this upper story is supported by large piers, which divide the nave from the aisles. The upper, or *clear* story, as it is called, has windows answering to those beneath. To form an interior roofing, which should at once hide the timbers above, and furnish an appropriate finish to the architrave, the same contrivance was resorted to ; and from this cause have proceeded those vast monuments of daring ingenuity, which, while they excite the admiration, have baffled the rival attempts of modern architects.

Having thus traced, we hope perspicuously and satisfactorily, the causes which gave rise to Gothic architecture, and led to its perfection, it will be proper, before discriminating between its several styles, to explain some of its leading principles, and those particulars in which it more especially differs from the better known principles of Greek and Roman architecture.

Of these, the first in importance is the pointed arch, of which there are three kinds. 1. The simple pointed arch, which is struck from two centres on the line of the impost. 2. The Tudor arch, or that which has four centres, of which two are on the line of the impost line, and the other two at any distance. 3. The ogee, which has likewise four centres, two on the impost line, and two on a line with the apex, the segments struck from which are reversed. This form is used only in tracery, or small work, except as a canopy, or drip-stone, over doors and windows. The pointed arch differs from the semi-circular, as employed by the Romans, besides its form, in having its soffit occupied by mouldings of various projections, instead of being flat, enriched with panels. The cause of this is its great breadth, having frequently to support a wall and roof, which required the piers to be of corresponding magnitude, to diminish the unpleasing effect of which, the architects surrounded them with slender shafts. The projections of these being carried into the arch, caused it to be of the form in question. It is scarcely necessary to add, that these piers are always undiminished. Arising from the general use of the arch is that of the buttress. In Norman work, this was avoided by the employment of walls of vast thickness, with very small windows; but when architecture began to assume a lighter character, the windows were enlarged and the thickness of the walls diminished. To compensate for this deficiency, the buttress was employed at once to resist the pressure of the arches within, and to prevent the necessity of the walls being of an unwieldy thickness. These are often divided into stages, each being of less projection than that beneath it, finished by pinnacles; and from the upper part of them spring insulated arches, serving as a projection for the clear story.

The next thing to be mentioned is the *steeple*, with its compound parts and accompaniments. When square-topped it is called a tower, which is often crowned with a spire. Slender and lofty towers are *turrets*, and are commonly attached either to the angles of a large tower, where they frequently contain staircases, or to the angles of a building. They are sometimes surmounted by spires, a beautiful example of which may be seen at Peterborough cathedral, in the turret at the north-west angle. In this exquisite and unique design the turret is square, and decorated at the angle with boltels, which are carried up beyond it, and finished by a triangular pinnacle. The spire in the centre is octagonal, and rectangularly placed within the square, four of its sides thus forming triangles with the angular boltels, which, being arched over, form grounds for pinnacles of the same form, which are carried up to about half of the height of the spire itself. The effect is beautiful beyond description, and merits the most attentive examination.

Next in importance are the *windows* of Gothic architecture ; but, as these differ so widely in the several styles as to form the readiest criterion for distinguishing them, they will be more properly noticed when we speak of these styles. We shall pursue the same plan with doors and other subordinate parts.

It may be proper, in this place, to say something of the *mouldings* of Gothic architecture. Of these, that which bears the most resemblance to the Roman mouldings is the *ogee*, distinguished by the same name, or that of cyma-reversa, in the nomenclature of the Italian school. A moulding used for the same purpose as the cyma-recta, and much resembling it, is also found, more frequently, perhaps, than any other. That which is most peculiar to the style is the *boltel*, or cylindrical and nearly detached moulding, often answered by a corresponding hollow. In the plate are delineated two forms of exterior drip-stones. (Plate 41, Cap figs. 4 and 7.)

We shall now delineate the different styles of Gothic architecture, with the peculiarities of each ; and, in so doing, follow the arrangement and nomenclature of Mr.

Rickman, the only writer who has attempted to give a clear and practical account of this beautiful, though neglected style. He distinguishes three variations, which may, without impropriety, be called the *orders* of Gothic architecture; differing, however, from the Greek and Roman orders in this particular circumstance, that while those are confined to one part of a building, or, at most, affect the rest only in regard to strength or delicacy, these extend through every part of the edifice. The first style, denominated by Mr. Rickman "Early English," commenced with the reign of Richard I., in 1189, and was superseded by the next, in 1307, the end of the reign of Edward I. It is principally distinguished by long, narrow windows, and bold ornaments and mouldings. The window, being so essential a mark of the style, claims to be considered in the first place.

The early English window is invariably long and narrow; its head is generally the lancet, or highly-pointed arch, but it is sometimes formed by a trefoil. In large buildings there are generally found two or more of these combined, with their drip-stones united. Three is the usual number, but sometimes four, five, seven, and, in one instance, — the east end of Lincoln cathedral, — eight are employed. When combined, there is usually a quatrefoil between the heads, and where there are many the whole is sometimes covered by a segmental pointed drip-stone, to which form the windows are adapted, by the centre one's being raised higher than the rest, which are gradually lowered on each side to the extremity. Sometimes, in late buildings, two windows have a pierced quatrefoil between them, and are covered by a simple pointed arch as a drip-stone; thus approaching so nearly the next style as not to be easily distinguished from it. This arrangement may be seen in the nave of Westminster Abbey. In large buildings, the windows are frequently decorated with slender shafts, which are usually insulated, and connected by bands with the wall. A fine example of this may be seen at the Temple Church, London, one of the purest buildings existing of this style.

The circular, rose, or catharine-wheel window is frequently found in large buildings of this style; in which, however, it did not originate, being found in Norman edifices. It appears to have received much attention from the architects of this period, being worked with great care.

The doors of this style are distinguished by their deep recess; columns usually insulated in a deep hollow, and a simple pointed arch, nearly equilateral in the interior mouldings, but in the exterior, from the depth of the door, approaching the semi-circle. They are also frequently ornamented by a kind of four-leaved flower placed in a hollow. In large buildings they are often divided by one or more shafts (clustered) in the centre, with one of the circular ornaments above.

To the steeples of this period were added, in many instances, spires, many of which are finely proportioned, and form a very characteristic and elegant finish to the buildings they accompany. They have usually ribs at the angles, which are sometimes crocketed; and in some instances they are still further enriched with bands of quatrefoils round the spire. The towers are usually guarded at the angles by buttresses, but octagonal turrets are sometimes met with, surmounted by pinnacles of the same plan. In small churches, the slope of the spire sometimes projects over the wall of the tower, which is finished by a cornice, and the diagonal sides of the spire, generally octagonal, are sloped down to the angles.

The arches of this style are chiefly distinguished by very numerous, though, for their size, bold mouldings, with hollows of corresponding depth. The lancet arch is chiefly used, though many are found much more obtuse. The form of the arch indeed, as Mr. Rickman observes, is by no means a criterion for the dimensions of the styles, each form being met with in buildings of each style, except the four-centred.

The piers are distinguished from those of the other styles, by being surrounded with bands which sometimes are confined to the shafts, and sometimes are continued on the pier. The capital is usually composed by plain bold mouldings, one of which is shown in the plate 41, figs. 4, 7, where is also delineated a base of this style; figs. 6, 9. The plan of these piers is shown in figs. 2, 5, of the same plate; the shaded part representing a section of the shaft, and the outline, a section of the base. A beautiful variation from Salisbury cathedral is seen in fig. 8.

The buttresses of this style are chiefly distinguished by their simplicity, having very few setts-off, and very rarely any ornament in their places. Frequently, indeed, as in Wells cathedral, a very early example of this style, they retain the Norman form, of very broad faces with slight projections, with a shaft inserted in the angles, and are continued no higher than the cornice. The flying buttress was not used till late in this style. The ornamental parts of the style now remain to be considered, which, till near its conclusion, were but sparingly used, and those, for the most part, of a very rude description. In the west front of Wells and Peterborough cathedrals may be seen specimens of the taste of the period in these particulars, which are wholly unworthy of imitation; but in the interior of Salisbury are many details, late in the style, which are very elegant, and will bear the most minute examination. It may be sufficient to mention, that in all the ornamental and minute details during this period, as well as in more important parts, the boldness and contempt of refinement, which are infallible marks of an early age, are very apparent; for which reason we shall defer the description of many ornamental details, which, nevertheless, were practised, and with success, in the latter part of this period, till the next style in which they were brought to perfection.

There is, however, one ornament peculiar to this style which it is necessary to notice, before we proceed further. It resembles a low pyramid, the sides of which are pierced in the form of curvilinear triangles, bending inwards. It is usually placed upon a hollow moulding, from which it is sometimes detached, except at the angles. It has, as yet, received no regular appellation, on account of its being so unlike any other object as to be described, or even delineated, with difficulty, and we believe it must be seen to be accurately comprehended. The only attempt at designation it has received is, the *toothed ornament.* The reason for applying such a name to it we leave for the ingenuity of the reader to discover.

The Early English style of Gothic architecture may, we think, without impropriety, be compared to the Doric order of the Greeks. Like that, it is the first attempt of a people emerging from barbarism; and, like that, it possesses all those qualities which it is natural to expect from such a state of society. Strength and simplicity are its predominating characteristics; ornament, except the more bold and artless, is foreign to its nature, and can never be introduced with propriety. For this reason, it may be employed with great advantage in churches, where the saving of expense is an object; as a finer effect may be produced by the use of this style than of any other whatever for equal expense. Of the fitness of Gothic architecture for ecclesiastical edifices, we presume it is now needless to say much. The circumstance of its having had its origin in Christian worship, and its consequent adaptation to its ceremonies, its fitness for the climate, and its devotional effect upon people in general, seem to point it out as peculiarly appropriate for this service.

In exterior effect Gothic architecture is very defective, and never more so than in this style. We have, indeed, scarcely one front which is at all reconcilable with good taste. That of Salisbury cathedral is generally admired, but we can see no reason for the preference. A consciousness of this defect of the style led the architect of that of Peterborough cathedral to make use of a singular expedient. Three ponderous arches, supported by triangular piers, receive the weight of three gables, and at each lateral extremity is a square turret, containing a staircase and surmounted by a spire, such as has already been described. The effect of the composition is grand, but it is not worthy of imitation. A field is thus offered for the exercise of modern invention, which, as this kind of architecture is better understood, it is hoped will not be neglected; much has been done, but something, we conceive, remains to be done, to render it a worthy and formidable competitor with the long-practised and deeply-studied architecture of Greece and Rome.

The Decorated English Style.

The style next in order to the Early English is denominated by Mr. Rickman *Decorated English*, as possessing a greater degree of delicacy than the former, without the excessive detail of the style which succeeded it. It ceased to be used soon after the death of Edward III., which happened in 1307. Its prominent feature is also found in its windows, with which, therefore, we shall commence our description.

The windows of this style are distinguished from those of the last by being larger, and divided into lights by slender upright stones, called mullions. Of decorated windows there are two descriptions. 1. Where the mullions branch out into geometrical figures, and are all of equal size and shape, and, — 2. Where they are dispersed through the head in curves in various descriptions, which is called flowing tracery, and are usually in windows of more than three lights, of different size and shape, the principal mullions forming simple figures, subdivided by the inferior ones. Sometimes the principal mullions are faced by slender shafts, with bases and capitals. The first description is considered the oldest; the principal example which contains this kind of window is Exeter cathedral, where they are very large, and nearly all composed of this kind of tracery. The flowing tracery, which composes the greater number of windows of this style, will be better understood by reference to the plate than by any description we could give; a small one is delineated at plate 42, fig. 1, of which the form is copied from one at Sleaford church, Lincolnshire. A specimen of the application of the same feature to larger windows may be seen in the view, in which the small one forms part of the composition. The architraves are commonly enriched by mouldings, which sometimes assume the form of columns, and the windows in composition frequently reach from pier to pier. The form of the arch is seldom more acute than that described on the equilateral triangle, and it is generally more obtuse. The richness of these windows invariably depends upon their size, the distance between the mullions being nearly the same in all; the largest, however, do not consist of more than nine lights. The drip-stone is, in this style, improved into an elegant canopy, the form of which is sometimes pedimental, and sometimes an ogee arch. It is decorated with *crockets* and a *finial*, and the space enclosed by it, and the exterior contour of the arch, is sometimes filled with tracery. The great west window of York cathedral, one of the finest in Great Britain, has a triangular one. The circular window was also brought to perfection in this style. A fine example in form, though not in detail, is now all that remains of the ancient palace of the Bishops of Winchester in Bankside, Southwark. This is of the geometrical description; one of the finest of flowing tracery is in the south transept of Lincoln cathedral.

The doors of this style are not so distinct as the windows from those of the former period; double doors are not so frequent, and the shafts are not detached from the mouldings, as in the Early English. In small doors there is frequently no column, but the mouldings of the arch are carried down the sides without interruption; there is frequently no base moulding, but a plain sloped face to receive the architrave. They are surmounted by the same sort of canopies as the windows.

The steeples of this period are distinguished from those of the last in little more than their windows, and a few unimportant details. The north-west spire of Peterborough cathedral, before described, decidedly belongs to it, though the tower beneath is Early English. The tower and spire of Newark church, Lincolnshire, are pointed out by Mr. Rickman as a peculiarly fine example.

The groining of the ceiling will be understood by referring to plate 41, where the groinings are seen springing from upper part of the caps, figs. 4 and 7. Fig 4 is the groining of the nave of York cathedral, the purest example of equal richness.

Most frequently, however, the nicely-decorated ribs are omitted, and the rib from pier to pier, with the cross springers, and the longitudinal and transverse ribs only are employed. At the intersection of these, bosses, or sculptured ribs, are almost invariably placed. The aisle-roofs are very rarely enriched with superfluous ribs, but those of Redcliff church, Bristol, are elegant exceptions.

Of arches little can be said. Of their forms it may be sufficient to observe, that the lancet arch is rarely to be met with; the Tudor never, but in one instance, — the nave of Westminster cathedral, — built, or rather cased, by the celebrated William of Wyckham; and it is here necessarily adopted on account of the form of the Norman arch it was employed to conceal. The mouldings are in general less numerous, and, consequently, less bold than those of the preceding style. In small works the ogee arch is frequently found, and decorated with crockets and a finial. One of these is shown in plate 42, fig. 2.

The piers of this style are, for the most part, square in their general form, and placed diagonally; two variations of these are shown in the plate 41, figs. 6, 9. That marked 3 is from Exeter cathedral, and 6, from the nave of that of York; both are pure and beautiful examples. The shafts are sometimes filleted; that is, a square and narrow face is continued vertically along its surface, projecting slightly from it. The capitals are frequently enriched with foliage, and the bases, in many instances, consist of reversed ogees, with square faces of various projections, and sometimes other mouldings. Decorated English buttresses are distinguished from those of the last style, which are most applicable to it, only by their greater richness, in buildings where decorations are not spared; and, consequently, in others they are perhaps the least characteristic parts of the composition. They are, however, usually finished by pinnacles, which are generally distinguished from those of the former style. The flying buttress is almost invariably used, and also surmounted by a pinnacle, which usually corresponds with the lower one. The buttresses of the aisles of Exeter cathedral are remarkable for being detached from the wall, the only support they afford to which is by the arches which connect them with it at the top.

The parapets of this style are sometimes horizontal, and sometimes embattled, each of which is frequently pierced in the form of cinquefoil headed arches, quatrefoils and triangles. Sunk panels are, however, more common. When plain embattled parapets are employed, the crowning mouldings are usually continued horizontally only, the face towards the opening being merely a vertical section.

As many of the ornamental parts of Gothic architecture were brought to perfection during this period, they cannot be better introduced than in this place. Among these, the use of crockets is a prominent feature; these are small bunches of foliage running up the side of the *gablet*, afterwards improved into the ogee canopy over doors, windows, and ornamental arches, and finished by a combination of two or more, called *finial*, which is separated from the rest by a small moulding. They are also used to decorate the angles of pinnacles. The upper part of a canopy of this description is shown in plate 42, fig. 2, from which these ornaments will be better understood than from any description. Another peculiarity of Gothic architecture is the *feathering* of windows, screen work, ornamental arches, panels, and sometimes doors. It is called trefoil, quatrefoil, or cinquefoil, according to the number of segments of circles, which are called cusps, of which it is composed. The method of drawing it may be seen from the window in the plate. A very beautiful door, thus ornamented, still exists in St. Stephen's chapel, Westminster, now the House of Commons.

Although the grotesque is the prevailing character of the sculpture employed in the decoration of Gothic architecture, many small ornaments are found, particularly in this style, designed with taste, and executed with the utmost delicacy. They are copied from the beautiful though humble flowers of the field, and are, in many instances, local.

We have compared the former style to the Doric of the Greeks, and the present may, with less propriety, be likened to the Ionic of the same people. Boldness and simplicity characterize the first; elegance and delicacy, the second. In both Greek and Gothic orders, ornament to profusion is allowable; yet in neither does it interfere with the composition, and may be entirely omitted. From this circumstance arises a universal applicability, belonging only to the far-famed *happy medium*, so often talked of, so seldom attained. In grandeur of composition, simplicity of arrangement, elegance of form, and *perfection* of capability, this style is, therefore, unrivalled, and may be used with advantage for every purpose of civil architecture. It is, however, peculiarly adapted for all churches whose size and situation render them of importance; and in such large buildings, where Gothic architecture may be thought desirable, as are of sufficient consequence to allow the architect to think of delicacy in the design of his details.

The Perpendicular Style.

The last of the grand divisions of Gothic architecture is the *Perpendicular* Style, introduced as the preceding fell into disuse, and finally overwhelmed by its own superfluity of decoration and uncompromising minuteness. It was not wholly lost sight of before the reign of James I., but few buildings were then erected without a mixture of Italian work.

The Perpendicular Style, like the others, is most readily distinguished by its windows, whence it also derives its appellation; the mullions of which, instead of being finished in flowing lines, or geometrical figures, are carried perpendicularly into the head. They are further distinguished by a *transom*, or cross-mullion, to break the height, under which is usually a feathered arch, and sometimes it is ornamented above by small battlements. The architraves of windows in this style have seldom shafts or mouldings, as in the former, but are worked plain, and, frequently, with a large hollow. Although these windows do not admit of any great variety in the disposition of the tracery, they are far more numerous than those of either of the other styles; few specimens of which remain that do not bear marks in their windows of the rage for alterations which appears to have prevailed during this period.

The doors of this style are remarkably varied from those of the preceding ones, by the arch's being finished by a horizontal moulding, which is continued down to the springing of the arch, and then shortly returned. This is called a *label.* The space enclosed by it and the exterior line of the arch is called the *spandrel*, which is commonly filled with a circle enclosing a quatrefoil and other circular ornaments.

The steeples of this style are, for the most part, extremely rich; spires are seldom met with, but lanterns are frequently used. A *lantern* is a turret placed above a building, and pierced with windows, so as to admit light into the space below. This is sometimes placed on the top of a tower, as at Boston, and supported with flying buttresses springing from it, and sometimes constitutes the tower itself, as at York, Peterborough, and Ely cathedrals, where it is placed at the intersection of the cross, and has a very fine effect. The exterior angles are frequently concealed by octagonal turrets containing staircases, but are usually strengthened by buttresses, either double or diagonal. A most beautiful finish for a steeple is found in that of the Church of Newcastle-upon-Tyne; where a small, square tower, each side of which is nearly occupied by a window, surmounted by a spire, is wholly supported by arch buttresses, springing from the pinnacle of the great tower. This is copied by Sir Christopher Wren, in the Church of St. Dunstan's in the East; which, though in workmanship and detail it is far inferior to the original, excels it in the proportion it bears to the rest of the composition.

Groining, in perpendicular work, assumes a new and more delicate character. A number of small ribs, diverging from a centre, are carried up in the form of one side of a pointed arch, and terminated equidistantly from that centre by a semi-circle.

As they recede from the point they are divided by smaller ribs or mullions, and these again are subdivided, according to the size of the roof, so as to make all the panels of nearly equal size. These panels are ornamented with feathered arches, &c., in the same manner as the windows, in conformity to which the whole is designed. The intervals between these semi circles are filled with tracery of the same description. This kind of roof is called *fan tracery;* it is exquisitely beautiful, and almost the only kind of groining used in this style, Another description of roof must now be mentioned, of very different character; this is the timber roof, of which Westminster Hall presents so magnificent an example. Here the actual timbers of the roof are so arranged as to form an architectural combination of great beauty; a wooden arch springs from each side of the building, supporting a pointed central one, finished downwards with pendants. The rest of the framing is filled with pierced panelling. This kind of roof is not found in churches; but it seems well adapted for large halls for public business, or any place intended for the occasional reception of large meetings.

The *arch,* in late perpendicular work, is generally low in proportion to its breadth, and is described from centres; this is called the Tudor arch, from its having been principally in use under the reign of two princes of that family. Besides this distinction in the form of the arch, there is an important one in the arrangement of the mouldings, which are carried down the architrave without being broken by a capital; and sometimes there is one shaft with the capital, and the others without.

The *piers* are remarkable for their depth in proportion to their width; frequently there is a flat face of considerable breadth in the inside of the arch, and a shaft in front running up to support the groining. The capitals, when there are any, are generally composed with plain mouldings; but there is sometimes a four-leaved square flower placed in the hollow.

The *buttresses* and *pinnacles* contain little remarkable, and are only distinguished from those of the last style by their extraneous ornaments, if they have any; the buttresses are sometimes panelled, and in some very late specimens the pinnacles are in the form of domes, of which the contour is an ogee arch.

The *parapets* of this style are generally embattled and pierced; they are worked with great delicacy, in the form of quatrefoil circles, &c.

The *ornament* of the Perpendicular Style is well characterized by the name, many buildings being, as Mr. Rickman observes, nothing but a series of vertical panelling. "For example," says he, "King's College chapel is all panel, except the floor; for the doors and windows are nothing but pierced panels, included in the general design; and the very roof is a series of them in different shapes." Monotony is inseparable from such an arrangement; grandeur is incompatible with it, and the appearance of it is a certain prognostic of decline in whatever is marked by its introduction. A beautiful small ornament, peculiar to this style, is the Tudor flower, which is a series of square flowers placed diagonally, and frequently attached, connected at the bottom by semi-circles; the lower interstices are filled with some smaller ornament. This is principally employed as a finish to cornices in ornamental work.

With whatever justice the preceding styles have been compared with the Doric and Ionic orders of Grecian architecture, the comparison does not hold between the present and the Corinthian. The former is a necessary gradation in the art, and is applicable to compositions of any size. The latter is not necessary, and is unpleasing, except in small works. The change from the graceful forms of the decorated windows to inelegant, artless, straight lines; the alteration in the form of the arch, which is a deviation from one of the leading principles of Gothic architecture; and, above all, that inordinate passion for ornament and minutiæ, which, like excessive refinement in other matters, is a certain mark of the decay of true taste; in short, almost every peculiarity in this style indicates approaching dissolution. These circumstances, however, which render the perpendicular style so objectionable for large buildings, make it peculiarly appropriate for small and confined parts of a building, such as chapels and domestic apartments, when Gothic architecture is preferred. For the latter purpose, we fear, indeed, it is ill adapted in any shape; all its peculiarities seem to point at magnificence and imposing effect, with which magnitude is inseparably connected, as their ultimate objects and the most proper field for their display; and with these qualities it is well known domestic comfort has little in common. The confined space in which the latter can alone be enjoyed is ill reconcilable with the interminable vistas and lofty proportions by many considered as the perfection of the former, It is, however, not only proper, but necessary, in some cases, to employ the Gothic in the decoration of apartments, and where this happens this style is decidedly preferable.

It has been truly observed by an ingenious writer on the subject of English architecture, that it can in no case be advantageously blended with the Grecian, differing, as it does, so essentially in its component parts. The Grecian style is designated by horizontal lines supported on columns, and by the entablature and its component parts; while the Gothic is dependent on perpendicular lines, and arches variously decorated, for the leading feature in its composition, as may plainly appear by consulting the best Grecian examples, and comparing them with the Decorated English, justly bearing the appellation here given by that able writer on this subject, Mr. Rickman.

Architecture of America.

The architecture of our country is at present in a very undefined, we may almost say in a chaotic state, though it has, since the commencement of the nineteenth century, undergone much improvement. It is now but about two hundred years—not so long as many of the finest specimens of European architecture have been standing—since a band of Pilgrims, driven by persecution from their native country, landed upon these western shores, and found a vast expanse of wilderness, stretching from one ocean to the other in breadth, and in length almost from the northern to the southern pole. Our country was then literally the *new world.* It was in a perfect state of nature ; and art had left scarcely a foot-print on its soil. The savage, with barely skill enough to shape his rude bow, to break the flint to a point for his arrow-head, and to peel the bark from the forest-trees for his hut, was its only inhabitant. And those men, who, for freedom of opinion, had fled from civilized Europe, landed here in the commencement of a severe winter, bringing with them but few recollections which could endear them to the things they had left. The hardships and persecutions they had so long endured had chastened their spirits, and imbued them with a formal stiffness and austerity, which manifested itself in all their works, and in nothing more than in the simple severity of their architecture. They appear to have been desirous of entirely obliterating the memory of the magnificent churches and pompous ceremonials attendant on the worship of their oppressors ; and, in the meeting-house of the Puritans, we see not this division of nave, transept and choir ; chancel and altar are lost, as well as the clustering columns and intersecting arches, which seem as if

> "Some fairy's hand
> 'Twixt poplars straight the ozier wand
> In many a prankish knot had twined;
> Then framed a spell when the work was done,
> And changed the willow wreaths to stone."

Those beauties of England's Gothic churches, as well as the more chaste and simple, and yet more enduring elegance of the Grecian temples, were never copied by them. And there were other reasons why the beauties of ornamental architecture have, in our country, been so long neglected. The landing of the Puritans on our shores made an era in the annals of the world, a luminous point in the path of civilization, whence we may date the commencement of an *age;* and the spirit of this new age is an enterprising spirit. Men leave their homes, plunge into the dense forest, find a stream whose banks, perhaps, the foot of a white man never before trod, erect a mill whose plashing wheel and whizzing saws soon tell that the forester's axe has found work abroad; and the mill, in turn, makes busy the echoing hammer, which now reigns throughout the village, from early morn to dewy eve; and, in a few days, we may say, a mimic city has arisen, where no dwelling but the Indian hut was ever before seen. True, it is a city of shingle palaces, erected to endure but for a generation. But the spirit of the age is locomotive. The people of this age are a transient people, flitting from place to place; and each builds a hut for *himself*, not for his successors. Railways and canals are fast spanning the continent. Our sons and daughters live abroad, and look out for rapid vehicles rather than abiding dwelling-places. Naught is here heard of those immense fortunes which have been accumulating for centuries in one family, and which, invested in massive castles or gorgeous palaces, with park and forest, have descended, entailed, from generation to generation, and been renewed, added to, and beautified, by each successive occupant. Fortunes are here, as it were, made and lost in a day; and funds invested in real property, though safe, are slowest in turning. Indeed, building has never been a favorite mode with our people for investment; and domestic architecture has, therefore, suffered much. But it is already beginning to improve, as many chaste and beautiful specimens in our immediate neighborhood testify. This spirit of improvement, however, is principally manifested in the designs and materials of our public buildings; among which we have many that might challenge the admiration of the European connoisseur. We want not now for models to be found in our own country of the purest Grecian, or the more beautiful *Gothic;* and surely we want not for materials. Among our public buildings, the Capitol at Washington is deserving of notice. Simple and elegant in its interior, its exterior is beautiful and imposing.

The domes over the wings rise with an elegant and graceful curve, and may be considered almost perfect specimens of that most difficult branch of ornamental architecture. Were the same graceful elevation given to the centre dome, it would add much to the beauty of the building. In Philadelphia we have the United States Bank, a faultless specimen of the pure Doric; classic, chaste, and simple in its proportions, it is a building of which we may well be proud. Philadelphia may also boast of her Exchange, and the Mint; both of which, built of white marble, in a style to suit the material, have a very imposing appearance.

The Girard College, at Philadelphia, is a magnificent specimen of the Corinthian order. The Custom House, at New York, built of white marble in the Grecian style, is the finest building in the city; and the new building for the University is a beautiful specimen of the Gothic style. In Boston we have many beautiful buildings, but few of pure architecture. Trinity Church, in Summer-street, is built of rough granite in the Gothic style. The front is beautiful, massive and imposing in its appearance, but the sides belong to an age of the Gothic different from the front; the interior excels that of any other church in our city in beauty; the walls painted in fresco, the graceful and well-proportioned clusters of pillars, the oaken wood-work, and the ornamented chancel, give it a magnificent appearance. But the central arch of the roof is altogether out of proportion, and, if constructed of any heavy material, could not support its own weight; it certainly adds no beauty, but rather takes from that of the other portions. The new building for the Library, and the Unitarian Church, at Cambridge, are among our best specimens of Gothic architecture, and we can only wish the church had been built of more durable materials. We have many graceful and elegant spires, both upon our city churches and those in our vicinity. That of the Federal-street Church, which is built in the Gothic style, is a model much to be admired. Among our specimens of Doric worthy of mention, are the new Custom House, the United States Branch Bank, the

Hospital at Rainsford Island, the Washington Bank, and Quincy Market, a plain but noble structure of hewn granite, about five hundred feet in length, constructed by, and an honor to, our city. The Stone Chapel, at the corner of School and Tremont streets, is our oldest specimen of the Ionic order. We have also, of the same order, St. Paul's Church, the Suffolk Bank, and Tremont Temple. The facade of the Temple is chaste and dignified. The front of Central Church, in Winter-street, and the rotunda of the Merchants' Exchange, are of the Corinthian style.

We have already trespassed on the limits usually assigned to a preface, but we hope not unnecessarily so. Want of space prevents our saying as much on *domestic* architecture as we would wish, in this part of the volume. But that is a branch of the art which is yet in its infancy among us, and a part upon which, if we should only write a page or two here, the little contained in that page or two would only serve to show the need of more.

We would only suggest, that, in constructing a dwelling-house, the convenience and comfort of the interior should ever receive more attention than the exterior elegance and symmetry; and that the beauty of a private house consists not so much in the nearness of its resemblance to a Grecian temple, a Chinese pagoda, or a Gothic church, as in its fitness for the purpose for which it is designed. It is necessary, above all things, to remember that houses are made to live in, and the convenience of their inmates is the first thing to be considered; after that, ornament may be added.

It has been our design, in preparing this work for the press, to add the little in our power towards establishing a pure and correct taste in our domestic architecture; and, if we have succeeded in that, we shall consider ourselves more than repaid, in the sense that we have done our duty in paying the debt which every man owes to his profession.

PART III.

THE ARRANGEMENT AND CONSTRUCTION OF DWELLING-HOUSES AND BUILDINGS IN GENERAL.

We now offer a few remarks on Domestic Architecture.

With respect to the situation of a house, where choice is allowed, it is obvious that the most desirable must be that which combines the advantages of pure air, and protection from cold winds, with a plentiful supply of water, convenient access, &c. As these observations, however, must present themselves to every one, we shall not here dwell upon them, but proceed to consider those essential parts of a house, *rooms*. And, first, their effect upon the exterior figure of a house.

The form which gives the largest area with the least circumference is evidently a circle; but this figure, when divided into apartments, is very inconvenient, from the numerous acute angles and broken curves which must necessarily compose them. Nearly the same objections apply to the triangle, which has the further disadvantage of occupying a smaller area with respect to its circumference than any other figure. Rectangular forms, therefore, are best adapted for houses in general; since, within them, the divisions of apartments may be made with the greatest regularity and least waste. As rectangles are most readily divided into rectangles, this is also the figure which may be employed to the greatest advantage in the rooms themselves. As to the proportions of these, the length may range from one to one and a half breadth. If larger than this, the room partakes too much of the gallery form. The usual rule for the height of a room is, if it be oblong, to make it as high as it is broad; and if square, from four-fifths to five-sixths of the side is a good proportion. With regard to health, however, no room should be less than ten feet in height. It is obvious, that on a floor where there are many rooms, they must be of various sizes, and to regulate them all by architectural rules would be productive of much inconvenience. As, therefore, the apparent height of a flat ceiled room is greater than that of a coved one of equal altitude, it is usual, in these cases, to make the larger rooms with flat ceilings, and the smaller ones with coved or domes. Apartments of state of unusual size may occupy two stories.

With regard to the decoration of ceilings, a great diversity of taste exists. At one period, no ceiling was thought to be sufficiently ornamented unless it was covered with paintings, chiefly representing allegorical subjects. This taste was carried to a great excess, and was the subject of much ridicule. Of late years, ornament of any description has been thought superfluous, and the ceiling has been usually left completely bare. This is, however, giving way to the geometrical decorations prevalent during the middle and latter part of the last century, which certainly give an enriched effect to a room, and possess this advantage over every other method of decoration, that they are capable of any degree of simplicity or richness, both in form and detail, according to the size of the apartment, or quantity of decoration in it. For rooms which are small, and the ceiling consequently near the eye, these ornaments should be delicately worked; but in those of larger size they require to be bolder. The angles formed by the ceiling and walls are concealed by cornices, the enrichment of which will of course depend upon the delicacy or simplicity observed in the embellishments of the room.

Doors.

The proportion for doors is somewhat over twice the breadth in height, as three and seven feet. Entrance doors, three, four and seven feet. In case of larger doors, for folding or sliding in partitions, or those for public houses, they should vary according to the height of stories, where they are required not to exceed twelve feet in width.

Doors for apartments should be as near the centre of partitions as convenient. For a suite of rooms, the doors should be nearly opposite; but in no case should they be placed near the fireplace, or so as to open opposite the bed, excepting those which connect the dressing-room with the bed-chamber.

The usual method of ornamenting doors is to finish the two sides and top with architraves, or fancy pilasters — corner block at the upper angles — or an entablature, frieze, and cornice; outside ones with pilasters, or attached columns, entablature, and cornice.

Windows.

It is obvious that, in arranging the windows of an apartment, it will first be necessary to decide on the quantity of light required to be admitted. Sir William Chambers observes that in the course of his own practice he has generally added the depth and height of rooms on the principal floors together, and taken one-eighth part thereof for the width of the window.

The height of the aperture in the principal floor should not much exceed double the width. In the other stories, they are necessarily lower in proportion, the width containing the same. The windows in modern houses are frequently brought down to the floor, in imitation of the French; but where this is not the case, the sills should be from two feet four to two feet six inches from the floor. The windows of the principal floor are generally the most enriched, and the usual manner of decorating them is by an architrave, surrounding them with a frieze and cornice, and sometimes a pediment. When they are required to be more simple, the frieze and cornice are omitted. In a front, the pediments are, for the sake of variety, often made triangular, and curved alternately, as in the banqueting-house at Whitehall.

When windows are required to be very broad in proportion to their height, the Venetian window is frequently employed, which consists of three contiguous apertures, the centre one being arched. The usual mode of executing this is by dividing the apertures by columns, and placing corresponding ones at the extremities of the opening; the side apertures are covered by an entablature, and the centre by a semi-circular architrave, of which the entablature forms the impost. In modern times, they are finished without columns and impost moulding, or arch, but have a straight cap; the centre, three lights wide, and one on each extremity.

Chimney-Pieces.

The necessary remarks on chimneys, as a part of *building*, will be more properly introduced in another place; we have here only to consider them as parts of a room and its decoration.

With respect to the situation of chimney-pieces, we have already mentioned that they should be sufficiently removed from the door. Sir William Chambers further advises that they should be "so situated as to be immediately seen by those who enter, that they may not have the persons already in the room, who are seated generally about the fire, to search for." Whether the worthy knight had experienced personal inconvenience from a maldisposition in this respect, we cannot tell, but do not conceive it to be an evil of the first magnitude.

The standard proportion of the chimney-piece is a square; in larger rooms somewhat lower, and in smaller, a little higher; its size will, of course, depend on the quantity of space to be heated, but the width of the aperture should not be less than three feet, nor more than five feet six inches. When the size of the apartment is considerable, it is better to make two fireplaces.

In the decoration of chimney-pieces, the utmost wildness of fancy has been indulged, but it is certainly proper to regulate their ornaments by the style of the building to which they belong. Those in which the Roman style predominates are designated much in the same manner as the windows, except where magnificence is attempted, in which case caryatides, termini, &c., are employed. In modern taste little is done by way of decoration; their richness consists principally of beautiful specimens of variegated marble columns or pilasters, and entablature.

Stairs.

"Staircases," says Palladio, "will be commendable if they are clear, ample, and commodious to ascend, inviting people, as it were, to go up. They will be clear, if they have a bright and equally diffused light; they will be sufficiently ample, if they do not seem scanty, and narrow, to the size and quality of the fabric, but they should never be less than three feet in width, that two persons may pass each other; they will be convenient in respect to the whole building, if the arches under them can be used for domestic purposes; and, with respect to persons, if their ascent is not too steep and difficult, to avoid which, the steps in breadth should be nearly once and a half the height of the rise." In modern dwellings the number of the steps depends on the height of the story they are intended to ascend, as galleries of less height are omitted for convenience of room and style of composition.

The rise should not exceed eight inches, nor be less than six inches in height; their top surfaces are sometimes inclined, for greater ease in ascending. The ancients were accustomed to make the number of steps of an odd number, that they might arrive at the top with the same foot that they began the ascent with; this arose from a superstitious idea of devotion in entering their temples. Palladio directs that the number of steps should not exceed thirteen before arriving at a resting-place; the present number of steps in flights is between thirteen and nineteen.

Staircases are either rectilinear or curvilinear in their forms; the former are most usual in dwelling-houses, as being more simple, and, in general, executed with less waste of material; but the latter, which may be either circular or elliptical, admit of greater beauty, if large, and greater conveniency, if small. Small staircases of this description are generally circular, and have a column, called a newel, in the middle; they are constructed with great simplicity, the newel being composed of one end of the successive steps, while the other rests in the wall. They are found in all our country churches. When ornament is studied, the steps may be made curved, which has a very pleasing effect. Modern staircases are finished with a newel at the foot of the first step, from six to eight inches diameter, richly carved. Where ample room is allowed, it is usual to put on a curtail step and scroll-rail, supported with an iron newel, and up the rail are several iron balusters to secure the same. In large designs, however, the elliptical is generally preferred, and is capable of very grand effect, which Sir William Chambers has sufficiently shown in one of the staircases at Somerset Place (that belonging to the Royal Society, and Society of Antiquaries), which, without any superfluous decoration, is a design of uncommon magnificence, and excelled by few of the kind. The newel being of a very unpleasing form in this kind of staircase, is an objection to its use where it is of a small size.

Those staircases which are open in the centre are generally lighted from the top, but where this is impracticable the light is admitted by windows in the most advantageous position the situation will allow.

Grecian Doric.

PLATES.

I have here made use of the Grecian example, given by Vitruvius, from the temple of Minerva, on the Acropolis at Athens, built under the administration of Pericles, the representation of which is found in

Plate 1.

Fig. 1. The proportional figures from the scale of the column. Divide the lower end into two equal parts; each is called a *module;* divide the module into thirty parts, which are called minutes as figured on the order; under the column *H* is the height of each member, and under the column *P* their projections from a line drawn perpendicular through the centre of this column, the entire height of the order.

Fig. 2. The scale of diameter.

Fig. 3. The lower part of the same.

Fig. 4. The whole height of the order; the letters on the same are references to the introduction.

Plate 2.

Fig. 1. A section of the entablature showing the manner of finish and the form of the mouldings inside of the portico.

Fig. 2. A section of the column at both ends, with twenty flutes and the manner of striking them: divide the circumference into twenty equal parts; trace lines to the centre; with the dividers draw a line, for the circumference of the top, intersected by the radius *a*, *b;* extend the dividers from *c* to *d*, and for the circumference of the lower diameter, to *g;* and from *e*, describe the curve for the flute *e*, *f;* and, in like manner, for the upper diameter, as shown by *g*, *e*, *f*.

Fig. 3. Represents the planceir with the mutules, having three rows of pins, six in each row, which are said to have arisen from the idea of the ends of rafters forming the roof.

Fig. 4. The elevation of the triglyphs containing two whole and two half channels.

Fig. 5. Shows a section of the guttæ, or drops, that are formed under the triglyph, or under the fillet of the architrave.

Fig. 6. The capital of column; *a*, *b*, the annulets formed on the lower part of the ovolo.

Plate 3.

Fig. 1. Grecian antæ: the width, when connected with columns, is governed by the diameter at the end of the column; they both being equal, the projection of each will not materially differ; but, on the outside of buildings, the breadth may be fifty-five minutes; on the external angles of porticos, they may be twenty-seven and a half minutes each, and leaving twenty-four minutes between the shaft; this will have a very good effect in large works. The projections from the wall are one-fifth, and, when inserted disconnected with columns, one-fourth to one-half may be the projections; when the composition is purely classical, one-half will be in the best taste.

Fig. 2. The projection from the wall one-fifth.

Fig. 5. The proportion of the capital, as figured for practical use.

Fig. 3. The mensuration of another cap.

Fig. 4. The projection from the wall.

Fig. 6. The proportion of the cap, as figured at large.

PLATE 4.

Fig. 1. Grecian frontispiece for outside doors, caps of pilasters, from plate 3, fig. 6.

Fig. 2. A vertical section showing the return of pilaster, panel, projection of imposts, doors, &c.: *b*, the threshold; *a*, *a*, *a*, steps, &c.; *j*, the return of pilasters; *c*, the panel and recess; *d*, the ceiling and the recess, with moulded panel; *p*, the architrave and width of soffit; *f*, the frieze of entablature; *g*, the portion, backing up from stone-work, shown by dotted lines; *e*, the floor timber, fastened by timber-clasps.

PLATE 5.

Fig. 1. The elevation of interior door. This style of inside doors, although very plain, is much admired on account of the smooth surface for paint, the durability, and the ease with which it is kept clean; thereby rendering it one principal reason for adopting it for common use. Drawn one inch to a foot; *H*, the architrave, with quatrefoil rosette let into the middle angle three-eighths of an inch; *I*, the style; *J*, the panel; *K*, the munnion; *N*, *N*, the plinth.

Fig. 2. Horizontal section: *a*, *a*, the jambs; *b*, *b*, the blocking-space; *c*, *c*, the back jamb; *d*, *d*, furring.

Fig. 3. The vertical section, full thickness: *M*, the rail; *L*, the panel.

PLATE 6.

Fig. 1. A horizontal section of one of the jambs, full size: *C*, *C*, the jamb and stop; *D*, *D*, the grounds; *E*, *E*, the lath and plastering; *F*, *F*, the architrave; *G*, the door.

PLATE 7.

Fig. 1 is a horizontal section of a window-frame, designed for a frame-house, with board and sheathed walls, the outside casing flush, the blinds shut flush with the casing; and, when painted a stone-color, has a very pleasing effect for a Doric house, and, at a little distance, resembles stone in color, as well as in the style of finish. *A*, the pulley-style; *B*, rough boarding; *C*, outside casing; *D*, stud; *E*, parting-slip; *F*, parting-bead; *G*, sash and blind-stop; *H*, sash-bead; *I*, inside casing; *J*, back lining; *K*, furring; *L*, shutter-stop; *M*, lath and plastering; *N*, pilaster or architrave; *O*, *O*, shutters.

Fig. 2. A section of a window designed for brick or stone wall: *a*, brick wall; *b*, outside moulding; *c*, outside casings; *d*, pulley-style; *e*, parting-slip; *f*, parting-bead; *g*, sash-bead; *h*, box-casing; *i*, back-casing; *j*, furring; *k*, edge-casing; *l*, ground; *m*, lath and plastering; *n*, architrave.

Fig. 3. *a*, soffit-bed; *b*, top sash-rail; *c*, style; *d*, sash-bead; *e*, outside of box; *f*, wall moulding; *g*, *g*, meeting rails; *h*, bottom-rail; *i*, *i*, middle rails; *j*, wood sill; *k*, stone sill; *C*, back.

Plate 8.

Fig. 1. The elevation of a French window: *a, a, a, a,* sash-styles; *b, b,* top rails; *c, c,* bottom rails.

Fig. 2. Vertical section of one side, sills, &c.

Fig. 3. A portion of the style, full thickness: *a,* style; *b,* brass plate, the dotted semi-circle, the portion of wood hollowed out; *c,* the perforation through the plate to admit the pivot at the end of *d; d* is a circular drop extending the entire width of the fold, each end playing in a plate each side, the pin or pivot to play loosely, as the plate *d,* by opening or shutting, is moved over the sill; and, as the sash closes, the plate *d* drops in and rests on the bottom, and cuts off the pressure of wind and water; *e,* the rabbet.

Plate 9.

Fig. 1. A geometrical elevation of a Grecian Doric house, on a scale of fifteen feet to an inch, designed for a gentleman's residence, in our republican country. The site is on the summit of a gentle eminence, which gives to it a peculiarly picturesque view, and a free circulation of air.

Fig. 2. The first floor: *a,* the entrance hall; *b, b,* parlors, with slide-doors; *c,* sitting-room; *d,* china-room; *e,* dining-room; *f,* back staircase; *g,* principal staircase; *H, H,* chimneys; *I, I, I, I,* columns of portico. It is intended to have the kitchen, pantry, store-room, &c., under the dining-room; in such cases, it will be necessary to open an area on the outside, eight feet wide, the whole length of the back side, with steps down at each end, and a back entrance to the same.

SPECIFICATION.

The excavation should be sufficient to admit the passage of workmen both sides of the walls, and to secure an equal density of bottom, either by beetling, by inverted arches, or by driving piles; in most cases, the beetling *only* will be necessary, especially in a location like this.

FOUNDATION-WALLS.

The first course should be two and a half feet broad, and one foot deep, with stones as long as convenient; the other courses, rising to within four inches of the intended grading of the ground, may be one foot ten inches in thickness, and properly levelled, the inside faced to batter one inch.

UNDERPINNING.

Fine hammered granite, three feet eight inches in height, the thickness one foot ten inches, as follows:

Offset inside for floors, one and a half inch.

Thickness of wall, one foot.

Thickness of pilasters, six inches.

Outside wash, one and a half inch.

Top of underpinning projects one inch.

The wall of the building, on the area, should be fine hammered granite, one foot nine inches thick, with splays, or bevels, cut for window-shutters; this wall should be perpendicular, faced on both sides; the bank wall for the area, at least three feet thick at bottom, faced up inside to batter one inch, five feet in height, and topped with a fixed stone for iron work; to have one flight of hammered granite steps at each end of the area; at the upper back entrance of the house, a stone passage over the area six feet wide, with cast-iron fence each side, and five steps to descend to the lawn; buttresses for front door-steps, three feet six inches high, to project from underpinning five feet ten inches, being one foot eight inches thick; five steps, six and a half feet long, eight inches rise, and one foot two inches in width of steps; project from the underpinning of end wall of house eleven feet six inches; the buttresses at the ends of porticos, three feet two inches broad, three feet six inches high, eleven feet six inches long. Steps, thirty-six feet two inches long, eight inches rise, one foot two inches tread ; the floor of porticos of fine hammered granite ; if convenient, make the length and breadth in one stone, thirty-six feet two inches long, and eight feet wide ; or if not, divide the length into three equal parts. The walls of principal, second, and attic stories, of fine hammered granite stone facings, from four to six inches thick, in regular courses, sixteen inches wide, of proper length ; beds and bells hammered ; returns, quoins and ravines, lined or backed up with bricks, making the thickness one foot ; iron clamps inserted in each of the horizontal joints, once in three feet in length. For details of caps, entablature, cornice, &c., see plates for the same ; gutters, sheet copper ; battlements, stone. The roof is intended to be covered with galvanized iron or tin — either will answer a good purpose ; copper trunks on the inside of the walls ; chimneys laid up as per plan, plate 9, fig. 2 ; brick trimmers turned ; hearths all laid ; marble slabs for first and second stories ; marble tiles for the attic. Chimney-pieces for parlors, cost fifty dollars each ; for dining and sitting rooms, forty dollars each ; for chambers, twenty-five dollars each. Lay up brick partition walls in the cellar. Partitions of entrance-hall to rest on the same, piers and arches for chimneys ; lathing and plastering.

FRAMING.

First floor, plank, two by twelve inches. Trimmers, three by twelve inches ; floor plank, sixteen inches from centre to centre. Second floor, two by eleven inches ; the second and attic, distance as on the first floor ; frame partitions fitted for twelve-inch nailings. Studs, three by four inches ; proper trusses and door-jambs ; the roof framed with trusses to support covering ; joists not exceeding seven feet for the bearing ; the trusses to extend transversely across the building ; the centre ridge to rise four feet above the gutter at the eaves. The covering joists, or rafters, three by five inches, not to exceed two feet apart, and spiked on transversely over the trusses ; the portico's roof to have two sections of rafters, each joist four by five inches, two feet apart, the roof well covered with matched boards, and fitted for the iron or tin covering.

FLOORS.

The under floors, straight edges well nailed down, to be deepened by plastering three-fourths of an inch thick, with screeds to level the same; the screeds to be taken out, and the space filled with mortar after the first plaster is dry, to preserve the mortar from giving away; cover the top with a thick coat of paste, and a layer of thick paper; it will, when dry, produce a hard surface; then lay the top floors, for the best rooms, with one and a half inch clear lumber, not to exceed six inches wide, grooved and tongued, perfectly seasoned, to be keyed up and blind-nailed; the other floors laid with inch boards got to a width and thickness, properly laid level and smoothed.

FURRING.

All of the walls, ceilings and partitions, to be furred for one foot nailing. The furrings for the windows with shutters, in first and second story, are to be one and three-fourths inch plank; the jambs for doors and windows, to have suitable ground. The walls, plastered down to the under floors.

WINDOWS,

To have box-frames double hung, for all except the French windows, first story, in the porticos; those to swing in two parts, each one light in width, see plate 8, figs. 1, 2, and 3; the thresholds rabbetted — see *e*, fig. 3; the width of opening, three feet six inches; the other windows three feet four inches; twelve lights each, cherry-wood sash; first story, glass, twelve by twenty inches; second, twelve by sixteen; the attic, eleven by fifteen. For the first two stories, provide, hang, and fasten box-shutters and sash; also box-shutters for the kitchen, fourfold, hung in two parts; the French windows, cherry sash-frames, properly hung, with butt hinges;

in the kitchen, stool casings, also stool and edge casing in the attic story; the first and second stories to have backs, elbows, back-linings and soffits, panelled shutters, pilasters for window and doors; first story with cap, pilasters, &c.

DOORS.

The outside ones two inches thick, three feet four inches by seven feet four inches; inside, first story, three by seven feet; one and three-fourths inch thick. Second story, two feet ten inches by six feet ten inches, one and a half inch thick; all doors two panels. See plan of door, plate 5. Butt hinges and mortise locks for all the doors; cut glass knobs for doors and shutters of the first and second stories; for attic and kitchen, rosewood knobs. The average price of Robinson's locks is one dollar and twenty-five cents. Pilasters, first story in regular proportions, support the stucco entablature; second story, fancy pilasters and corner blocks. The attic and kitchens, plain pilasters and corner blocks; all doors to have hard-wood thresholds.

STAIRS,

To be built as per plan, in the hall one flight, circular-framed carriages, curtail step and scroll, mahogany rail and balusters, noosing-step returned, framed gallery, skirtings, &c.; a turned iron newel to support the rail; *f* represents the common staircase, leading from the basement floor to the attic, framed carriage and newels, the newels turned; newels and rails of cherry-wood, round pine balusters, noosing-steps returned, the steps and risers grooved to receive the plinths, proper ease off, &c.; the stairs lighted from a sky-light through the roof; casings for rooms, where pilasters are introduced for doors and windows, should show only the plinth between; you may have the attic base for the pilasters and sub-plinth; for details, pilasters and capitals, see plate 3, fig. 1 or 2.

SHEATHING.

The kitchen and store-room, in the basement story, sheathed up with boards from five to six inches wide, four feet from the floor; sheath also the bathing-room, plate 10, fig. 2, at *f;* also provide and put up water-closet in the same, with such conveniences as are used in the first-class houses; have bathing-tub and water-tank fitted to use warm and cold water at pleasure; shower-bath, and proper apparatus for the same.

LATHING AND PLASTERING.

Lath and plaster all the walls; ceiling and partitions to be lathed and plastered with good lime and hair mortar, two coats, and finished with one coat of fine stuff. Whiten the ceiling, and prepare the walls for painting. The floors to be deepened by plastering on the under floors. Set cooking-range with cast-iron back, cast hollow for heating water. See article on warming.

WARMING.

This house is intended to be warmed by heated water. Perkins' patent is upon a principle that will bear investigation. The cooking-range in the kitchen is made with a hollow cast-iron back, to hold from four to five gallons, with copper pipes introduced, one at the bottom and one at the top of this back, extending near three feet from the boiler, one and a half to two inches, calibre, then lead pipe of the same size to be carried to the rooms to be warmed; there lay a coil of about forty feet of pipe; the coil may be enclosed in a chamber to imitate a piece of furniture, thence carried to all the apartments in the house, and returned to the under pipe connected with the hollow back, having the whole tightly closed by soldering; then introduce an aperture at the highest point, made convenient for filling with water. When filled, close the aperture, when, by the common use of the range, a current is produced in the water within the pipe, passing from the upper pipe heated, and returning through the lower pipe to renew the revolution. There being no escape for steam, one filling will last considerable time without renewing the water.

Another, and, as we think, a still better method of warming houses, or other buildings, by means of heated water, is that of Mr. Dexter, of this city. The following is a description of this method, as exemplified in the house of Mr. S. K. Williams, No. 68 Boylston-street.

A chamber of brick-work is built in the cellar, under the front entry, containing 360 cubic feet; under, and near the centre, is a grate similar to those used for Bryant and Herman's furnaces, over which is set a copper boiler, holding thirty-two gallons; on one side of the boiler are fifty-four copper tubes, four inches in diameter and four feet long, set perpendicular, and resting upon a table of brick-work, three and a half feet above the bottom of the cellar; connected by six semi-cylindrical pipes, five feet in length, entering from the boiler, parallel to each other, and uniting with the boiler at the bottom. The upper ends of the tubes are united with each other in a transverse direction. The boiler is a cylinder, set upright above the brick-work four feet in height, and extends nearly to the height of the tubes. In the entry above is set a copper vessel with a lid to shut tight, containing sixteen gallons; a tube three-fourths of an inch in diameter enters near the bottom, passing down through the air-chamber into the boiler, for the purpose of filling by a force-pump; a stop-cock is inserted in the vessel at top, to supply the boiler with cold water. The heated water is drawn from the same boiler for warm baths, and from this air-chamber are funnels, registers and dampers, entering parlors, entry, &c. To communicate direct heat to the chambers, there is a wooden box ten by fourteen inches square, set perpendicular against the wall of the entry, passing up to the entry above, or communicating with the rooms by horizontal pipes and registers through the floor. At one side of the grate is a projection of brick-work, enclosing a metallic cylinder, fourteen or fifteen inches in diameter and about four and a half feet perpendicular, the top of which communicates with a register by a horizontal pipe. Near the bottom of this cylinder is a horizontal branch to admit the heated air from the large chamber to the small one. The smoke-pipe passes from the grate into the large chamber, entering the perpendicular cylinder through the lower branch, thence through one side of the cylinder, horizontally, to the chimney-flue ; thus leaving sufficient space to admit the heat from the long chamber into the cylinder, around the smoke-pipe. To admit cold air into the chamber, a flue is provided twelve inches square, entering in a downward direction under the front door-steps. This flue passes horizontally under the cellar floor, rises in a perpendicular direction, and enters the chamber near the top. The cold air finds its way through the hot air in the chamber, and becomes sooner rarefied than when entering near the bottom of the chamber. This experiment, by Mr. Dexter, is highly successful. It is secure against any eruption from the boiler or pipes, to the injury of the house or of its occupants. The rarefied air thus obtained produces a sensation similar to that produced by sitting in a room, with the windows up, in the month of June. In effect, winter is thus changed into summer.

Plate 10.

Fig. 1 exhibits a perspective view of plate 9: the windows, first story in the porticos, are intended for long French style, to open down upon thresholds as a door. See plate 8.

Fig. 2. Plan of chamber floors: *a*, the chamber entry ; *e*, *e*, *e*, *e*, bed-chambers; *d*, *d*, closets ; *h*, staircase continued ; *f*, the bathing-room.

Plate 11.

Fig. 1 is a geometrical elevation of a very genteel residence, with a piazza in front, the entrance on the right-hand side ; this house may be built of wood, framed walls, floors and roof, the roof slated or shingled as may best suit the proprietor ; the walls boarded and sheathed.

Fig. 2. The principal floor: *a*, the entrance-hall, ten feet wide; *b*, *b*, parlors with sliding-doors; *c*, principal stair-case; *d*, china-room; *g*, kitchen; *i*, pantry; *j*, wood-house; *h*, back stairs; *e*, the piazza. Scale, fifteen feet to an inch.

PLATE 12.

Fig. 1. A perspective view of plate 11, fig. 1.

Fig. 2. The second floor: *a*, *b*, *d*, *e*, *f*, bed-chambers; *h*, dressing or bathing room; *g*, the back staircase; *i*, the front stair-landing; *c*, *c*, closets. The estimate for building this house, all above the cellar, is two thousand dollars; done in a plain manner, according to the design here given.

PLATE 13.

Fig. 1. The elevation of a cottage, very convenient for a small, genteel family; drawn for French windows in the piazza; to be built of wood, fourteen feet length of posts, ten feet first story, three feet eight inches upright walls in the attic; attic story, eight feet in clear height.

Fig. 2. The principal floor. Scale, fifteen feet to an inch. Estimated cost, one thousand and four hundred dollars.

PLATE 14.

Fig. 1. A perspective view of the front, and one end of plate 13, fig. 1.

Fig. 2. Second floor, dimensions of the rooms figured on the plan.

Grecian Ionic.

From the temple on the Ilyssus, at Athens. In this example I have omitted the human figures in the entablature, the adoption of which, by many, is considered superfluous and absurd; and have selected only those ornaments which essentially belong to the order, strictly preserving the proportions.

PLATE 15.

Fig. 1 shows the proportions of the order in minutes, figured from the lower diameter of the column. Take two modules of thirty minutes each, or sixty minutes, for the diameter.

Fig. 2 is the attic base, which is used in common to the orders. The column of figures under the letter *H* shows the height of the members, and under *P*, the projections from a line drawn perpendicularly through the centre, the entire height of the order.

Fig. 3. The entire height of the order as figured on the margin, with a full column.

PLATE 16.

Fig. 1. The inverted section of the capital at one of the angles of the building.

Fig. 2. The elevation of the capital.

Fig. 3. One of the scrolls, on which is shown the method of drawing the same. Make the whole height forty minutes of the order; then drop a plumb-line indefinitely from the lesser projection of the echinus. Take nineteen and a half minutes from *A* to *B*. From *B* draw indefinitely the line *B*, *c*, at right angles with *A*, *B*. From *B* set off on *B*, *c*, three minutes to *D*. From *D* drop indefinitely the perpendicular *D*, *E*. On *D*, *E*, set off three minutes to *F*. From *F* draw indefinitely the horizontal line, *F*, *G*. On *F*, *G*, set off three minutes, to 7, making the square *B*, *D*, *F*, 7. By diagonal lines find the centre of this square which will be the centre of the eye. To describe the curves of the volute, extend your dividers from *B* to *A*, and describe the quadrant, *A*, *c*. On the point *D*, describe *c*, *E*. On the point *F*, describe *E*, *G*. On the point 7, describe *G*, *I*. This completes the first revolution. For the second revolution: divide each side of the square *B*, *D*, *F*, 7, into six equal parts, or half-minutes. On each side of this square set off one half-minute, and draw indefinitely the line 1, 3, 2, parallel to *B*, *D*, *c*; 3, 4, 5, parallel to *D*, *F*, *E*; 5, 0, 6, parallel to *F*, 7, *G*; and *o*, 1, 8, parallel to 7, *B*, *A*. Now, on point 1, describe the quadrant *I*, 2. On point 3, describe the quadrant 2, 4. On point 5, describe 4, 6. On point *o*, describe 6, 8. This completes the second revolution. For the third revolution, take another half-minute on the square *B*, *D*, *F*, 7, and proceed as before. All the mouldings, of each quadrant, will of course be described from the same central points.

PLATE 17.

Fig. 1. The example from the temple of Minerva Polias, leaving the ornamented mouldings for those who prefer to make use of them in more expensive structures. The proportional measures are given on the margin in height and projections.

Fig. 2. The Ionic base.

Fig. 3. Elevation of the order. See figures on the margin. This style of base, the attic, or the base on pilasters, plate 18, fig. 1, may be used as may be most appropriate for the structure into which they are introduced. The Ionic base may be most proper for common use.

PLATE 18.

Fig. 1. A pilaster or anta to the Ionic column: the cap may be changed for *e*, plate 19.

Fig. 2. The original cap figured in the columns *H*, *P*.

Fig. 3. Base. See figures for proportions.

Fig. 4. Dentils, as figured for cornice, plate 17.

Fig. 5. Part of the elevation of cap to column, plate 17, fig. 1.

Fig. 6. Method of drawing raking mouldings to coincide in *B*, *A*, *c*. At *A*, draw a right angle to *B c;* divide the depth of the moulding into four equal parts, as 1, 2, 3, 4; draw parallel lines through 1, 2, 3, 4, to *d*, *f*, *h*. At the square, raise a perpendicular to *o*. From *b*, *d*, *f*, *h*, points of intersection, draw lines intersecting this, at right angles, at *a*, *c*, *e*, *g*. Now transfer *b*, *a*, to 4, 4; *d*, *c*, to 3, 3; *f*, *e*, to 2, 2; *h*, *g*, to 1, 1. Transfer the same to *c*, as *a*, *b;* *c*, *d;* *e*, *f;* *g*, *h*. Draw curved lines through each point of intersection, making the form of the moulding, which will conform to the same mould on the level cornice, on the flanks, when cut on the same mitre, raising the raking part to its intended angle.

MOULDINGS.

The original Grecian mouldings are best adapted for classical works, and produce, in my opinion, the best effect; invariably preserving the elliptic or conic sectional form, while the Roman are composed of parts of regular circles; and the modern taste seems to have varied from both, inasmuch as straight lines have taken the place of circles and ellipses, as shown in plate 20, *b*, *c;* while *a*, *d*, *e*, *f*, *g*, preserve Grecian forms.

PLATE 19.

Figs. *a*, *b*, *c*, retain the principal curve of a Grecian cavetto, with additions or combinations of other moulded forms; this, in some cases, may be executed, and considered as an improvement. Mouldings, as here shown, may be executed in common to each of the Grecian orders, although their combination differs somewhat in each of the Grecian examples; *d* is for a Grecian Doric impost or pilaster; *e* is intended for the Ionic or Corinthian, where foliage is not introduced.

PLATE 20.

Figs. *a*, *b*, *c*, the Grecian quirk, ovolo and variations; *d*, *e*, *f*, cyma-reversa, and variations for the sake of variety; *g*, cyma-recta; *h*, bed-mould; *i*, cyma-recta and addition of quirk and quarter round, which, in some cases, may be used with good effect, at near a level with the eye.

PLATE 21.

Fig. 1. The elevation of a cottage, very convenient for a small genteel family; drawn for French windows in front. To be built of wood, fourteen feet length of posts, ten feet first story, three feet upright walls in the attic. Attic story, eight feet in clear height.

Fig. 2. The principal floor: dimensions figured on the plan. Estimated cost, one thousand and four hundred dollars. Scale, fifteen feet to an inch.

PLATE 22.

Fig. 1. A perspective view of the front and one end.

Fig. 2. Second floor: dimensions of rooms figured on the plan.

PLATE 23.

This villa is designed for a genteel dwelling in a village or country town, to be erected on the summit of a gentle eminence. It is intended for comfort and convenience rarely met with in any dwelling; as dwelling-houses depend much on their location for comfort, health, and pleasure.

Fig. 1. A geometrical elevation: height of stories — first, eleven feet, second, ten feet.

Fig. 2. The first floor: *a*, entrance hall; *b* and *c*, parlors; *d*, dining-room; *e*, sitting-room; *f*, back entry and stairs; *h*, kitchen; *i*, closet; *j*, bathing-room; *g*, back passage; *k*, wood-house. Scale, fifteen feet to an inch.

PLATE 24.

Fig. 1. Perspective view of plate 23.

Fig. 2. Second floor: dimensions of rooms figured.

PLATE 25.

Fig. 1. Geometrical elevation, with French windows and frontispiece. This house is intended for a professional gentleman. *a*, vestibule; *b*, dining-room; *c*, parlor; *d*, *e*, ante-rooms; *f*, china-closet; *g*, kitchen; *h*, back entrance to staircase.

PLATE 26.

A perspective view of plate 25, designed for long French windows, to swing in from a threshold at the floor.

Fig. 2. The second floor, with four bed-chambers: dimensions marked on the plan. The roof on either side would be very convenient for enjoying an airing after a hot summer day. Scale, fifteen feet to an inch.

Plate 27.

The elevation of an Ionic house, having the Ionic proportions, but the Doric dressings; Egyptian style of windows. The windows and doors, sash and glass; each fold of sash to swing in, containing two widths of glass of fourteen inches each, four lengths in height, of one foot nine inches each; the window in the frontispiece will serve well for a door, and as a window to light the vestibule. The roof to be covered with galvanized tin, with copper eave-gutters, &c.

Fig. 2. *a*, vestibule; *d*, *e*, ante-rooms; *b*, parlor; *c*, dining-room; *f*, staircase; *g*, kitchen; *h*, pantry.

Plate 28.

Fig. 1. The perspective elevation of plate 27.

Fig. 2. Plan of second floor, with five sleeping-chambers, and bathing-room, with a water-closet, &c.

Plate 29.

Fig. 1. Elevation of a dwelling-house, two stories: a low basement and cellar; for the basement it should be walled up, an open area with stone steps to descend from the bank, to give a pass to this story outside the exterior walls. Fine hammered granite facings, backed up with brick; the partitions, walls, and chimneys, laid of brick, and a metallic covering for the roof.

Fig. 2. The principal floor: this house is designed for two families, with front entrances right and left. See elevation.

Plate 30.

Fig. 1. A different front for plate 29, fig. 2. Although the style of this front, in its peculiar characteristic, is omitted, it still preserves the Ionic proportion, and is well adapted for a house planned as plate 29, fig. 2.

Fig. 2. A third front elevation for the same. This elevation essentially differs from the other two, and approaches nearer the ancient English style. Its effect is rather picturesque than otherwise. The second floor may be arranged very similar to the principal one. The two designs on this plate are intended for an attic story.

Grecian Corinthian.

This order seems to have taken rise in the flourishing days of Corinth, a celebrated city of Greece. The proportions of the order resemble the graceful figure of a virgin, more delicate than the more mature age of the matron, which has given rise to the Ionic proportions. The composition of foliage is considered the leading character of the Corinthian capital, which is arranged in two annular rows of leaves, so that each leaf in the upper row grows up between those of the lower row, in such a manner that a leaf of the upper row will stand in the middle of each face of the capital, and from each leaf of the upper row three stocks spring with volutes, two of them meeting under the angle of the abacus, and two in the centre of the side, touching or interwoven with each other. A capital thus constructed is called Corinthian.

Plate 31.

This example is from the lantern of Demosthenes, otherwise called the monument of Lysicrates. With some variation in the entablature and dentils, it may be considered a beautiful specimen of the Grecian art, and may be imitated with success when elegance is required in the composition.

Fig. 1 represents the entablature and cap of the column.

Fig. 2. The base: dimensions of height and projections figured under *P*, *H*, from a scale of sixty minutes for the diameter of the column at the base.

Fig. 3. The full-length column, entire height of the order.

Plate 32.

Fig. 1. A design for antæ for the columns, plate 31. The face of this anta, or pilaster, is equal to the diameter of the column at the neck, and equal in width at top and bottom; thus avoiding the difficulty of increasing the projection of the capital beyond that of the column to which it may be attached.

Fig. 2. The capital of column, plate 31, fig. 1. Inverted and horizontal section of the column and flutes at the neck.

Fig. 3. The cornice, inverted.

The Romans, adopting the general features of this order, introduced into it some variations from the Greek specimens.

PLATE 33.

This example is taken from the Pantheon, at Rome; although considered somewhat plainer than that from the temple of Jupiter, it is, notwithstanding, beautiful and chaste; it is considered an excellent example of the Roman style.

Fig. 1. Elevation of the order; proportions figured to a scale of minutes of the order from the diameter of the column; *H*, the height; *P*, the projections.

Fig. 2. The elevation of the base.

Fig. 3. The entire height of the order figured in modules and minutes.

PLATE 34.

Fig. 1. Elevation of the cap. The leaves are shown in outline before cutting the raffles, stalks, veins, &c.

Fig. 2. The capital of fig. 1, inverted, in which are shown the projections of the abacus, leaves, &c.

Fig. 3. Elevation of one of the leaves, with the requisite raffles, stalks, and veins.

Fig. 4. The side elevation of a modillion and its appropriate ornament.

Fig. 5. Modillion inverted.

PLATE 35.

Fig. 1. Corinthian frontispiece. Scale, three-eighths of an inch to a foot.

Fig. 2. The steps and floor for the column to rest upon.

Fig. 3 shows the flank of frontispiece, or portico.

PLATE 36.

Figs. 1, 2, 3 and 4, are designs for stucco cornices.

Fig. 5. Scale of inches which will answer for height. Fig. 1, for twenty feet; fig. 2, for sixteen feet; fig. 3, for twelve feet; and fig. 4, for eleven feet.

Fig. 6. Single architrave for the Doric order.

Fig. 7. Single architrave for the Ionic order.

Fig. 8. Single architrave for the Corinthian order.

Fig. 9. Section of the finish of doors. See plate 6.

PLATE 37.

Fig. 1 exhibits a perspective view of a Corinthian house. Although the modillions and other enrichments are omitted, the Corinthian proportions are preserved, which may be added where expense is not limited.

Fig. 2. Geometrical elevation of the principal front. This design, carried out in full Corinthian order, will produce a very beautiful effect. It contains most of the conveniences required in a gentleman's dwelling of the first class.

PLATE 38.

This plate exhibits the first floor. The dimensions are figured on the several apartments; — the closets in each corner. In the back rooms, the corners will serve well for closets, dressing-rooms, &c.; in the front ones, for water-closets, or for other conveniences, as may be required. These projections produce a very good effect in the exterior composition, and form fit recesses for the porticos. The introduction of the pier and anta, at each end of the portico, prevents the naked appearance that would be produced by the insulated column. Parlors, sixteen by eighteen feet; sitting-room, sixteen by sixteen; dining-room, sixteen by sixteen; front entrance-hall, fifteen feet wide; back entrance, six feet wide; kitchen, sixteen by sixteen;

wash-room, nine by thirteen; bathing-room, six by eight; wood-house, eight by thirty-four.

Plate 39.

This plate represents the framing of the first floor. Sills, eight by twelve inches; hearth-trimmers, three by twelve; floor-plank, two by twelve inches; kitchen hearth-trimmers, four by twelve; one foot from centre to centre.

Plate 40.

This plate shows the framing of the second floor as per plan; sixteen inches from centre to centre; girders, seven by eleven inches; hearth and stair trimmers, three by eleven; plank, two by eleven; the principal rooms are to have two tiers of bridging.

Gothic.

Plate 41.

Figs. 1, 4 and 7, represent columns, or piers. Fig. 1 is intended for exterior decoration; figs. 4 and 7 for interior; to support the ceiling of churches, where vaulted arches are introduced. The parts rising above the caps show the spring of the arches and their curves; the perpendicular lines, the transverse groins, which, as they rise, and are intersected by the embossed ribs springing from the other piers or columns, are sometimes spread out. They are occasionally ornamented with rosettes, or various kinds of foliage.

Figs. 2, 5 and 8, are sections of piers or columns. Fig. 2 shows the position of the four small reeds introduced in the curvilinear form of the main shaft. Fig. 5 is from the nave of York cathedral, and fig. 8, from Exeter cathedral. These examples are beautiful. The general form of figs. 5 and 8 being square, and placed diagonal to the face and spring of the arches, and clustered with reeds, makes a good support at the base line from which the arches spring. The splay of the arches with bold mouldings has a very beautiful effect. Figs. 3, 6 and 9, are intended for the bases which are represented in sections; 2, 5 and 8, the outline curves, represent the larger reeds, while the smaller ones are continued through the base to the plinth.

Plate 42.

Fig. 1 represents a window from Sleyford church, Lincolnshire, England, but reduced for a smaller window. The arch is formed on an equilateral triangle, and is sometimes filled with flowing tracery, and quatrefoils, and cinctures. See the figure. The deep curved hollow within the columns forms a very good drip-stone in the arch, and a deep shade on the sides; which effect is good. Scale, three-eighths of an inch to a foot; it may be used to advantage for churches, or other public buildings of this style of architecture.

Fig. 2 is a window used in the centre of the front of churches when a tower is introduced in the composition. Its effect is decidedly good. The head of this window being the ogee arch, the canopy is ornamented with crockets and a finial.

Plate 43.

Fig. 1 is the outline drawing of a large size for fig. 2.

Fig. 2. The spandrell-head window, as frequently used for small windows for Gothic dwellings. This cap forms a very good drip-stone; the top being level, the sides drop at right angles with the top and ends, but are sometimes continued on a level, to stop against the pilaster, or to form a connection with the adjoining windows.

Fig. 3. A vertical section of fig. 2. Figs. 4 and 5 are sectional styles of sash-frames.

Plate 44.

Fig. 1. A design for a door, with finish appropriate for the exterior.

Fig. 2 is intended for the interior of a Gothic dwelling, the finish forming the architrave, to project one-half the width of the face. The architrave, whose section forms one-half of an octagon figure, is admired for its smooth and clean surfaces.

Fig. 3. A part of the door-head of fig. 1 enlarged.

Fig. 4. The raking cornice for the gables of Gothic dwellings.

Plate 45.

Fig. 1. Geometrical elevation of a Gothic dwelling, having two upright stories.

Fig. 2. Plan of principal floor. The dimensions of rooms are figured on the plan. This house may afford conveniences over many others. The exterior, properly carried out, gives quite a picturesque appearance. Scale, fifteen feet to an inch. Estimated cost of building, four thousand and five hundred dollars.

Plate 46.

Fig. 1. A perspective view of plate 45, fig. 1.

Fig. 2. The chamber floor, containing four bed-chambers, and a bathing-room, six by seven feet. Dimensions figured on the plan.

Plate 47.

Fig. 1. Geometrical elevation of a dwelling built for David Sears, Esq., in Brookline, Mass. This house was built of brick ; the cellar of stone ; slate and galvanized tin roof-covering ; copper gutters and trunks ; cooking-range in kitchen ; bathing-room, water-closet, &c., in the second story ; and a Bryant and Herman's furnace set in the cellar ; also a well and cistern. Exterior walls painted and sanded ; free-stone caps and sills. The cost of this building was eight thousand dollars.

Fig. 2. A plan of the principal floor : dimensions figured on the plan. Scale, fifteen feet to an inch.

Plate 48.

Fig. 1. A perspective view of plate 47, fig. 1.

Fig. 2. Chamber floor, containing six bed-chambers, bathing-room, &c. Dimensions figured on the plan.

Groined Arches and Vaulting.

Plate 49

Shows a method for striking the centres for semi-circular and elliptical arches, with the groins or hips to coincide with each other; also, the covering of the vaulting.

OPERATION.

Fig. 1. Draw the lines O, X, intersecting at L; draw the cord of the semi-circle, I; find the centre line 7; extend this line to the intersection at L; divide one-half of the semi-circle into seven equal parts, on each side, as figured; divide K in the same manner as I. Draw lines from 1, 2, 3, 4, 5, 6, to intersect X at 1, 2, 3, 4, 5, 6. From 1, 2, 3, &c., on X, draw lines at right angles with X, indefinitely. Transfer the distance between 1, 2, 3, &c., on the semi-circle and its chord, to these last-drawn perpendicular lines at *a*, *b*, *c*, &c.; and a line passing through these several points, 1, *a;* 2, *b;* 3, *c*, &c., will give the curve of the hip or groin.

COVERING OF CENTRES.

Divide the whole length of the hip, *a*, *b*, *c*, *d*, *e*, *f*, *g*, into seven equal parts; draw the centre line, *K*, *L*, *H*, from the chord in *H;* take six of the seven parts of the hip; lay off on the centre line; divide into seven equal parts. Extend the lines of intersection from *a*, *b*, *c*, *d*, *e*, *f*, *g*, in *K*, through 1, 2, 3, 4, 5, 6, on *X;* then through the cord *H*, intersecting 1, 2, 3, 4, 5, 6, 7, in *H*, at *a*, *b*, *c*, *d*, *e*, *f*, *g;* trace a curve line through these intersections. This will form the curve to cut the covering of the centres. *H*, *I*, may be performed as the above, *K*, *H;* — *a*, *a*, *a*, *a*, &c., represent sections of the piers from which the arches are formed.

Fig. 2. The elevation of the piers: *a*, *a*, *a*, *a*, *b*, *b*, the frame for front centring; there should be two thicknesses of stuff to break joints, and nailed together or bolted, in larger works.

IONIC DETAILS FOR PLATES 29 AND 30.

Plate 50.

Fig. 1. Perspective sketch of the elevation of the Ionic capital.

Fig. 2. Base of the same.

Fig. 3. Principal cornice for elevation. Plates 29 and 30.

Fig. 4. Frieze, fillet and architrave for the same.

Fig. 5. Front elevation of truss, for Venetian window.

Fig. 6. Side elevation of the same.

Fig. 7. Cap of antæ.

Fig. 8. Architrave around the window.

Fig. 9. Stone-work for balcony of window. Plate 30, fig. 1.

Fig. 10. Section of rail for the same.

Fig. 11. Cap of pilaster to same elevation.

Fig. 12. Base to the same.

Fig. 13. Cornice for front parlor.

Fig. 14. Cornice for back parlor.

Fig. 15. Principal bed-room cornice.

Fig. 16. Second, ditto.

DETAILS FOR GOTHIC HOUSE. PLATE 30, FIG. 2.

Fig. 17. Stone cap.

Fig. 18. Head of window.

Fig. 19. Mullion of the same.

Fig. 20. Sill of the same.

Fig. 21. Elevation of chimney-pot, or stone turret.

Fig. 22. Plan of the same, showing iron fly, or smoke ventilator.

Fig. 23. A section of stone gutter, cornice, and portion of roof. *A*, cornice ; *B*, gutter; *C*, wall-plate; *D*, rafter; *E*, ceiling-joist; *F*, brick-work; *G*, plaster and cornice; *H*, battens and slate.

Fig. 24. Plan of stone jambs, frame and door for principal entrance. *A*, stone-jamb; *B*, door-frame; *C*, door; *D*, architrave.

Church Architecture.

In this enlightened and Christian country, where the arts and sciences are daily applied to the comfort and convenience of the whole people, this branch of architecture has hitherto been very much neglected. In regard to the elegance and costliness of its structures devoted to the worship of God, our country can bear no comparison with the civilized nations of Europe. There are many obvious reasons why this is so.—First, the superior age, wealth and population of those countries, may be urged as reasons why we cannot hope, at present, to compete with them in erecting such magnificent edifices as adorn their principal cities. Our fathers came to these shores to escape the imposition of religious forms and doctrines which their consciences disapproved; and this, no doubt, prejudiced their minds against the "pomp and pride" of prelacy, as well as of royalty; and left as little desire to imitate the magnificent church structures they had left behind, as to copy the political forms of their father-land.

Again, the pecuniary depression under which our forefathers labored, the numberless sacrifices they made for the *true* dignity and honor of the religion of Christ, and their deep-seated aversion to ostentation of any kind, would alike forbid the erection of elegant structures, and account for the almost total neglect with which this department of architecture has hitherto met, in our country.

It would be very difficult, perhaps, in the present state of things among us, to imitate the highly enriched and expensive structures which have, for so long a time, been the pride and glory of the older world. But we cannot but indulge the hope, that, ere long, though we may not surpass or even equal those nations, the greater part of whose wealth and power has been in the hands of the church, in the grandeur and costliness of our religious edifices, we may yet equal them in regard to the taste and architectural simplicity of these structures ; qualities more in harmony with our republican form of government, and, as we cannot but think, with the simplicity of our faith and worship, than would be the cathedrals of York, Milan or Rome, even if we could reproduce them here.

After consulting convenience and strength, the next thing to be attended to in a religious edifice is the proportion and details of the building, which must all be made to harmonize with the general design ; or else the grand object — the adaptation of the structure to the purposes of public worship — is wholly lost. No one, who has within him a spirit that prompts him to worship God, can be insensible to an emotion nearly allied to that of religious reverence, when he approaches and enters a Gothic structure, built with due regard to the rules of the art. The lofty spire, pinnacles and finials, seem as so many fingers pointing upward to heaven, and directing his way thither. In the massive tower and battlements, the mind perceives an emblem of the stability of truth, and of the gracious promises of God, and is led to repose confidingly in Him. On entering, the mind swells with the feeling of sublimity, and seems, almost involuntarily, to rise in adoration of the Being who is himself so great, and has given to man the power to raise a temple so fit for His worship. Though, sometimes, we must confess, where the grandeur and ornament of the structure have been carried to the extreme point, which they attained, especially in Catholic countries, in those ages when the greatest attention was given to the magnificence of ecclesiastical buildings, our mind has been irresistibly withdrawn from the *object* to the *place* of worship ; and we have been profoundly impressed with the truth of those words of the great apostle to the Gentiles, which he spoke while standing upon Mars Hill, in the very shadow of the most beautiful, imposing, and architecturally perfect, of all the temples that have ever been raised by human hands for divine worship,—"God, that made the world, and all things therein, seeing that he is Lord of heaven and earth, dwelleth not in temples made with hands, neither is worshipped with men's hands as though he needed anything, seeing he giveth to all life, and breath, and all things." Still, in the severest notions that can be entertained of the spirituality of the object of our worship, or of the service that it is at once our duty and blessing to offer Him, there is nothing that forbids, but, rather, much that favors, a highly-cultivated taste, and the purest style of structure and ornament, in temples dedicated to the worship of God,—that Being who has given man a faculty to perceive and enjoy beauty and sublimity, in all their forms, and then surrounded him with such an endless variety of objects, the work of his own creative hand, by which that faculty may be exercised, cultivated and gratified.

Having spoken thus of the importance and effect of proportion, and of the general harmony of the parts with the design or object of the building, we would only observe, in addition, that this effect is greatly aided by an appropriate material for the structure, as also by the colors that are introduced into its various parts, and the degree of light or shade thrown over the interior.

Quincy granite is a material which, for the exterior of a church, is admirably adapted to its main purpose. Its great solidity, and consequent durability, and the gravity of its color, especially when unhewn, render it exceedingly fit, especially for a massive religious structure. And, for the interior finish, the native black walnut of our country harmonizes equally with its main object. The walls will require paint of a lighter tint, and the ceiling should be of a light stone-color.

PLATE 51.

Fig. 1. The front elevation of a Gothic church, for a village or country town; showing the steeple, pointed buttresses, arches and finials, with their proper ornaments; a basement for school-room, &c.

Fig. 2. The elevation of a Gothic church, with a low basement. The height of the principal story, twenty-five feet. This front has a tower and parapet; the tower with battlements and appropriate ornaments. The building, fifty-two feet by eighty, exclusive of the tower, which projects ten feet. Height of tower, seventy-five feet. Scale, twenty feet to an inch.

Plate 52.

Fig. 1. Side elevation of fig. 2, plate 51. Here is shown the spandrell window-caps, or drips, the turrets, the Tudor flower at the eaves, the trefoils and quatrefoils. The windows to have diamond sash; the belfry with a large quatrefoil window.

Fig. 2. The principal floor of elevation of fig. 2, plate 51, and of fig. 1, plate 52. This floor contains eighty-four pews, in which five hundred persons can be seated with comfort: *a*, the entry; *b*, *b*, staircases; *d*, *d*, side aisles; *c*, the broad aisle; *g*, the pulpit.

Figs. 3 and 4, the front and back ends. Fig. 3 is the entrance to the basement; *a*, front doorway; *b*, *b*, staircases; *d*, *d*, side aisles; *c*, the broad aisle. Fig. 4 shows the arrangement for the back end for the Episcopal form of worship: *a*, the altar; *b*, the broad aisle; *g*, *g*, side aisles; *e*, *f*, robing-rooms; *c*, the reading, and *d*, the sermon desk.

Fig. 5 shows the elevation of pews, reading-desk, stairs and altar. Each of these designs is drawn on a scale of twenty feet to an inch.

Plate 53

Represents the front elevation of a modern Gothic church, drawn to a scale of twenty-five feet to an inch; the columns octagon, with buttresses attached, and surmounted with pointed pinnacles, and finials; cornices with terret blocking; the windows Flemish arch; the tower above the roof thirty feet square; height from the entrance floor to the bell-deck, eighty-seven feet. Steeple at the base, twenty feet octagonal; height one hundred and twelve feet from the deck; eight octagon columns; height of the ground base four feet eight inches; whole height from the ground to the top of steeple, two hundred and three feet and eight inches.

PLATE 54.

This represents the side elevation of *plate* 53; scale twenty-five feet to an inch; six Gothic columns; also the tower two, and five windows in the body, and two in the tower the opposite side, to correspond with this as to the arrangement of columns, windows, and their respective details.

PLATE 55.

Fig. 1 represents the ground plan, sixty-two by eighty-four feet; tower projects in front nineteen feet; in the rear is a vestry, twelve by twenty-five feet. N. B.—The thickness of walls, and projection of columns and buttresses, to be added. The principal entrance and staircase, ten by sixty-two feet. The arrangement of pews and aisles is considered very convenient, and will accommodate one thousand seats on the first floor, and gallery three hundred.

Fig. 2 shows the gallery, the arrangement of pews and orchestra, the landing of the stairs on the second or gallery floor, and a section of two columns, on which the rear part of the tower is to be supported.

Fig. 3 represents the ceiling, the lines of the groined arches, and rosettes in their respective angles.

Fig. 4. Transverse section near the centre of the building, the inclination of the galleries, also the arrangement of the timbers in the roof, and the two columns to support the tower, also the form of the groined arches.

PLATE 56.

Fig. 1 is a portion of the front finish of galleries; on the right hand is represented a vertical section, with projections of the finish; this figure is drawn to a scale of one inch to a foot.

Fig. 2 is a longitudinal section, on which is the projection of stiles, and recess of panels, and thickness of the front wall of gallery front.

Fig. 3 shows the elevation of the front of pews, panels and scrole, also the section of caps.

Fig. 4 is a representation of a longitudinal section; through the centre is shown the groined arches, pendits, columns, windows and gallery.

Fig. 5 is a vertical section of the tower columns, and form of arching.

This plan of a church may be reduced by adopting a scale of twenty feet to the inch.

Stair Building.

This is one of the most important subjects connected with the art of building, and should be attentively considered, not only with regard to the situation, but as to the design and execution. The convenience of the building depends on the situation; and the elegance, on the design and execution of the workmanship. In contriving a grand edifice, particular attention must be paid to the situation of the space occupied by the stairs, so as to give them the most easy command of the rooms.

"Staircases," says Palladio, "will be commendable, if they are clear, ample and commodious to ascend; inviting, as it were, people to go up; they will be clear, if they have a bright and equally diffuse light; they will be sufficiently ample, if they do not seem scanty and narrow to the size and quality of the fabric; but they should never be less than four feet in width, that two persons may pass each other; they will be convenient with respect to the whole building, if the arches under them can be used for domestic purposes; and with respect to persons, if their ascent is not too steep and difficult, to avoid which, the steps should be twice as broad as high."

With regard to the lighting of a good staircase, a skylight, or rather lantern, is the most appropriate; for these unite elegance with utility—that is, admit a powerful light, with elegance in the design ; indeed, where the staircase does not adjoin the exterior wall, this is the only light that can be admitted. Where the height of a story is considerable, resting-places are necessary, which go under the name of *quarter-paces* and *half-paces*, according as the passenger has to pass one or two right angles ; that is, as he has to describe a quadrant or semi-circle. In very high stories, which admit of sufficient head-room, and where the space allowed for the staircase is confined, the staircase may have two revolutions in the height of one story, which will lessen the height of the steps ; but in grand staircases only one revolution can be admitted, the length and breadth of the space on the plan being always proportioned to the height of the building, so as to admit of fixed proportions.

The breadth of the steps should never be more than fifteen inches, or less than nine ; the height, not more than seven or less than five ; there are cases, however, which are exceptions to all rule. When the height of the story is given in feet, and the height of the step in inches, you may throw the feet into inches, and divide it by the number of inches the step is high, and the quotient will give the number of steps.

It is a general maxim, that a step of greater breadth requires less height than one of less breadth : thus a step of twelve inches in breadth will require a rise of five and a half inches, which may be taken as a standard, to regulate those of other dimensions.

Though it is desirable to have some criterion as a guide in the arrangement of a design, yet workmen will, of course, vary them as circumstances may require. Stairs are constructed variously, according to the situation and destination of the building.

Geometrical stairs are those which are supported by having one end fixed in the wall, and every step in the ascent having an auxiliary support from that immediately below it, and the lowest step from the floor.

Bracket stairs are those which have an opening, or well, with strings and newels, and are supported by landings and carriages ; the brackets are mitred to the ends of each riser, and are fixed to the string-board, which is moulded below like an architrave.

Dog-legged stairs are those which have no opening, or well-hole, and have the rail and baluster of both the progressive and returning flights falling in the same vertical planes, the steps being fixed to strings, newels and carriages, and the ends of the steps of the inferior kind terminating only upon the side of the string, without any nosing. In taking dimensions and laying down the plan and section of staircases, take a rod, and, having ascertained the number of steps, mark the height of the story by standing the rod on the lower floor ; divide the rod into as many equal parts as there are to be risers, then, if you have a level surface to work upon below the stair, try each of the risers as you go on, and this will prevent any excess or defect ; for any error, however small, when multiplied, becomes of considerable magnitude, and even the difference of an inch in the last riser will not only have a bad effect to the eye, but will be apt to confuse persons not thinking of any such irregularity. In order to try the steps properly by the story-rod, if you have not a level surface to work from, the better way will be to lay two rods on boards, and level their top surface to that of the floor ; place one of these rods a little within the string, and the other near or close to the wall, so as to be at right angles to the starting line of the first riser, or, which is the same thing, parallel to the plan of the string ; set off the breadth of the steps upon these rods, and number the risers ; you may set not only the breadth of the flyers, but that of the winders also. In order to try the story-rod exactly to its vertical situation, mark the same distances of the risers upon the top edges, as the distances of the plan of the string-board and the rods are from each other.

In bracket stairs, as the internal angle of the steps is open to the end, and not closed by the string as in common dog-legged stairs, and the neatness of workmanship is as much regarded as in geometrical stairs, the baluster must be neatly dove-tailed into the ends of the steps, two in every step. The face of each front baluster must be in a straight surface with the face of the riser, and, as all the balusters must be equally divided, the face of the middle baluster must stand in the middle of the face of the riser of the preceding step and succeeding one. The risers and heads are all previously blocked and glued together, and, when put up, the under side of the step nailed or screwed into the under edge of the riser, and then rough brackets to the rough strings, as in dog-legged stairs, the pitching pieces and rough strings being similar. For gluing up the steps, the best method is to make a templet, so as to fit the external angle of the steps with the nosing.

The steps of geometrical stairs should be constructed so as to have a very light and clean appearance when put up: for this purpose, and to aid the principle of strength, the risers and treads, when planed up, should not be less than one-eighth of an inch, supposing the going of the stair, or length of the step, to be four feet, and for every six inches in length another one-eighth may be added. The risers ought to be dove-tailed into the cover, and when the steps are put up the treads are screwed up from below to the under edge of the risers. The holes for sinking the heads of the screws ought to be bored with a centre bit, then fitted closely in with wood, well-matched, so as entirely to conceal the screws, and appear as one uniform surface. Brackets are mitred to the riser; and the nosings are continued round. In this mode, however, there is an apparent defect; for the brackets, instead of giving support, are themselves unsupported, and dependent on the steps, being of no other use, in point of strength, than merely tying the risers and treads of the internal angles of the step together; and from the internal angles being hollow, or a re-entrant angle, except at the ends, which terminate by the wall at one extremity, and by the brackets at the other, there is a want of regular finish. The cavetts, or hollow, is carried round the front of the riser, and is returned at the end, and mitred round the bracket; and if an open string, that is, the under side of the stairs open to view, the hollow is continued along the angle of the step and the risers.

The best plan, however, of constructing geometrical stairs is, to put up the strings, and to mitre the brackets to the risers, as usual, and enclose the soffits with lath and plaster, which will form an inclined plane under each flight, and a winding surface under the winders. In superior staircases, for the best buildings, the soffits may be divided into panels. If the risers are made from two-inch plank, it will add greatly to the solidity.

In constructing a flight of geometrical stairs, where the soffit is enclosed as above, the bearers should all be framed together, so that when put up they will form a perfect staircase. Each piece of farm-work, which forms a riser, should, in the partition, be well wedged at the ends. This plan is always advisable when strength and firmness are requisite, as the steps and risers are entirely dependent on the framed carriages, which, if carefully put together, will never yield to the greatest weight.

In preparing the string for the wreath part, a cylinder should be made of the size of the well-hole of the staircase, which can be done at a trifling expense; then set the last tread and riser of the flyers on one side, and the first tread and riser of the returning flight on the opposite side, at their respective heights; then on the centre of the curved surface of this cylinder mark the middle between the two, and with a thin slip of wood, bent round with the ruling edge, cutting the two nosings of these flyers, and, through the intermediate height marked on the cylinder, draw a line, which will give the wreath line formed by the nosings of the winders; then draw the whole of the winders on this line, by dividing it into as many parts as you want risers, and each point of division is the nosing of such winder. Having thus far proceeded and carefully examined your heights and widths, so that no error may have occurred, prepare a veneer of the width intended for your string, and the length given by the cylinder, and after laying it in its place on the cylinder, proceed to glue a number of blocks about an inch wide on the back of the veneer, with their fibres parallel to the axis of the cylinder.

When dry, this will form the string for the wreath part of the staircase, to be framed into the straight strings.

It is necessary to observe, that about five or six inches of the straight string should be in the same piece as the circular, so that the joints fall about the middle of the first and last flyers. This precaution always avoids a cripple, to which the work would otherwise be subject.

The branch of stair-building that falls under our next and last consideration is that of hand-railing, which calls into action all the ingenuity and skill of the workman.

This art consists in constructing hand-rails by moulds, according to the geometrical principles, that if a cylinder be cut in any direction, except parallel to the axis or base, the section will be an ellipsis; if cut parallel to the axis, a rectangle; and if parallel to the base, a circle.

Now, suppose a hollow cylinder be made to the size of the well-hole of the staircase, the interior concave, and the exterior convex, and the cylinder be cut by any inclined or oblique plane, the section formed will be bounded by two concentric similar ellipses; consequently, the section will be at its greatest breadth at each extremity of the larger axis, and its least breadth at each extremity of the smaller axis. Therefore, in any quarter of the ellipsis there will be a continued increase of breadth from the extremity of the lesser axis to that of the greater.

Now, it is evident that a cylinder can be cut by a plane through any three points; therefore, supposing we have the height of the rail at any three points in the cylinder, and that we cut the cylinder through these points, the section will be a figure equal and similar to the face-mould of the rail; and if the cylinder be cut by another plane parallel to the section, at such a distance from it as to contain the thickness of the rail, this portion of the cylinder will represent a part of the rail with its vertical surfaces already worked ; and again, if the back and lower surface of this cylindric portion be squared to vertical lines, either on the convex or concave side, through two certain parallel lines drawn by a thin piece of wood, which is bent on that side, the portion of the cylinder thus formed will represent the part of the rail intended to be made.

Though the foregoing only relates to cylindrical well-holes, it is equally applicable to rails erected on any seat whatever.

The *face-mould* applies to the two faces of the plank, and is regulated by a line drawn on its edge, which line is vertical when the plank is elevated to its intended position. This is called the *raking-mould.*

The *falling-mould* is a parallel piece of thin wood applied and bent to the side of the rail piece, for the purpose of drawing the back and lower surface, which should be so formed that every level straight line, directed to the axis of the well-hole, from every point of the side of the rail formed by the edges of the falling mould, coincide with the surface. In order to cut the portion of rail required out of the least possible thickness of stuff, the plank is so turned up on one of its angles, that the upper surface is nowhere at right angles to a vertical plane passing through the chord of the plane ; the plank in this position is said to be *sprung.*

The *pitch-board* is a right-angled triangular board made to the rise and tread of the step, one side forming the right angle of the width of the tread, and the other of the height of the riser. When there are both winders and flyers, two pitch-boards must be made to their respective treads, but, of course, of the same height, as all the steps rise the same.

The level by which the edge of the plank is reduced from the right angle, when the plank is sprung, is termed the *spring of the plank*, and the edge thus bevelled is called the *sprung edge.*

The bevel by which the face-mould is regulated to each side of the plank is called the *pitch.*

The formation of the upper and lower surface of a rail is called the *falling of the rail;* the upper surface of the rail is termed the *back.*

In the construction of hand-rails, it is necessary to spring the plank, and then to cut away the superfluous wood, as directed by the draughts, formed by the face-mould; which may be done, by an experienced workman, so exactly, with a saw, as to require no further reduction; and when set in its place, the surface on both sides will be vertical in all parts, and in a surface perpendicular to the plan.

In order to form the back and lower surface, the falling mould is applied to one side, generally the convex, in such a manner that the upper edge of the falling mould at one end coincides with the face of the plank; and the same in the middle, and leaves so much wood to be taken away at the other end as will not reduce the plank on the concave side; the piece of wood to be thus formed into the wreath or twist, being agreeable to their given heights.

To grade the front string of stairs, having winders in a quarter-circle at the top of the flight, connected with flyers at the bottom.—In Fig. 1, Plate 57, *a, b* represents the line of the facia along the floor of the upper story, *b, e, c* the face of the cylinder, and *c, d* the face of the front string. Make *g, b* equal to one-third of the diameter of the baluster, and draw the centre-line of the rail, *f, g, g, h, i,* and *i, j,* parallel to *a, b, b, e, c,* and *c, d;* make *g, k* and *g, l* each equal to half the width of the rail, and through *k* and *l* draw lines for the convex and the concave sides of the rails, parallel to the centre-line; tangical to the convex side of the rail, and parallel to *k, m,* draw *n, r, o;* obtain the stretch-out, *q, r,* of the semi-circle, *k, p, m;* extend *a, b* to *t,* and *k, m* to *s;* make *c, s* equal to the length of the steps, and *i, u* equal to eighteen inches, and describe the arcs *s, t* and *u,* 6, parallel to *m, p;* from *t,* draw *t, w,* tending to the centre of the cylinder; from 6, and on the line 6, *u, x,* run off the regular tread, as at 5, 4, 3, 2, 1, and v; make u, x equal to half the arc u, 6, and make the point of division nearest to x, as v, the limit of the parallel steps or flyers; make r, o equal to m, z; from o, draw o, a^3, at right angles to n, o, and equal to one rise; from a^3, draw a^2, s, parallel to n, o, and equal to one tread; from s, through o, draw s, b^2.

Then, from w, draw w, c^2 at right angles to n, o, and set up on the line w, c^2 the same number of risers that the floor, A, is above the first winder, B, as at 1, 2, 3, 4, 5 and 6; through 5, on the arc 6, u, draw d^2, e^2, tending to the centre of the cylinder; from e^2, draw e^2, f^2 at right angles to n, o, and through 5, on the line w, c^2, draw g^2, f^2 parallel to n, o; through 6 (on the line, w, c^2) and f^2, draw the line h^2, b^2; make 6, c^2 equal to half a rise, and from c^2 and 6 draw c^2, i^2, and 6, j^2, parallel to n, o; make h^2, i^2 equal to h^2, f^2; from i^2, draw i^2, k^2, at right angles to i^2, h^2, and from f^2 draw f^2, k^2, at right angles to f^2, h^2; upon k^2, with k^2, f^2 for radius, describe the arc f^2, i^2; make b^2, l^2 equal to b^2, f^2, and ease off the angle at b^2, by the curve f^2, b^2. Then from 1, 2, 3 and 4 (on the line w, c^2), draw lines parallel to n, o, meeting the curve in m^2, n^2, o^2 and p^2; from these points draw lines at right angles to n, o, and meeting it in x^2, r^2, s^2 and t^2; from x^2 and r^2 draw lines tending to u^2, and meeting the convex side of the rail in y^2 and z^2; make m, v^2 equal to r, s^2, and m, w^2 equal to r, t^2; from y^2, z^2, v^2 and w^2, through 4, 3, 2 and 1, draw lines meeting the line of the wall-string in a^3, b^3, c^3 and d^3; from e^3, where the centre-line of the rail crosses the line of the floor, draw e^3, f^3 at right angles to n, o, and from f^3, through 6, draw f^3, g^2; then the heavy lines f^3, g^2, e^2, d^2, y^2, a^2, z^2, b^3 v^2, c^3, w^2, d^3 and z, y, will be the lines for the risers, which, being extended to the line of the front string, b, e, c, d, will give the dimensions of the winders, and the grading of the front string, as was required.

To obtain the falling-mould for the twist of the last-mentioned stairs.—Make i^2, g^3 and i^2, h^3 (fig. 1, plate 57) each equal to half the thickness of the rail; through h^3 and g^3, draw h^3, i^3 and g^3, j^3, parallel to i^2, z; assuming k, k^3 and m, m^3, on the plan, as the amount of straight to be got out with the twists, make *n*, *q* equal to *k*, k^3, and *r*, l^3 equal to *m*, m^3; from *n* and l^3, draw lines at right angles to *n*, *o*, meeting the top of the falling-mould in n^3 and o^3; from o^3, draw a line crossing the falling-mould at right angles to a chord of the curve f^2, b^2; through the centre of the cylinder draw u^2, 8 at right angles to *n*, *o*; through 8 draw 7, 9, tending to k^2; then n^3, 7 will be the falling-mould for the upper twist, and 7, o^3 the falling-mould for the lower twist.

To obtain the face-mould of one-quarter of the cylinder, as in plate 57, *b*, *c*, extend the lines 1, 2, 3, &c., to the outer curve of the cylinder, transfer those ordinates to *x*, *z*, the pitch-line; the develop of one-quarter of the circle at right angles to *x*, *z* gives the face-mould for this section.

Plate 58.

Fig. 2. Nos. 1, 2 and 3, show the method of obtaining the face-mould, and the requisite thickness of material. No. 1, the ground plan, with ordinates, 1, 2, 3, &c. Transfer the ordinates to the pitch-line *k*, *f*, at right angles *k*, *f*, 1, 2, 3, &c., which gives the face-mould, and No. 3 shows the requisite thickness of plank. See *k*, *z* and *o*, *x*. No. 3.

To find the face-mould for Fig. 2, *Plate* 58.—Draw the base-line *c*, *d*; divide *c*, *d* into any convenient number of parts, as 1, 2, 3, 4, 5, 6, at right angles to *c*, *d*, and note their intersections with the concave and convex sides of the cylinder or ground plan; then extend these ordinates to any convenient distance at right angles to *c*, *d*, and parallel to each other; then ascertain the angle of the pitch-line *x*, *z*, then set off on a right angle to the pitch-line the transfers from the base *c*, *d*, which gives the curve of the face-mould required by tracing through the points noticed at the base. For the overease, see Plate 57, Fig. 2.

To find the falling-mould for the rail of winding stairs. — In Fig. 1, Plate 58, *a*, *c*, *b* represents the plan of a rail around half the cylinder, *A* the cap of the newel, and 1, 2, 3, &c., the face of the risers in the order they ascend. Find the stretch-out *e*, *f*, of *a*, *c*, *b*; from *e*, through the point of the mitre at the newel-cap, draw *o*, *s*; obtain on the tangent, *e*, *d*, the position of the points *s* and *h*, as at *t* and *m*; from *e*, *t*, *m* and *f*, draw *e*, *x*, *t*, *u*, *m*, *q* and *f*, *h*, all at right angles to *e*, *d*; make *e*, *g* equal to one rise, and *m*, *q* equal to twelve, as this line is drawn from the twelfth riser; from *g*, through *q*, draw *g*, *i*; make *g*, *x* equal to about *three-fourths* of a rise; draw *x*, *u* at right angles to *e*, *x*, and ease off the angle at *u*; at a distance equal to the thickness of the rail, draw *v*, *w*, *y* parallel to *x*, *u*, *i*; from the centre of the plan *o*, draw *o*, *l* at right *angles* to *e*, *d*; bisect *h*, *n*, *m*, *p*, and through *p*, at right angles to *g*, *i*, draw a line for the joint; in the same manner, draw the joint at *k*; then *x*, *i*, *y*, *w*, will be the falling-mould for that part of the rail which extends from *s* to *b*, on the plan.

To describe the scroll for a hand-rail over a curtail step.—Plate 58. Let *a*, *b*, fig. 3, be the given breadth, one and three-fourths the given number of revolutions, and let the relative size of the regulating square to the eye be one-third of the diameter of the eye. Then, by the rule, one and three-fourths, multiplied by four, gives seven; and three, the number of times a side of the square is contained in the eye, being added, the sum is ten. Divide *a*, *b*, therefore, into ten equal parts, and set one from *b* to *c*; bisect *a*, *c*, in *e*; then *a*, *e* will be the length of the longest ordinate (1 *d* or 1 *e*). From *a* draw *a*, *d*, from *e* draw e^1, and from *b* draw *b*, *f*, all at right angles to *a*, *b*; make e^1 equal to *e*, *a*, and through 1 draw 1 *d*, parallel to *a*, *b*; set *b*, *c* from 1 to 2, and upon 12 complete the regulating square; divide this square as at fig. 3; then describe the arcs that compose the scroll, as follows: upon 1, describe *d*, *e*; upon 2, describe *e*, *f*; upon 3, describe *f*, *g*; upon 4, describe *g*, *h*, *&c.*; make *d*, *l* equal to the width of the rail, and upon 1, describe *l*, *m*; upon 2, describe *m*, *n*, *&c.*; describe the eye upon 8, and the scroll is completed.

Plate 58.

To obtain the falling-mould for the raking part of the scroll.—Tangical to the rail at *h*, fig. 3, plate 58, draw *h*, *k* parallel to *d*, *a*; then *k*, a^2 will be the joint between the twist and the other part of the scroll. Make *d*, e^2 equal to the stretch-out of *d*, *e*, and upon *d*, e^2 find the position of the point *k*, as at k^2: at Fig. 4, make *e*, *d* equal to e^2, *d* in Fig. 3, and *d*, *c* equal to *d*, *k*, in that figure ; from *c*, draw *c*, *a* at right angles to *e*, *c*, and equal to one rise ; make *c*, *b* equal to one tread ; and from *b*, through *a*, draw *b*, *j*, bisect *a*, *c* in *l*, and through *l* draw *m*, *q*, parallel to *e*, *h* : *m*, *q* is the height of the level part of a scroll, which should always be about three and one-half feet from the floor ; ease off the angle *m*, *f*, *j*, and draw *g*, *w*, *n*, parallel to *m*, *x*, *j*, and at a distance equal to the thickness of the rail ; at a convenient place for the joint, as *i*, draw *i*, *n* at right angles to *b*, *j*; through *n*, draw *j*, *h* at right angles to *e*, *h*; make *d*, *k* equal to *d*, k^2, in Fig. 3, and from *k* draw *k*, *o* at right angles to *e*, *h*; at Fig. 3, make *d*, h^2 equal to *d*, *h* in Fig. 4, and draw h^2, b^2 at right angles to *d*, h^2; then *k*, a^2 and h^2, i^2 will be the position of the joints on the plan, and at Fig. 4, *o*, *p* and *i*, *n*, their position on the falling-mould ; and *p*, *o*, *i*, *n* (fig. 4) will be the falling-mould required.

To describe the face-mould.—Plate 58. At Fig. 3, from *k*, draw *k*, r^2 at right angles to r^2, *d*; at Fig. 4, make *h*, *r* equal to h^2, r^2, in Fig. 3, and from *r* draw *r s* at right angles to *r*, *h*; from the intersection of *r*, *s* with the level line *m*, *q*, through *i*, draw *s*, *t*; at Fig. 3, make h^2, b^2 equal to *q*, *t* in Fig. 4, and join b^2 and r^2; from a^2, and from as many other points in the arcs a^2, *l* and *k*, *d*, as is thought necessary, draw ordinates to r^2, *d* at right angles to the latter ; make *r*, *b* (Fig. 6) equal in its length and in its divisions to the line r^2, b^2 in Fig. 3 ; from *r*, *n*, *o*, *p*, *q* and *l* draw the lines *r h*, *n d*, *o a*, *p e*, *q f* and *l c*, at right angles to *r b*, and equal to r^2, *k*, d^2, s^2, f^2, a^2, &c., in Fig. 3 ; through the points thus found, trace the curves *k l* and *a c*, and complete the face-mould, as shown in the figure. This mould is to be applied to a square-edged plank, with the edge *l*, *b* parallel to the edge of the plank. The rake lines upon the edge of the plank are to be made to correspond to the angle *s*, *t*, *h*, in Fig. 4. The thickness of the stuff required for this mould is shown at Fig. 4, between the lines *s*, *t* and *u*, *v*—*u*, *v* being drawn parallel to *s*, *t*.

To describe the scroll for a curtail step. — Plate 58, Fig. 3. Bisect *d*, *l*, Fig. 3, in *o*, and make *o*, *v* equal to one-third of the diameter of a baluster; make *v*, *w* equal to the projection of the noosing, and *e*, *x* equal to *w*, *l;* upon 1 describe *w*, *y*, and upon 2 describe y^2; also upon 2 describe *x*, *i*, upon 3 describe *i*, *j*, and so around to 2; and the scroll for the step will be completed.

General rule for finding the size and position of the regulating square. — Plate 58, Fig. 5. The breadth which the scroll is to occupy, the number of its revolutions, and the relative size of the regulating square to the eye of the scroll being given, multiply the number of revolutions by four, and to the product add the number of times a side of the square is contained in the diameter of the eye, and the sum will be the number of equal parts into which the breadth is to be divided. Make a side of the regulating square equal to one of these parts. To the breadth of the scroll add one of the parts thus found, and half the sum will be the length of the longest ordinate.

To find the proper centres in the regulating square. — Let *a*, 2, 1, *b*, Fig. 5, be the size of a regulating square, found according to the previous rule, the required number of revolutions being one and three-fourths. Divide two adjacent sides, as *a*, 2 and 2, 1, into as many equal parts as there are quarters in the number of revolutions, as seven; from those points of division, draw lines across the square at right angles to the lines divided; then, 1 being the first centre, 2, 3, 4, 5, 6 and 7 are the centres for the other quarters, and 8 is the centre for the eye; the heavy lines that determine these centres being each one part less in length than its preceding line.

To determine the position of the balusters under the scroll. — Bisect *d*, *l*, Fig. 3, in *o*, and upon *l*, with 1, *o* for radius, describe the circle *o*, *r*, *u;* set the baluster at *p* fair with the face of the second riser, *k*, and from *p*, with half the tread in the dividers, space off as at *o*, *q*, *r*, *s*, *t*, *u*, &c., as far as *A;* upon 2, 3, 4 and 5, describe the centre-line of the rail around to the eye of the scroll; from the points of division in the circle *o*, *r*, *u*, draw lines to the centre-line of the rail, tending to the centre of the eye, 8 ; then, the intersection of these radiating lines with the centre-line of the rail will determine the position of the balusters, as shown in the figure.

NOTE.—The figures 1, 2, 3, &c., on the left of Fig. 3, represent a method of getting the size or proportion of a scroll. Divide the face, *a*, *c*, into eleven parts ; then five and one-half of these parts will form the inside of the regulating square, 1, 2, as explained in Fig. 3.

To apply the face-mould to the plank.—In Plate 57, Fig. 2, *A* represents the plank with its best side and edge in view, and *B* the same plank turned up so as to bring in view the other side and the same edge, this being square from the face. Apply the tips of the mould at the edge of the plank, as at *a* and *o* (*B*), and mark out the shape of the twist ; from *a* and *o* draw the lines *a*, *b* and *o*, *c* across the edge of the plank, the angles, *e*, *a*, *b* and *e*, *o*, *c;* turning the plank up as at *B*, apply the tips of the mould at *b* and *c*, and mark it out as shown in the figure. In sawing out the twist, the saw must be moved in the direction *a*, *b;* which direction will be perpendicular when the twist is held up in its proper position.—In sawing by the face-mould, the sides of the rail are obtained ; the top and bottom, or the upper and the lower surfaces, are obtained by squaring from the sides, after having bent the falling-mould around the outer or convex side, and marked by its edges. Marking across by the ends of the falling-mould will give the position of the butt-joint.

To find the falling-mould of a rail for a staircase with a semi-cylinder at each end, beginning on the gallery of the first flight and continued to the gallery of the second flight.—Draw the width of your rail on Fig. 1, Plate 59, then take a limber strip of wood and bind round the inside of your rail on Fig. 1, and mark the width of your treads on the noosing ; then lay out your falling-mould, as shown in Fig. 2. Setting up the height of your rise and using your limber strip for the width of your treads, draw a line to cut the top corner of your noosings, and make your eases from the winders down on to the flyers, and from the flyers on to lower winders, and then on to gallery, setting up on gallery one-half of your rise; make your joints on your falling-mould, say four inches by the circle on the gallery and in the centre of the well-room, and over the sixth and sixteenth risers, as shown in Fig. 2.

To obtain the position of butt-joints for the falling-mould, with a semi-cylinder at each end with winders, and a portion of the centre with flyers.—Select for the bearing point that position which will make the most graceful ease in the angles; it may in some cases vary a little, in the distance from the pitch line of the risers, when the rail is to bear equal on the noosing of steps, or when fitting the joints. The joint may be so arranged as to bring the butt-joint all on the extreme curve of the ease; consequently the straight part will require less thickness of material, but the curve part will require more thickness than if the position had been more equally divided.

To find the position of the butt-joints.—Set up on the front of the rise next below the bearing point lines *a, b, c* equal to the depth of the rail, perpendicular to the plan, at the intersection of the rail, *k, l, m;* then draw the line *k, z,* tending to the centre, which gives the position of the butt-joint, as is also shown in Fig. 1, Plate 58.

To find the face-mould for an overease.—Find *c*, the centre of the stretch-out, on the inside of the rail, in Fig. 1; draw a line from *a* through that point; then in Fig. 2 draw a perpendicular line to cut the joint on the top side of falling-mould, from *b* to *c*. Then draw a level line to cut the lower side of the joint of the falling-mould on the gallery, from *c* to *d*, find the centre of that line, and draw a perpendicular line to intersect the lower side of falling-mould, from *e* to *f;* then draw a level line from *f* to *g;* then draw a line from *b*, through *f* to *h;* take the distance from *c* to *h*, and set off on Fig. 4, from *a* to *i;* draw a line from *i*, to cut the inside of the joint at *j;* then draw a line from *j* at right angles with the last line from *l* to *m;* then draw a line from *a* to *n*, which is the height line. Take the height on Fig. 2, from *b* to *c;* set up that from *l* to *n;* then draw your pitch line from *n* to *m*. Draw as many lines as convenient to prick off your mould, from your cord line, *l, m,* parallel with your height line, *a*, *r*, through your ground plan ; then, lay your board for your mould by your pitch line, and square your ordinates across your board ; to prick off your mould, take the distance from *l* to *a*, and set off from *n* to *o*, and in like manner with all the other ordinates ; then draw a line from *o* to *p*, which is your spring line on the level of your plank.

The lines for an underease are drawn the same as an overease, as shown in fig. 3.

Plate 60.

When the falling-mould is curved, as described in Plate 60, Fig. 1, *s*, *r*, *d*, *b*, the joints at each end of the ground plan of one-quarter of a cylinder, make *a*, *c* equal to the stretch-out of the concave side *s*, *b*, divide *a*, *c* and *s*, *b* each into the like number of equal parts on *a*, *c*, and from each point of division, *a*, *k*, *c*, *l*, at right angles to *a*, *c*, as *e*, *f*, *g*, *h*, *i*, intersecting the pitch line, *k*, *j*; then draw lines, *k*, *l*, *m*, *n*, *o*, *p*, from those intersections parallel to *a*, *c* and *r*, *d*, on the corresponding pitch line *w*, *y*, *z*, *t*, and *j*, *k*, the falling-mould. From the points of division in the arc dividing the arc *r*, *d*, in the same proportion as *s*, *b* and *d*, *r*, through *b*, draw *d*, *t* and *b*, *u* at right angles to *a*, *d*, and from *j* and *v* draw *j*, *u* and *v*, *w* at right angles to *j*, *c*; then *x*, *t*, *u*, *w* will be the vertical projection of the joint *d*, *b*, when the radiating lines on the plan, *s*, *r* and *d*, *b*, corresponding to the vertical lines, *k*, *j*. To represent a joint, find their vertical projection as at 1, 2, 3, 4, 5 and 6, through the corners of the parallelograms trace the curve lines shown in the figure, then 6, *u* will be the helinet or vertical projection of *s*, *r*, *d*, *b*. To find the necessary thickness of plank to work out this part of the rule, draw the lines *z*, *t* and *w*, *y*, which distance apart gives the thickness of plank required.

Plate 60, Fig. 4. Join *b*, *c*, and from *o* draw *o*, *h* at right angles to *b*, *c*; upon the stretch-out *d*, *g*, as *d*, *f*, draw *b*, *j* and *c*, *b* at right angles to *b*, *c*; make *b*, *j*, *c*, *l*, from *l*, *j*, draw *l*, *m*, *c*; from *h* draw *h*, *n* parallel to *c*, *b*; from *n* draw *n*, *r* at right angles to *b*, *c*, and join *r* and *s* through the lowest corner of the plan, as *p*; draw *v*, *e* parallel to *b*, *c*, *a*, *e*, *u*, *p*, *k*, *t*, and from as many other points as is thought necessary draw ordinates to the base line *v*, *e*, parallel to *r*, *s;* through *h* draw *w*, *x* at right angles to *m*, *l*, upon *n;* with *r*, *s* for radius, describe an intersecting arc at *x*, and join *n* and *x* from the points at which the ordinates meet the line *m*, *l* at right angles to *v*, *e*, and from points of intersection *m*, *l* draw corresponding ordinates parallel to *n*, *x;* make the ordinates which parallel to *n*, *x* of the corresponding lengths to *r*, *s*, and through the points thus found trace the face-mould.

Plate 60, Fig. 3, shows the process to obtain the helinet top and bottom joint of the butts *j*, *k*, the vertical lines; — draw *j*, *k* to *w*, *h*, and join *w* and *h;* then *w*, *h* is the proper representative of the helinet of *j*, *k*, on the plan it being the line of joint; *e*, *m* therefore is projected also by *i*, *b*, on the top of the helinet, and the line *d*, *o* by *c*, *a*—*a*, *i* and *i*, *b* coincide with *c*, *b*, the line of the joint on the convex side of the rail.

Plate 60, Fig. 2. *To find the butt-joint when the middle height is below a line joining the other two.* The lower twist of the rail, Fig. 1, Plate 57, is of this nature; the face-mould for the same is Fig. 2, Plate 60; the plan of the rail at the bottom of the Fig. is supposed to lay perpendicular under the face-mould at the top, and each end unite at the top, and each over the corresponding ones at the base, *r*, *s*, the ordinates 1, 2, 3, 4 and 5; diagonal from those points raised perpendicular lines to the intersection of *j*, *l*, at the same diagonal, through the points of which trace the concave side of the face-mould.

Plate 61.

We present on Plate 61 a design in elevation for a store which may be constructed of cast iron. The inside of the front wall should be lined up with brick, or the piers supported as the work may require, by hollow cast-iron posts, 4x12 inches square. Fig. 1 shows the elevation, and Fig. 2 a plan of the ceiling of the entrance story. The patterns for the castings may be constructed in their several parts, so as to give a depth of sinkage to the panels, &c., as the taste of the builder may require. The patterns should be made so as to produce castings of about one-quarter of an inch in thickness. The elevation is drawn at a scale of one-eighth of an inch to a foot, and it is thought from this the different parts of the work may be delineated, so as to produce the desired result.

Fig. 3 shows the main cornice, bracket, &c., on a scale of one inch to a foot.

Fig. 4 shows a horizontal section of the wall through the windows of the second and third stories, on a scale of one-half an inch to a foot.

Plate 62.

Fig. 1 shows a design for a store, which may be of either stone or brick: this, like the one which precedes it, is drawn to a scale of one-eighth of an inch to a foot, and will be understood without further explanation.

On the elevation at Fig. 1 will be observed the horizontal lines at each of the two upper stories; these breaks may be formed by breaking out the stones in the form of a belt; the projections need not be more than one inch. Should the building be constructed of bricks, the projections may be omitted, and the whole surface be made plain. The design of the projections in the stone being to give a better effect to the joints, if the joints are dispensed with, as would be the case were the building constructed of bricks, the projections would not be needed.

Fig. 2 shows a plan of the ceiling of the entrance story.

Fig. 3 shows the store-doors, at a scale of one-half an inch to a foot.

Fig. 4 shows the method of constructing the meeting-stiles of the show-case, or internal sash, at the store-windows, and

Fig. 5 shows the stiles to which the sashes are hung, and are drawn full size.

Plate 63.

Shows at Fig. 1 in elevation, and at Fig. 2 in plan, an Oriel Window, designed to be constructed on a level with the second story of a dwelling-house. The scale for delineating the respective parts of the same will be seen on the plate.

Plate 64.

Fig. 1 shows the front elevation of a villa, in the Italian style.

Fig. 2 shows a transverse section of the same.

Figs. 3 and 4, the plans.

The design is drawn at a scale of fifteen feet to an inch, and will be readily understood, without further explanation.

This villa may be constructed of bricks, if desired, and covered with cement. The walls should be twelve inches thick, and should be made vaulted, or hollow. They may be so constructed, by laying one course in width on the outside face of the wall, and another on the inside, allowing as much space to intervene as will make the wall twelve inches in thickness.

All the angles should be made solid, and one course of brick should be laid up at the sides of the frames of the windows. At distances of every two feet in height and thirty inches apart, the outer and inner parts of the walls should be tied together, to make the work secure. This may be done with bricks, or by pieces of sheet-iron of any width (more than one inch), and short enough to come within the faces of the walls. These pieces need not be bent in any way, but simply laid in the wall as the work progresses. The weight of the bricks above them will retain them in their position, and, by omitting to turn down the ends of them on either face of the wall, we avoid the rust which would come from them were they exposed to the action of the atmosphere. Should the building be left uncemented, the wall should be *eight* inches thick on the outside, with a space of three inches, and then a wall of four inches, or the width of a brick. By constructing the walls in this manner, we make the building both warm and dry, and thus avoid that serious objection to a brick building, namely, dampness.

The idea in regard to thickness of walls of buildings left without cement, namely, that the exterior wall should be eight inches instead of four inches, was not advanced, in consideration that the cement would impart to the wall a strength which would not exist without it, but comes from the fact that water will pass through the joints of a four-inch wall in a storm, and the extra four inches are needed to remedy a defect which would not exist in a wall covered with cement. A wall constructed hollow, and properly tied as directed, is much stronger than a solid wall; and as dampness cannnot pass over an air space, the interior wall must be much drier than it could be was there a medium for the conduction of dampness, as brick and mortar. The remarks made in regard to the construction of brick dwelling-houses will apply with equal force to brick basements of wooden dwelling-houses. A basement of brick may be made to be as dry as though constructed of wood, if the precaution be taken to build them with a vault or air space, as directed. The wall will be stronger, will give a better support to the sills of the building, and may be made at nearly the same cost as though they were built solid.

In ordinary cases, where the building is not too large, the wall need not be more than ten inches thick, making two inches of vaulting between the walls. Coming so near the ground, storms could not produce the effect on them which would be produced on a high structure, and therefore would be obviated the necessity of making them as thick as proposed for uncemented buildings.

GLOSSARY

OF

ARCHITECTURAL TERMS.

Abacus. The upper member of the capital of a column, whereon the architrave rests. Scammozzi uses this term for a concave moulding in the capital of the Tuscan pedestal, which, considering its etymology, is an error.

Abutment. The solid part of a pier from which an arch springs.

Acanthus. A plant, called in English *Bear's breech*, whose leaves are employed for decorating the Corinthian and Composite capitals. The leaves of the acanthus are used on the bell of the capital, and distinguish the two rich orders from the three others.

Accompaniments. Buildings, or ornaments, having a necessary connection or dependence, and which serve to make a design more or less complete; a characteristic peculiarity of ornaments.

Accouplement. Among carpenters, a tie, or brace; sometimes the entire work when framed.

Acroteria. The small pedestals placed on the extremities and apex of a pediment.

Admeasurement. Adjustment of proportions; technically, an estimate of the quantity of materials and labor of any kind used in a building.

Alcove. The original and strict meaning of this word, which is derived from the Spanish *Alcoba*, is that part of a bed-chamber in which the bed stands, and is separated from the other parts of the room by columns or pilasters.

Amphiprostyle. In ancient architecture, a temple with columns in the rear as well as in the front.

Amphitheatre. A double theatre, of an elliptical form on the ground plan, for the exhibition of the ancient gladiatorial fights and other shows.

Ancones. The consoles or ornaments cut on the keys of arches, sometimes serving to support busts or other figures.

Annulet. A small, square moulding, which crowns or accompanies a larger. Also that fillet which separates the flutings of a column. It is sometimes called a *list*, or *listella*, — which see.

Antæ. A name given to pilasters attached to a wall.

Apophyge. That part of a column between the upper fillet of the base and the cylindrical part of the shaft of the column, which is usually curved into it by a cavetto.

Aræostyle. That style of building in which the columns are distant four, and sometimes five, diameters from each other; but the former is the proportion to which the term is usually applied. This columnar arrangement is suited to the Tuscan order only.

Arcade. A series of arches, of apertures, or recesses; a continued covered vault, or arches supported on piers, or columns, instead of galleries. In Italian towns the streets are lined with arcades, like those of Covent Garden and the Royal Exchange.

Arch. An artful arrangement of bricks, stones, or other materials, in a curvilinear form, which, by their mutual pressure and support, perform the office of a lintel, and carry superincumbent weights, the whole resting at its extremities upon piers, or abutments.

Arch-buttress, or *Flying-buttress.* (In Gothic architecture) an arch springing from a buttress, or pier, and abutting against a wall.

Archeion. The most retired and secret place

in Grecian temples, used as a treasury, wherein were deposited the richest treasures pertaining to the deity to whom the temple was dedicated.

Architect. One who designs and superintends the erection of buildings.

Architrave. The lower of the primary divisions of the entablature. It is placed immediately upon the abacus of the capital.

Astragal. From the Greek word for a bone in the foot, to which this moulding was supposed to bear a resemblance. A small moulding, whose profile is semi-circular, and which bears also the name of *Talon*, or *Tondino.* The astragal is often cut into beads and berries, and used in ornamental entablatures, to separate the faces of the architrave.

Attic. A term that expresses anything invented or much used in Attica, or the city of Athens. A low story erected over an order of architecture, to finish the upper part of the building, being chiefly used to conceal the roof, and give greater dignity to the design.

Attic Base. [See Base.]

Attic Order. An order of low pilasters, generally placed over some other order of columns. It is improperly so called, for the arrangement can scarcely be called an order.

Auriel or *Oriel.* (In Gothic architecture) a window projecting outwards for private conference; whence its appellation.

Balcony. A projection from the surface of a wall, supported by consoles or pillars, and surrounded by a balustrade.

Baluster. A small pillar, or pilaster, serving to support a rail. Its form is of considerable variety, in different examples. Sometimes it is round, at other times square; it is adorned with mouldings, and other decorations, according to the richness of the order it accompanies.

Balustrade. A connected range of a number of balusters on balconies, terraces around altars, &c. [See Baluster.]

Band. A term used to express what is generally called a *Face*, or *Facia.* It more properly means a flat, low, *square-profiled* member, without respect to its place. That from which the Corinthian, or other modillions, or the dentils project, is called the modillion band, or the dentil band, as the case may be.

Bandelet. A diminutive of the foregoing term, used to express any narrow, flat moulding. The tænia on the Doric architrave is called its Bandelet.

Banker. A stone bench, on which masons cut and square their work.

Banquet. The footway of a bridge raised above the carriageway.

Barrel Drain. A drain of the form of a hollow cylinder.

Base. The lower part of a column, moulded or plain, on which the shaft is placed.

Basement. The lower part, or story, of a building, on which an order is placed, with a base, or plinth, die and cornice.

Basil. A word used by carpenters, &c., to denote the angle to which any edged tool is ground and fitted for cutting wood, &c.

Basin, en Coquille, that is, shaped like a shell.

Basin is likewise used for a dock.

Basket. A kind of vase in the form of a basket filled with flowers or fruits, serving to terminate some decoration.

Bassilica. A town or court hall, a cathedral, a palace, where kings administer justice.

Basso Relievo, or *Bas Relief.* The representation of figures projecting from a background, without being detached from it. Though this word, in general language, implies all kinds of relievos, from that of coins to more than one-half of the thickness from the background.

Bath. A receptacle of water appropriated for the purpose of bathing.

Batten. A scantling of stuff, from two to six inches broad, and from five-eighths to two inches thick, used in the boarding of floors; also upon walls, in order to secure the lath on which the plaster is laid.

Batter. When a wall is built in a direction that is not perpendicular.

Battlements. Indentations on the top of a parapet, or wall, first used in ancient fortifications, and afterwards applied to churches and other buildings.

Bay. (In Gothic architecture) an opening between piers, beams, or mullions.

Bay Window. [See Auriel.]

Bead and Flush work. A piece of panel work with a bead run on each edge of the included panel.

Bead and But work. A piece of framing in which the panels are flush, having beads stuck or run upon the two edges with the grain of the wood in their direction.

Bed-Mouldings. Those mouldings in all the orders between the corona and frieze.

Billet-Moulding. (In Gothic architecture) a cylindrical moulding, discontinued and renewed at regular intervals.

Boltel. (In Gothic architecture) slender shafts, whether arranged round a pier, or attached to doors, windows, &c. The term is also used for any cylindrical moulding.

Boss. (In Gothic architecture) a sculptured protuberance at the interjunction of the ribs in a vaulted roof.

Bossage. (A French term.) Any projection left rough on the surface of a stone for the purpose of sculpture, which is usually the last thing finished.

Boultin. A name given to the moulding, called the egg, or quarter-round.

Broach. (In Gothic architecture) a spire, or polygonal pyramid, whether of stone or timber.

Bracket. (In Gothic architecture) a projection to sustain a statue, or other ornament, and sometimes supporting the ribs of a roof.

Bulk. A piece of timber from four to ten inches square, and is sometimes called ranging timber.

Buttress. (In Gothic architecture) a projection on the exterior of a wall, to strengthen the piers and resist the pressure of the arches within.

Cabling. The filling up of the lower part of the fluting of a column, with a solid cylindrical piece. Flutings thus treated are said to be cabled.

Caisson. A name given to the sunk panels of various geometrical forms, symmetrically disposed in flat or vaulted ceilings, or in soffits, generally.

Canopy. (In Gothic architecture) the ornamented dripstone of an arch. It is usually of the ogee form.

Canted. (In Gothic architecture) any part of a building having its angles cut off is said to be canted.

Capital. The head, or uppermost part of a column or pilaster.

Carpenter. An artificer whose business is to cut, fashion and join timbers together, and other wood, for the purpose of building; the word is from the French *charpentier*, derived from *charpentie*, which signifies timber.

Carpentry, or that branch which is to claim our attention, is divided into three principal heads, namely, Constructive, Descriptive, and Mechanical; of these, Descriptive carpentry shows the lines, or methods for forming every species of work in *plano*, by the rules of geometry; Constructive carpentry, the practice of reducing the wood into particular forms, and joining the forms so produced so as to make a complete whole, according to the intention of the design; and Mechanical carpentry displays the relative strength of the timbers, and the strains to which they are subjected by their disposition.

Cartouch. The same as modillions, except that it is exclusively used to signify those blocks or modillions at the eaves of a house. [See Modillion.]

Caryatides. Figures of women, which serve instead of columns, to support the entablature.

Casement. The same as Scotia, — which see. The term is also used for a sash hung upon hinges.

Cauliculus. The volute or twist under the flower in the Corinthian capital.

Cavetto. A hollow moulding, whose profile is a quadrant of a circle, principally used in cornices.

Cell. [See Naos.]

Cincture. A ring, list or fillet, at the top or bottom of a column, serving to divide the shaft of a column from its capital and base.

Chamfer. (In Gothic architecture) an arch, or jamb of a door, canted.

Champ. (In Gothic architecture) a flat surface in a wall, or pier, as distinguished from a moulding, shaft, or panel.

Cinque-foil. (In Gothic architecture) an ornamental figure, with five leaves, or points.

Column. A member in architecture of a cylindrical form, consisting of a base, a shaft, or body, and a capital. It differs from the pilaster, which is square on the plan. Columns should always stand perpendicularly.

Composite Order. One of the orders of architecture.

Cope, Coping. (In Gothic architecture) the stone covering the top of a wall or parapet.

Corbel. (In Gothic architecture) a kind of bracket. The term is generally used for a continued series of brackets on the exterior of a building supporting a projecting battlement, which is called a *Corbel table.*

Corinthian Order. One of the orders of architecture.

Cornice. The projection, consisting of several members, which crowns or finishes an entablature, or the body or part to which it is annexed. The cornice used on a pedestal is called the cap of the pedestal.

Corona. Is that flat, square, and massy member of a cornice, more usually called the drip, or larmier, whose situation is between the cymatium above and the bed-moulding below. Its use is to carry the water, drop by drop, from the building.

Corridor. A gallery, or open communication to the different apartments of a house.

Corsa. The name given by Vitruvius to a platband, or square facia, whose height is more than its projecture.

Crenelle. (In Gothic architecture) the opening of an embattled parapet.

Crest. (In Gothic architecture) a crowning ornament of leaves running on the top of a screen, or other ornamental work.

Crocket. (In Gothic architecture) an ornament of leaves running up the sides of a gable, or ornamented canopy.

Cupola. A small room, either circular or polygonal, standing on the top of a dome. By some it is called a lantern.

Cushioned. [See Frieze.]

Cusp. (In Gothic architecture) a name for the segments of circles forming the trefoil, quatrefoil, &c.

Cyma, called also *Cymatium*, its name arising from its resemblance to a wave. A moulding which is hollow in its upper part, and swelling below.

Decagon. A plain figure, having ten sides and angles.

Decastyle. A building having ten columns in front.

Decempeda. (*Decem*, ten, and *pes*, foot, Latin.) A rod of ten feet, used by the ancients in measuring. It was subdivided into twelve inches in each foot, and ten digits in each inch; like surveyors' rods used in measuring short distances, &c.

Decimal Scale. Scales of this kind are used by draftsmen, to regulate the dimensions of their drawings.

Decoration. Anything that enriches or gives beauty and ornament to the orders of architecture.

Demi-Metope. The half a metope, which is found at the retiring or projecting angles of a Doric frieze.

Dentils. Small, square blocks, or projections used in the bed-mouldings of the cornices in the Ionic, Corinthian, Composite, and sometimes Doric orders.

Details of an Edifice. Drawings or delineations for the use of builders, otherwise called working plans.

Diagonal Scale is a scale subdivided into smaller parts by secondary intersections, or oblique lines.

Diameter. The line in a circle passing from the circumference through the centre.

Diamond. A sharp instrument formed of that precious stone, and used for cutting glass.

Diapered. (In Gothic architecture) a panel, or other flat surface, sculptured with flowers, is said to be diapered.

Diastyle. That intercolumniation, or space between columns, consisting of three diameters — some say four diameters.

Die, or *Dye.* A naked square cube. Thus the body of a pedestal, or that part between its base and cap, is called the die of the pedestal. Some call the abacus the die of the capital.

Dimension. (*Dimetier*, Latin.) In Geometry is either length, breadth, or thickness.

Diminution. A term expressing the gradual decrease of thickness in the upper part of a column.

Dipteral. A term used by the ancients to express a temple with a double range of columns in each of its flanks.

Dodecagon. A regular polygon, with twelve equal sides and angles.

Dodecastyle. A building having twelve columns in front.

Dome. An arched or vaulted roof, springing from a polygonal, circular, or elliptic plane.

Doric Order. One of the five orders of architecture.

Dormant, or *Dormer Window.* (In Gothic architecture) a window set upon the slope of a roof or spire.

Dooks. Flat pieces of wood of the shape and size of a brick, inserted in brick walls, sometimes called plugs, or wooden bricks.

Door. The gate, or entrance of a house, or other building, or of an apartment in a house.

Dormitory. A sleeping room.

Drawing or *Withdrawing Room.* A large and elegant apartment, into which the company withdraw after dinner.

Dressing-Room. An apartment contiguous to the sleeping-room, for the convenience of dressing.

Drip. (In Gothic architecture) a moulding much resembling the cymatium of Roman architecture, and used for the same purpose as a canopy over the arch of a door or window.

Drops. [See Guttæ.]

Echinus. The same as the ovolo, or quarter round; but perhaps it is only called Echinus with propriety.

Edging. The reducing the edges of ribs or rafters, that they may range together.

Elbows of a Window. The two panelled flanks, one under each shutter.

Elevation. A geometrical projection drawn on a plane perpendicular to the horizon.

Embankments are artificial mounds of earth, stone, or other materials, made to confine rivers, canals, and reservoirs of water, within their prescribed limits; also, for levelling up of railroads, &c.

Embrasure. (In Gothic architecture) the same as *Crenelle*, — which see.

Encarpus. The festoons on a frieze, consisting of fruits, flowers, and leaves. [See Festoon.]

Entablature. The assemblage of parts supported by the column. It consists of three parts, the architrave, frieze, and cornice.

Entail. (In Gothic architecture) delicate carving.

Entasis. The slight curvature of the shafts of ancient Grecian columns, particularly the Doric, which is scarcely perceptible and beautifully graceful.

Entresol. [See Mezzanine.]

Epistylum. The same as architrave, — which see.

Eustyle. That intercolumniation which, as its name would import, the ancients considered the most elegant, namely, two diameters and a quarter of a column. Vitruvius says this manner of arranging columns exceeds all others in strength, convenience, and beauty.

Facade. The face or front of any considerable building to a street, court, garden, or other place.

Facia. A flat member in the entablature or elsewhere, being, in fact, nothing more than a band, or broad fillet.

Fane, Phane, Vane. (In Gothic architecture) a plate of metal, usually cut into some fantastic form, and turning on a pivot, to determine the course of the wind.

Fastigium. [See Pediment.]

Feather-edged Boards are narrow boards made thin on one edge. They are used for the facings or boarding of wooden walls.

Festoon. An ornament of carved work, representing a wreath or garland of flowers or leaves, or both, interwoven with each other.

Fillet. The small, square member which is placed above or below the various square or curved members in an order.

Finial. (In Gothic architecture) the ornament, consisting usually of four crockets, which is employed to finish a pinnacle, gable, or canopy.

Flank. The least side of a pavilion, by which it is joined to the main building.

Flatning, in inside house painting, is the mode of finishing without leaving a gloss on the surface, which is done by adding the spirits of turpentine to unboiled linseed oil.

Flight of Stairs is a series of steps, from one landing-place to another.

Floors. The bottoms of rooms.

Flutings. The vertical channels on the shafts of columns, which are usually rounded at the top and bottom.

Flyers are steps in a series, which are parallel to each other.

Folding Doors are made to meet each other from opposite jambs, on which they are hung.

Foliage. An ornamental distribution of leaves or flowers on various parts of the building.

Foreshorten. A term applicable to the drawings or designs in which, from the obliquity of the view, the object is represented as receding from the opposite side of the plane of the projection.

Foundation. That part of a building or wall which is below the surface of the ground.

Foot. A measure of twelve inches, each inch being three barleycorns.

Frame. The name given to the wood work of windows, enclosing glass, and the outward work of doors or windows, or window shutters, enclosing panels; and in carpentry, to the timber work supporting floors, roofs, ceilings, or to the intersecting pieces of timbers forming partitions.

Fret. A kind of ornamental work, which is laid on a plane surface; the Greek fret is formed by a series of right angles of fillets, of various forms and figures.

Frieze, or *Frize.* The middle member of the entablature of an order, which separates the architrave and the cornice.

Frontispiece. The face or fore front of a house; but it is a term more usually applied to its decorated entrance.

Front. A name given to the principal interior facade of a building.

Frustum. A piece cut off from a regular figure; the frustum of a cone is the part that remains when the top is cut off by an intersection parallel to its base, as the Grecian Doric column without a base.

Furrings are flat pieces of timber, plank or board, used by carpenters to bring dislocated work to a regular surface.

Fust. The shaft of a column. [See Shaft.]

Gable. (In Gothic architecture) the triangularly-headed wall which covers the end of a roof.

Gable Window. (In Gothic architecture) a window in a gable. These are generally the largest windows in the composition, frequently occupying nearly the whole space of the wall.

Gablet. (In Gothic architecture) a little gable. [See Canopy.]

Gage. In carpentry, an instrument to strike a line parallel to the straight side of any board or piece of stuff.

Gain. The bevelled shoulder of a binding joist.

Garland. (In Gothic architecture) an ornamental band surrounding the top of a tower or spire.

Glyphs. The vertical channels sunk in the triglyphs of the Doric frieze.

Gola, or *Gula.* The same as Ogee, — which see.

Gorge. The same as Cavetto, — which see.

Gouge. A chisel of a semi-circular form.

Granite. A genus of stone much used in building, composed chiefly of quartz, feldspar and mica, forming rough and large masses of very great hardness.

Groin. (In Gothic architecture) the diagonal line formed by the intersection of two vaults in a roof.

Groined Ceiling. A surface formed of three or more curved surfaces, so that every two may form a groin, all the groins terminating at one extremity in a common point.

Groove, or *Mortise.* The channel made by a joiner's plane in the edge of a moulding, style or rail, to receive the tenon.

Ground Floor. The lowest story of a building.

Ground Plane. A line forming the ground of a design or picture, which line is a tangent to the surface of the face of the globe.

Ground Plot. The ground on which a building is placed.

Grounds. Joiners give this name to narrow strips of wood put in walls to receive the laths and plastering.

Guttæ, or *Drops.* Those frusta of cones in the Doric entablature which occur in the architrave below the tænia under each triglyph.

Gutters are a kind of canals in the roofs of houses, to receive and carry off rain water.

Halving. The junction of two pieces of timber, by inserting one into the other; in some cases to be preferred to mortising.

Hand-Railing. The art of forming hand-rails round circular and elliptic well-holes without the use of the cylinder.

Hanging-Stile, of a door. Is that to which the hinges are fixed.

Heel of a Rafter. The end or foot that rests upon the wall plate.

Helical Line of a Hand-Rail. The line, or spiral line, representing the form of the hand-rail before it is moulded.

Helix. The curling stalk under the flower in the Corinthian capital. [See Cauliculus.]

Hem. The spiral projecting part of the Ionic capital.

Hexastyle. A building having six columns in front.

Hood-Mould. (In Gothic architecture.) [See Drip.]

Hook-Pins. The same as *Draw Bore-Pins*, to keep the tenons in their place, while in the progress of framing: the pin has a head, or notch, in the outer end, to draw it at pleasure.

Hypæthral. Open at top; uncovered by a roof.

Hyperthyron. The lintel of a doorway.

Hypotrachelium. A term given by Vitruvius to the slenderest part of the shaft of a column where it joins the capital. It signifies the part under the neck.

Inchnography. The transverse section of a building, which represents the circumference of the whole edifice; the different rooms and apartments, with the thickness of the walls; the dimensions and situation of the doors, windows, chimneys; the projection of columns, and everything that could be seen in such a section, if really made in a building.

Impost. The layer of stone or wood that crowns a door-post or pier, and which supports the base line of an arch or arcade; it generally projects, and is sometimes formed of an assemblage of mouldings.

Inch. The twelfth part of a foot. For the purpose of reckoning in decimal fractions, it is divided into ten parts, or integers.

Inclined Plane. One of the mechanical powers used for raising ponderous bodies, in many instances of immense weight; a declivity of a hill, &c.

Insular Column is a column standing by itself.

Insulated. Detached from another building.

Intaglio. Any thing with figures in relief on it.

Intercolumniation. The distance between two columns.

Intrados. The under curved surface or soffit of an arch.

Inverted Arches. Such as have their intrados below the centre, or axis.

Ionic Order. One of the orders of architecture.

Jack Plane. A plane about 18 inches long, to prepare for the trying. plane.

Jack Rafters. The Jack timbers, which are fastened to the hip rafters and the wall plates.

Jambs. The side pieces of any opening in a wall, which bear the piece that discharges the superincumbent weight of such wall.

Joinery, in building, is confined to the nicer and more ornamental parts.

Jointer. A tool used for straightening and preparing stuff for joints, &c. This jointer is about two feet eight or ten inches long.

Kerf. The slit or cut in a piece of timber, or in a stone, by a saw.

King Post. The middle post in a section of rafters.

Label. (In Gothic architecture) a name for the drip, or hood moulding of an arch when it is returned square.

Lacunar, or *Laquear.* The same as Soffit.

Lantern. (In Gothic architecture) a turret or tower placed above a building, pierced either with windows to admit. light, or holes to let out steam.

Larmier. Called also Corona, — which see.

Lath. A narrow slip of wood, $1\frac{1}{4}$ to $1\frac{1}{2}$ inches wide, $\frac{1}{4}$ to $\frac{3}{8}$ inch thick, and four feet long, used in plastering.

Leaves. Ornaments representing natural leaves. The ancients used two sorts of leaves, natural and imaginary. The natural were those of the laurel, palm, acanthus, and olive; but they took such liberties with the form of these, that they might almost be said to be imaginary, too.

Level. A surface which inclines to neither side.

Lining. Covering for the interior, as casing is covering for the exterior surface of a building.

Lintel. A piece of timber or stone placed horizontally over a door, window, or other opening.

List, or *Listel.* The same as fillet, or annulet.

Listing. The cutting the sapwood out from both edges of a board.

Loop. (In Gothic architecture) a small, narrow window.

Louvre. (In Gothic architecture.) [See Lantern.]

Luffer Boarding. The same as blind slats.

Machicolations. (In Gothic architecture) small openings in an embattled parapet, for the discharge of missile weapons upon the assailants. Frequently these openings are underneath the parapet, in which case the whole is brought forward and supported by corbels.

Mechanical Carpentry. That branch of carpentry which teaches the disposition of the timbers according to their relative strength, and the strains to which they are subjected.

Mediæval Architecture. The architecture of England, France, Germany, &c., during the middle ages, including the Norman and early Gothic styles.

Members. (*Membrum,* Latin.) The different parts of a building; the different parts of an entablature; the different mouldings of a cornice, &c.

Metope. The square space between two triglyphs of the Doric order. It is sometimes left plain, at other times decorated with sculpture.

Mezzanine. A low story introduced between two principal stories.

Minerva Polias. A Grecian temple at Athens.

Minute. The sixtieth part of the diameter of a column. It is the subdivision by which architects measure the small parts of an order.

Mitre. An angle of forty-five degrees, a half of a right angle.

Modillion. An ornament in the entablature of richer orders, resembling a bracket.

Module. The semi-diameter of a column. This term is only properly used when speaking of the orders. As a semi-diameter it consists of only thirty minutes. [See Minute.]

Mosaic. A kind of painting representing cubes of glass, &c., and is formed of different colored stones, for paving, &c. Specimens of this kind have been found among the ruins of antiquity.

Mouldings. Those parts of an order which are shaped into various curved or square forms.

Mouth. The same as Cavetto, — which see.

Mutule. A projecting ornament of the Doric cornice, which occupies the place of the modillion in imitation of the ends of rafters.

Mullion. (In Gothic architecture) the framework of a window.

Naked. The unornamented, plain surface of a wall, column, or other part of a building.

Naos, or *Cella.* The part of a temple within the walls.

Newel. The solid, or imaginary solid, when the stairs are open in the centre, round which the steps are turned about.

Niche. A square or cylindrical cavity in a wall, or other solid.

Obelisk. A tall, slender frustum of a pyramid, usually placed on a pedestal. The difference between an obelisk and a pyramid, independent of the former being only a portion of the latter, is, that it always has a small base in proportion to its height.

Octastyle. A building with eight columns in front.

Ogee, or *Ogive.* The same as Cyma, — which see.

Order. An assemblage of parts, consisting of a base, shaft, capital, architrave, frieze, and cornice, whose several services, requiring some distinction in strength, have been contrived, or designed, in five several species, — Tuscan, Doric, Ionic, Corinthian, and Composite; each of which has its ornaments, as well as general fabric, proportioned to its strength and character.

Ordonnance. The arrangement of a design, and the disposition of its several parts.

Orle. (*Ital.*) A fillet or band under the ovolo of the capital. Palladio applies the term also to the plinth of the base of the column or pedestal.

Ovolo. A moulding sometimes called a quarter-round, from its profile being the quadrant of a circle. When sculptured it is called an Echinus, — which see.

Panel. A thin board having all its edges inserted in the groove of a surrounding frame.

Parapet. From the Italian Parapetto, breast high. The defence round a terrace, or roof of a building.

Parastatæ. Pilasters standing insulated.

Pavilion. A turret or small building, generally insulated, and comprised beneath a single roof.

Pedestal. The substruction under a column or wall. A pedestal under a column consists of three parts, — the base, the die, and the cornice, or cap.

Pediment. The low, triangular crowning ornament of the front of a building, or of a door, window, or niche.

Pend. (In Gothic architecture) a vaulted roof without groining.

Pendant. (In Gothic architecture) a hanging ornament in highly-enriched vaulted roofs.

Pinnacle. (In Gothic architecture) a small spire.

Peripteral. A term used by the ancients to express a building encompassed by columns, forming, as it were, an aisle round the building.

Peristylium. In Greek and Roman houses, a court, square, or cloister.

Perspective. Is the science which teaches us to dispose the lines and shades of a picture so as to represent, on a plane, the image of objects exactly as they appear in nature.

Piazza. A continued archway, or vaulting, supported by pillars or columns; a portico.

Pier. A solid between the doors or the windows of a building. The square, or other formed mass, or post, to which a gate is hung.

Pilaster. A square pillar engaged in a wall.

Pile. A stake or beam of timbers, driven firmly into the ground.

Pillar. A column of irregular form, always disengaged, and always deviating from the proportions of the orders; whence the distinction between a pillar and a column.

Platband. A square moulding, whose projection is less than its height or breadth.

Plinth. The square solid under the base of a column, pedestal, or wall.

Porch. An arched vestibule at the entrance of a church, or other building.

Portico. A place for walking under shelter, raised with arches, in the manner of a gallery; the portico is usually vaulted, but has sometimes a flat soffit, or ceiling. This word is also used to denote the projection before a church or temple, supported by columns.

Post. A piece of timber set erect in the earth. Perpendicular timbers of the wooden frame of a building.

Posticum. The back door of a temple ; also the portico behind the temple.

Principal Rafters. The two inclined timbers which support the roof.

Profile. The contour of the different parts of an order.

Projecture. The prominence of the mouldings, and members beyond the naked surface of a column, wall, &c.

Proscenium. The front part of the stage of the ancient theatres, on which the actors performed.

Prostyle. A building or temple with columns in front only.

Purlins. Pieces of timber framed horizontally from the principal rafters, to keep the common rafters from sinking in the middle.

Pycnostyle. An intercolumniation equal to one diameter and a half.

Pyramid. A solid with a square, polygonal, or triangular base, terminating in a point at top.

Quarter Round. [See Ovolo and Echinus.]

Quatrefoil. (In Gothic architecture) an ornament in tracery, consisting of four segments of circles, or cusps, within a circle.

Quirk Mouldings. The convex part of Grecian mouldings, when they recede at the top, forming a reënticent angle with the surface which covers the moulding.

Quoins. The external and internal angles of buildings or of their members. The corners.

Radius, in Geometry, is the semi-diameter of a circle, or a right line drawn from the centre to the circumference ; in mechanics, the spoke of a wheel.

Rails, in framing, the pieces that lie horizontal; and the perpendicular pieces are called stiles, in wainscoting, &c.

Raking. A term applied to mouldings whose arrises are inclined to the horizon.

Relievo, or *Relief.* The projecture of an architectural ornament.

Resistance, in mechanics, that power which acts in opposition to another, so as to diminish or destroy its effect.

Reticulated Work. That in which the courses are arranged in a net-like form. The stones are square, and placed lozengewise.

Return. (*Fr.*) The continuation of a moulding, projection, &c., in an opposite direction, as the flank of a portico, &c.

Rib. (*Sax.*) An arched piece of timber sustaining the plasterwork of a vault, &c.

Ridge. The top of the roof which rises to an acute angle.

Ring. A name sometimes given to the list, cincture, or fillet.

Roman Order. Another name for the Composite.

Rose. The representation of this flower is carved in the centre of each face of the abacus in the Corinthian capital, and is called the rose of that capital.

Rustic. The courses of stone or brick, in which the work is jagged out into an irregular surface. Also, work left rough, without tooling.

Sagging. The bending of a body in the middle by its own weight, when suspended horizontally by each end.

Salon. An apartment for state, or for the reception of paintings, and usually running up through two stories of the house. It may be square, oblong, polygonal, or circular.

Saloon. (*Fr.*) A lofty hall, usually vaulted at the top, with two stages of windows.

Sash. The wooden frame which holds the glass in windows.

Scaffold. A frame of wood fixed to walls, for masons, plasterers, &c., to stand on.

Scantling. The name of a piece of timber, as of quartering for a partition, when under five inches square, or the rafter, purlin, or pole-plate of a roof.

Scapus. The same as Shaft of a Column, — which see.

Scarfing. The joining and bolting of two pieces of timber together transversely, so that the two appear but as one.

Scotia. The name of a hollowed moulding, principally used between the tori of the base of columns.

Severy. (In Gothic architecture) a separate portion of a building.

Shaft. That part of a column which is between the base and capital. It is also called the Fust, as well as Trunk of a column.

Shank. A name given to the two interstitial spaces between the channels of the triglyph in the Doric frieze.

Shooting. Planing the edge of a board straight, and out of winding.

Shoulder. The plane, transverse to the length of a piece of timber from which a tenon projects.

Shutters. The boards or wainscoting which shut up the aperture of a window.

Sill. The timber or stone at the foot of a window or door; the ground timbers of a frame which support the posts.

Skirtings. The narrow boards which form a plinth round the margin of a floor.

Socle. A square, flat member, of greater breadth than height, usually the same as plinth.

• *Soffit.* The ceiling or underside of a member in an order. It means also the underside of the larmier or corona in a cornice; also, the underside of that part of the architrave which does not rest on the columns. [See also Lacunar.]

Sommer. The lintel of a door, window, &c.; a beam tenoned into a girder, to support the ends of joists on both sides of it.

Spandrel. (In Gothic architecture) the triangular space enclosed by one side of an arch, and two lines at right angles to each other, one horizontal, and on a level with the apex of the arch, the other perpendicular, and a continuation of the line of the jamb.

Spiral. A curve line of a circular kind, which in its progress recedes from its centre.

Steps. The degrees in ascending a staircase.

Stereobata, or *Stylobata.* The same as Entasis.

Strap. An iron plate to secure the junction of two or more timbers, into which it is secured by bolts.

Stretching Course. Bricks or stones laid in a wall with their longest dimensions in the horizontal line.

Surbase. The mouldings immediately above the base of a room.

Systyle. An intercolumniation equal to two diameters.

Table. (In Gothic architecture) any surface, or flat member.

Tæni. A term usually applied to the lastel above the architrave in the Doric order.

Templet. A mould used by bricklayers and masons for cutting or setting the work; a short piece of timber sometimes laid under a girder.

Tenon. A piece of timber the thickness of which is divided into about three parts. The two outside parts are cut away, leaving two shoulders; the middle part projects, and, being fitted to a mortise, is usually termed a tenon.

Terrace Roofs. Roofs which are flat at the top.

Tetrastyle. A building having four columns in front.

Torus. A moulding of semi-circular profile, used in the bases of columns.

Tracery. (In Gothic architecture) a term for the intersection, in various forms, of the mullions in the head of a window or screen.

Transom. (In Gothic architecture) a cross mullion in a window.

Trefoil. (In Gothic architecture) an ornament consisting of three cusps in a circle.

Triglyph. The ornament of the frieze in the Doric order, consisting of two whole and two half channels, sunk triangularly on the plan.

Trimens. Pieces of timber framed at right angles with the joints against the wall, for chimneys, and well-holes for stairs.

Trimmer. A small beam, into which are framed the ends of several joists. The two joists into which each end of the trimmer is framed are called *trimming joists.*

Trough Gutter. A gutter below the dripping eaves, to convey the water to the pipe by which it is discharged.

Trunk. [See Shaft.] When the word is applied to a pedestal it signifies the dado, or die, or body of the pedestal answering to the shaft of the column.

Truss. When the girders are very long, or the weight the floors are destined to support is very considerable, they are *trussed.*

Tuscan. One of the orders of architecture.

Tusk. A bevelled shoulder made above a tenon, to strengthen it.

Tympanum. The space enclosed by the cornice of the sloping sides of a pediment, and the level fillet of the corona.

Vault. An arched roof, so contrived that the stones, or other materials of which it is composed, support and keep each other in their places.

Vestibule. An ante-hall, lobby, or porch.

Vice. (In Gothic architecture) a spiral staircase.

Volute. The scroll which is appended to the capital of the Ionic order.

Wall-plates. Pieces of timber which are so placed as to form the supports to the roof of a building.

Well. The space occupied by a flight of stairs; the space left in the middle, beyond the ends of the steps, is called the *well-hole.*

Zigzag. (In Gothic architecture) an ornament so called from its resemblance to the letter.

THE PLATES

Pl. 1

GRECIAN DORIC

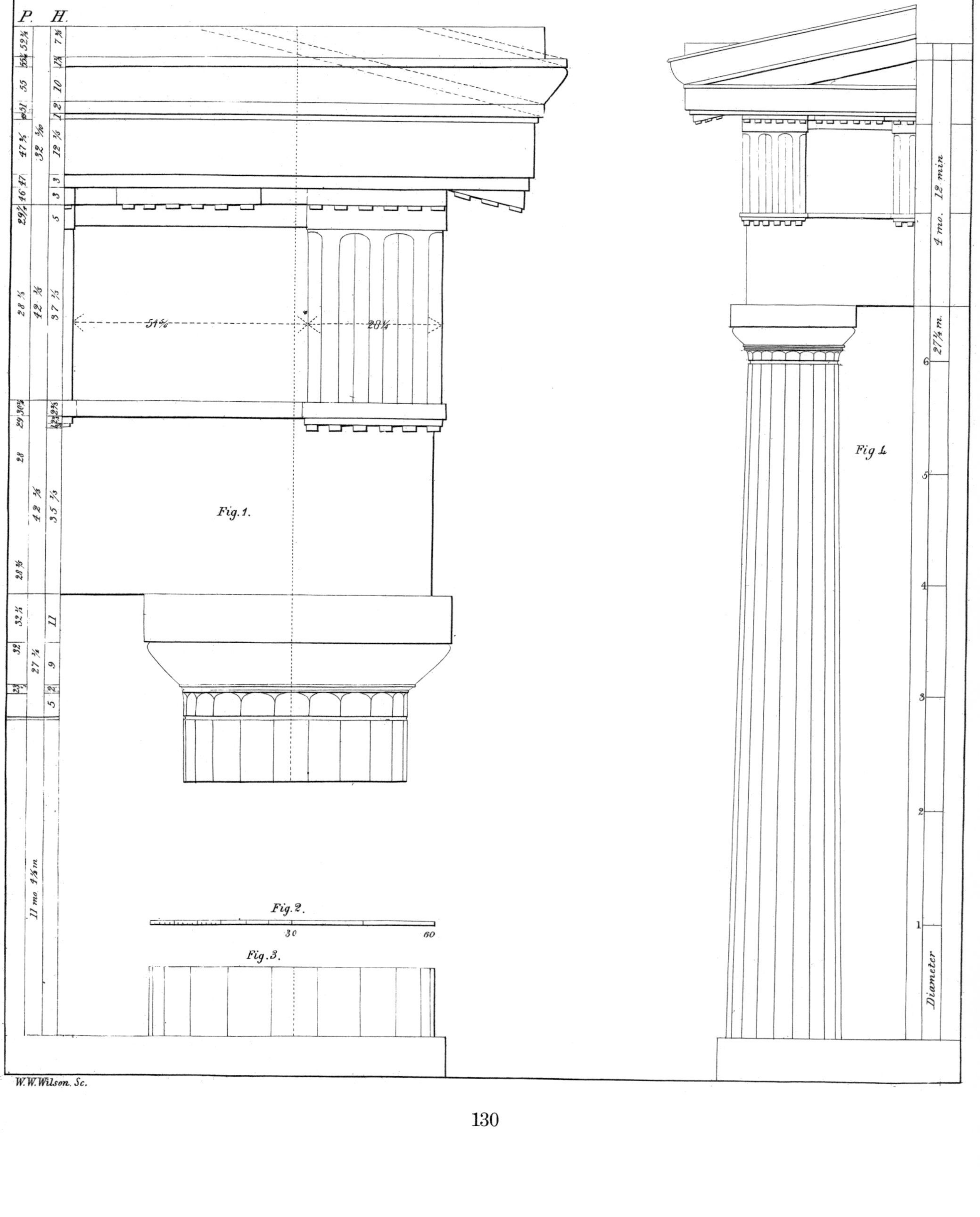

W. W. Wilson. Sc.

Pl. 2

GRECIAN DORIC.

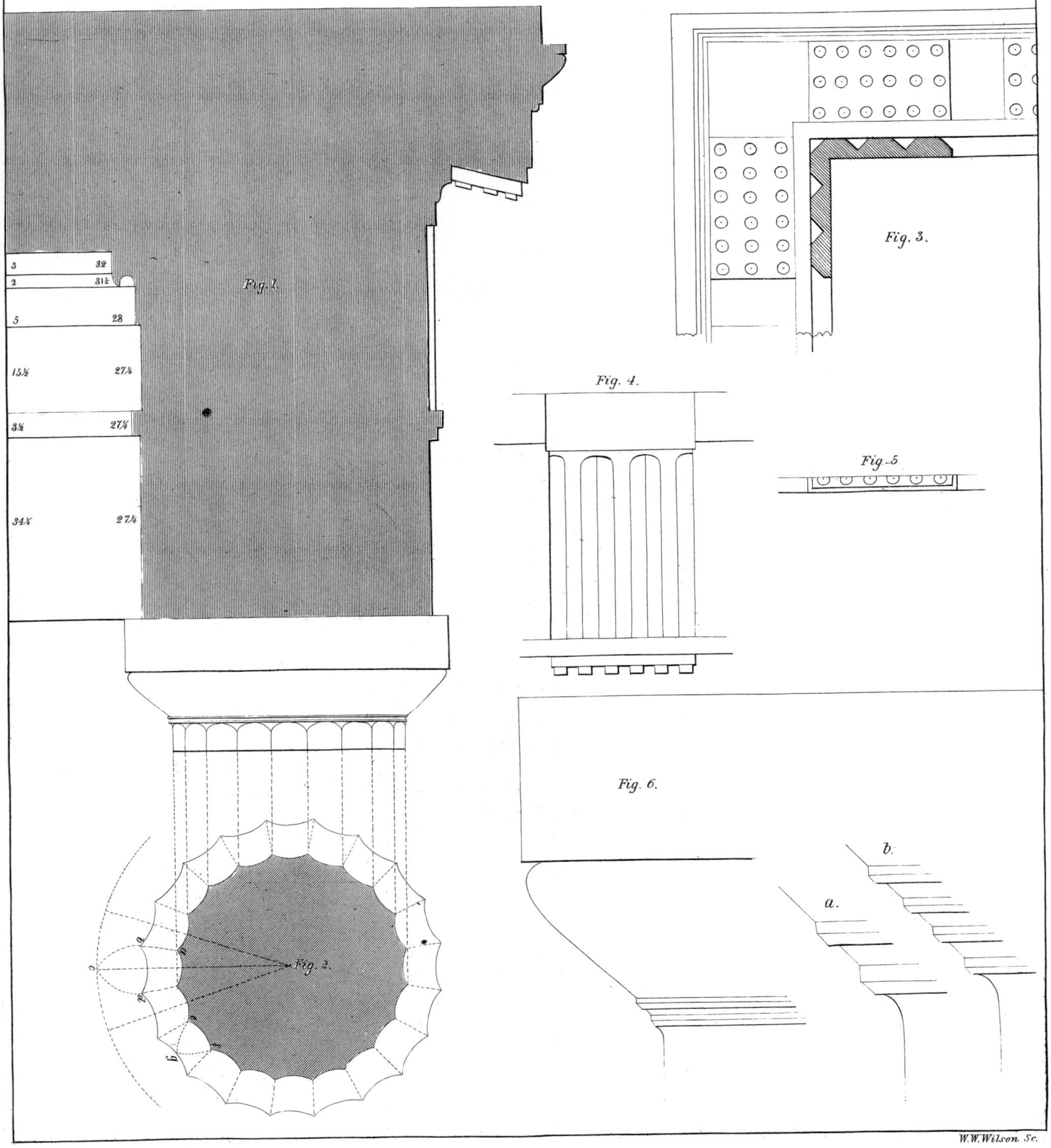

W.W. Wilson Sc.

Pl. 3

GRECIAN DORIC.

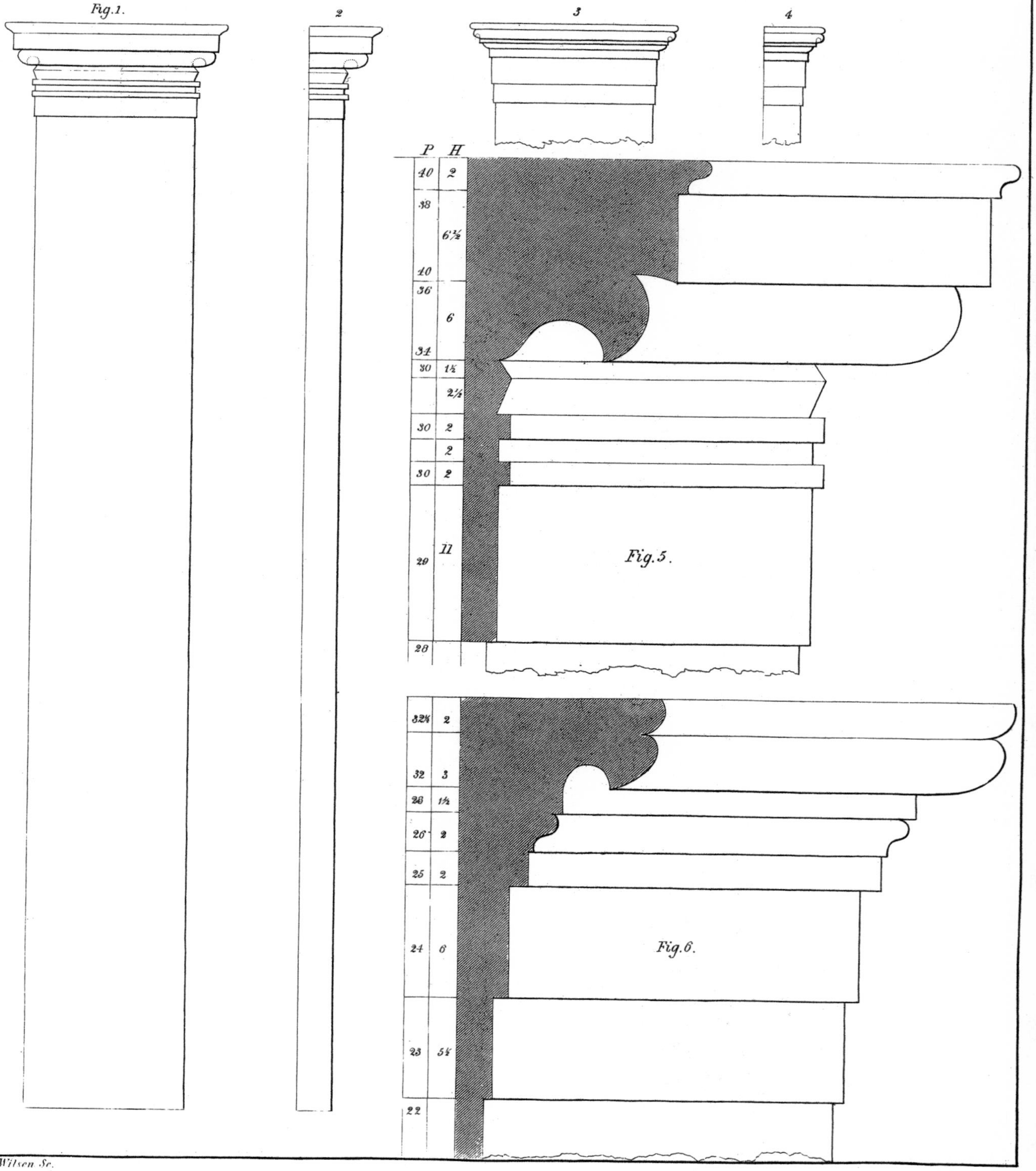

W. W. Wilson Sc.

GRECIAN FRONTISPIECE.

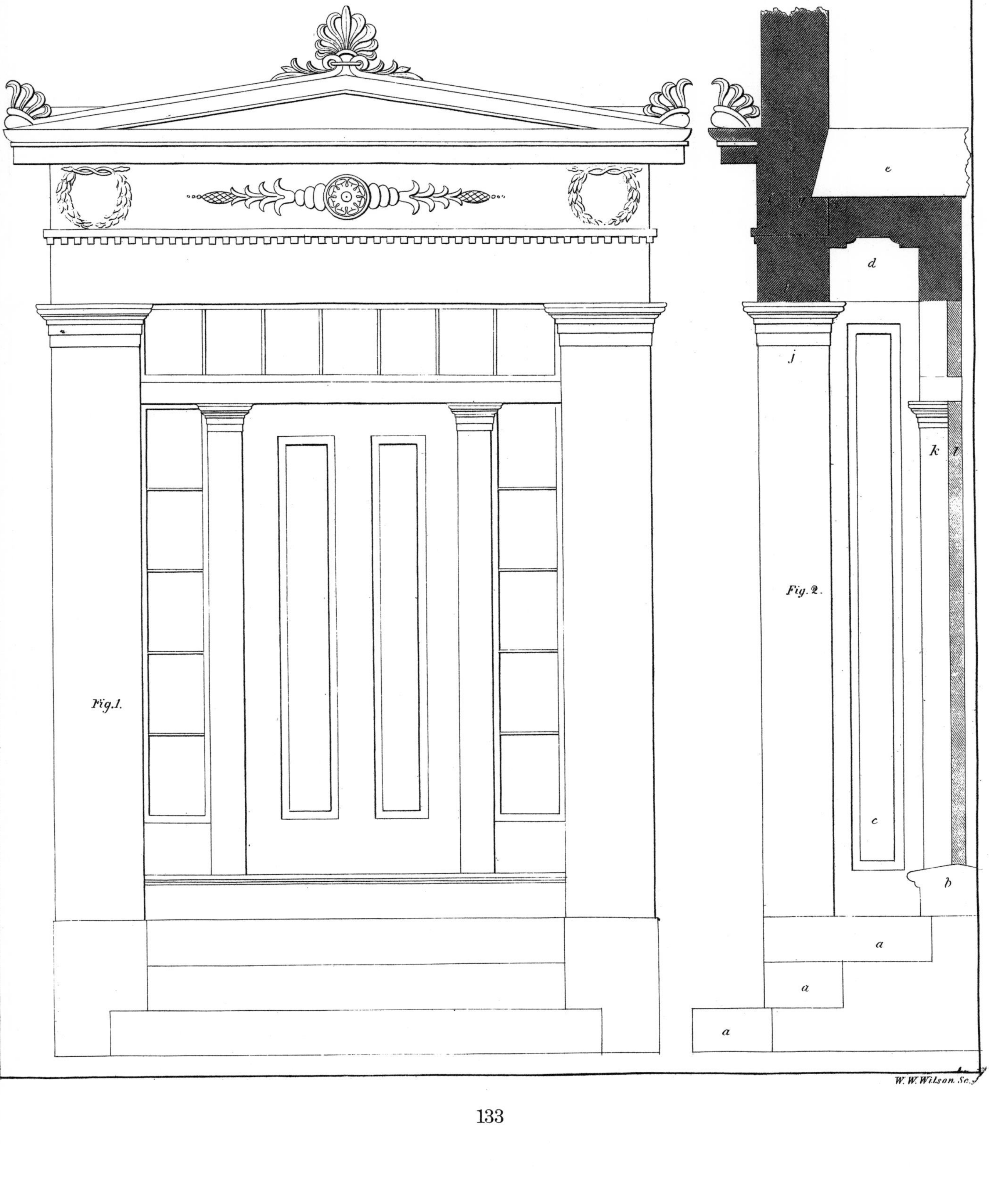

W. W. Wilson Sc.

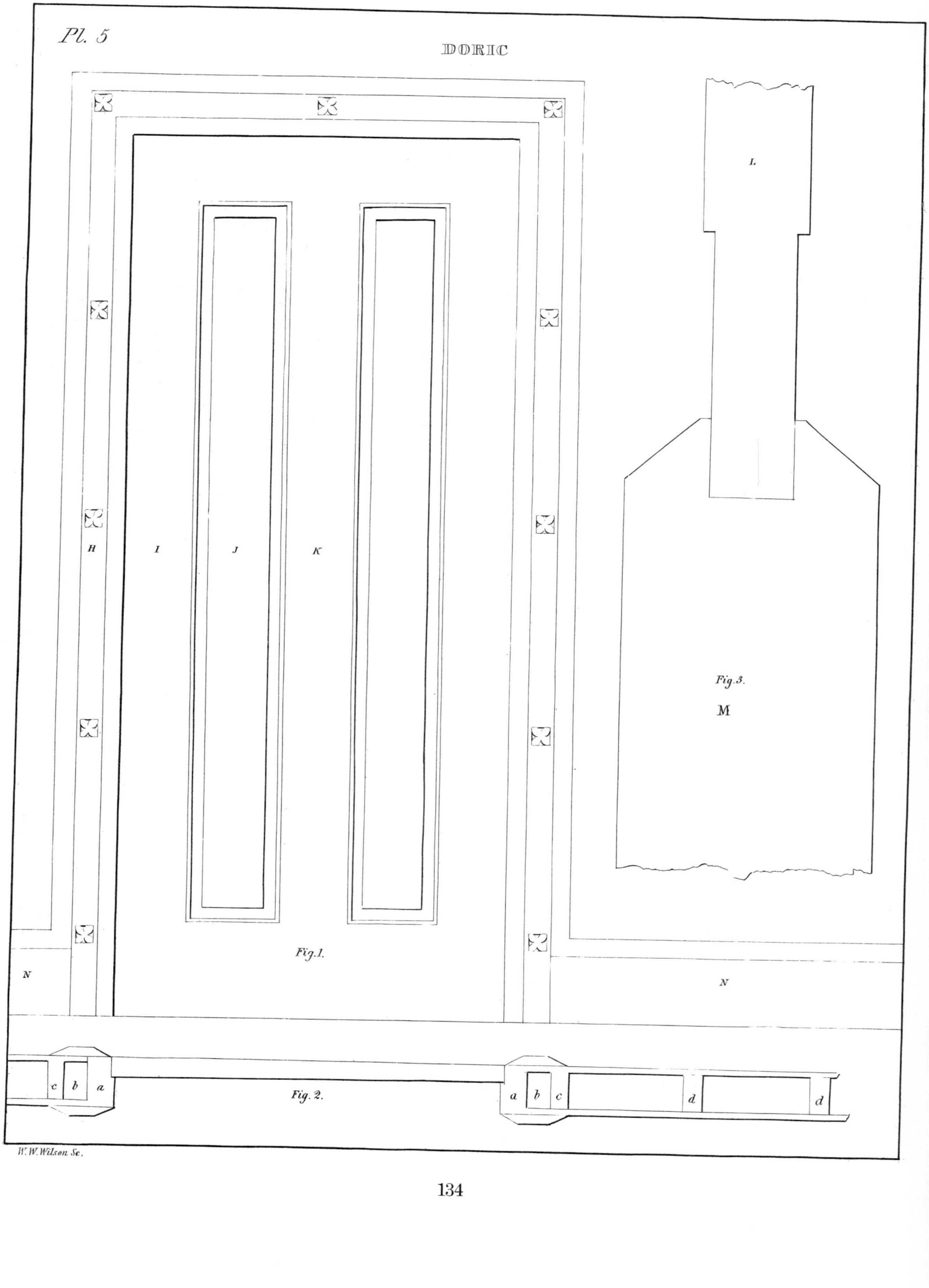
Pl. 5
DORIC
L
H
I
J
K
Fig. 3.
M
Fig. 1.
N
N
c
b
a
Fig. 2.
a
b
c
d
d
W. W. Wilson Sc.

DORIC

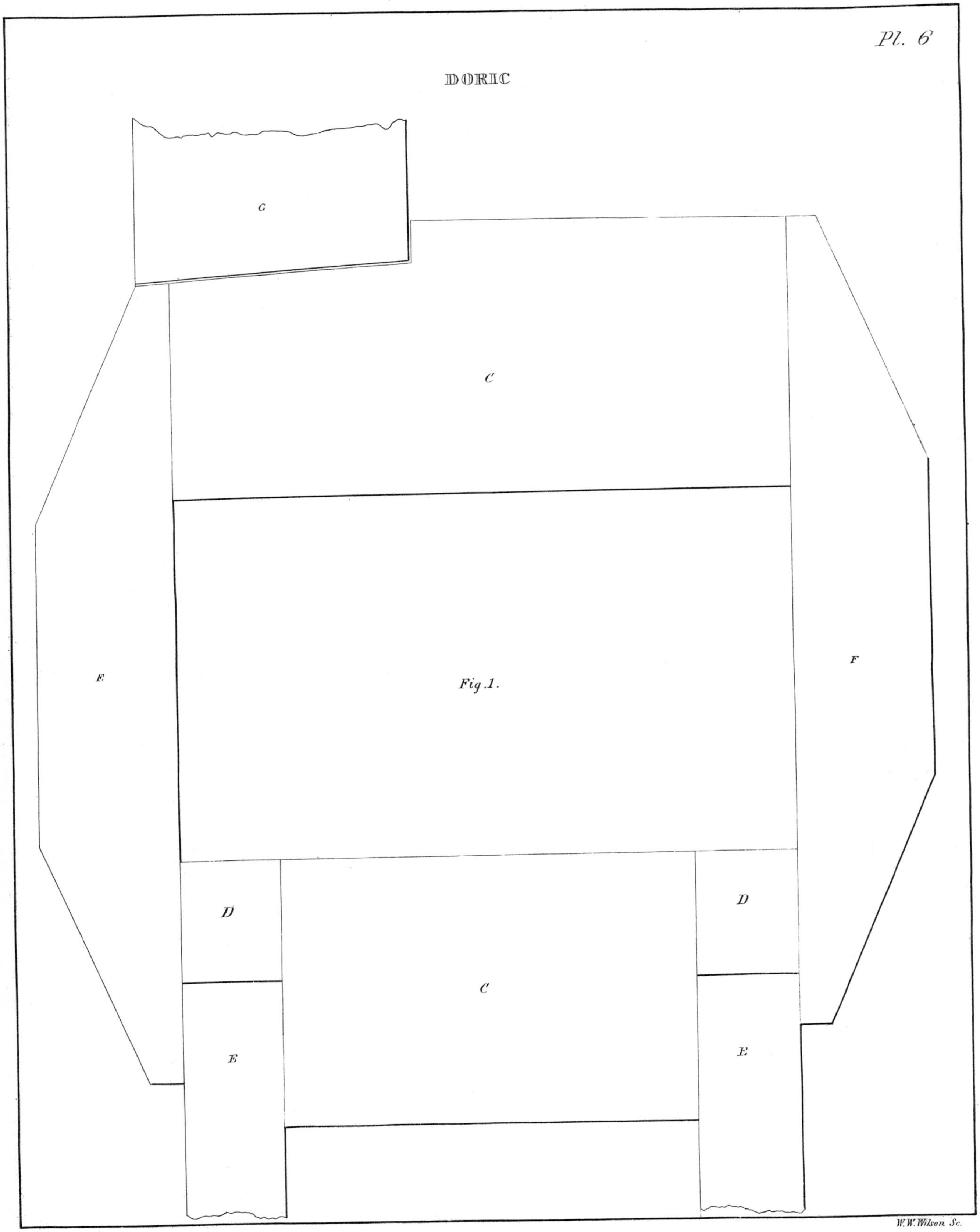

W. W. Wilson Sc.

Pl. 7

DORIC

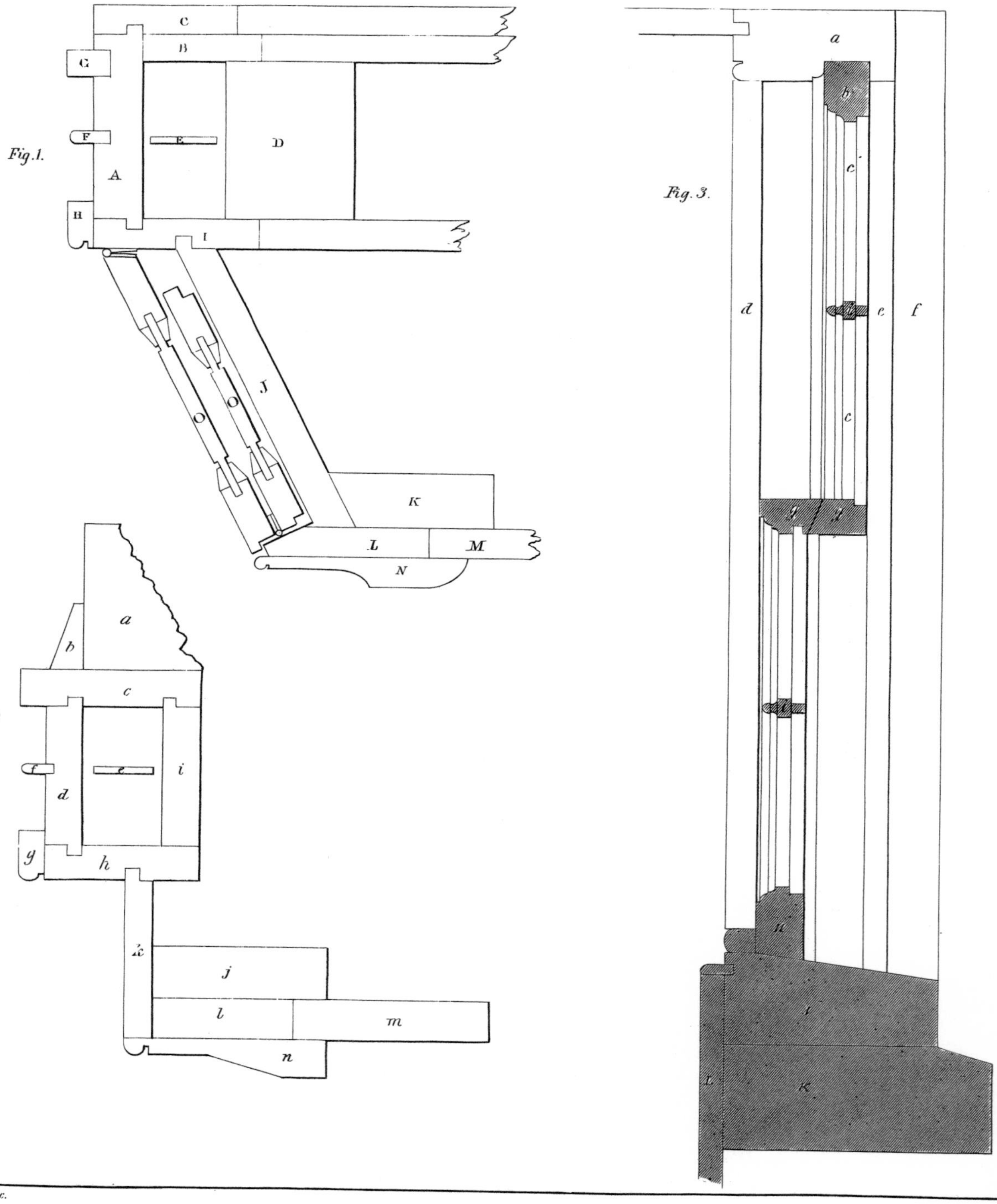

W. W. Wilson Sc.

Pl. 8

DORIC

Fig. 1.

W. W. Wilson Sc.

Pl. 9

DORIC

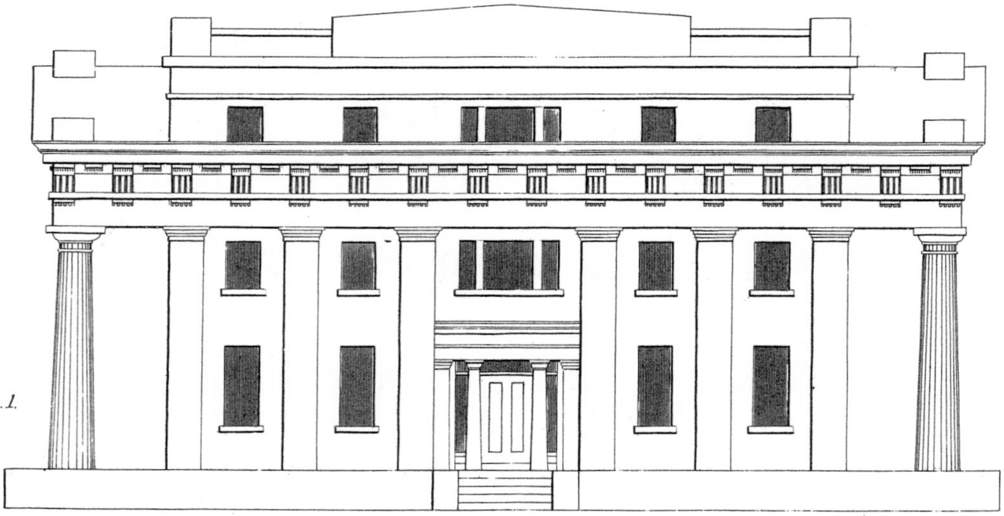

Fig. 1.

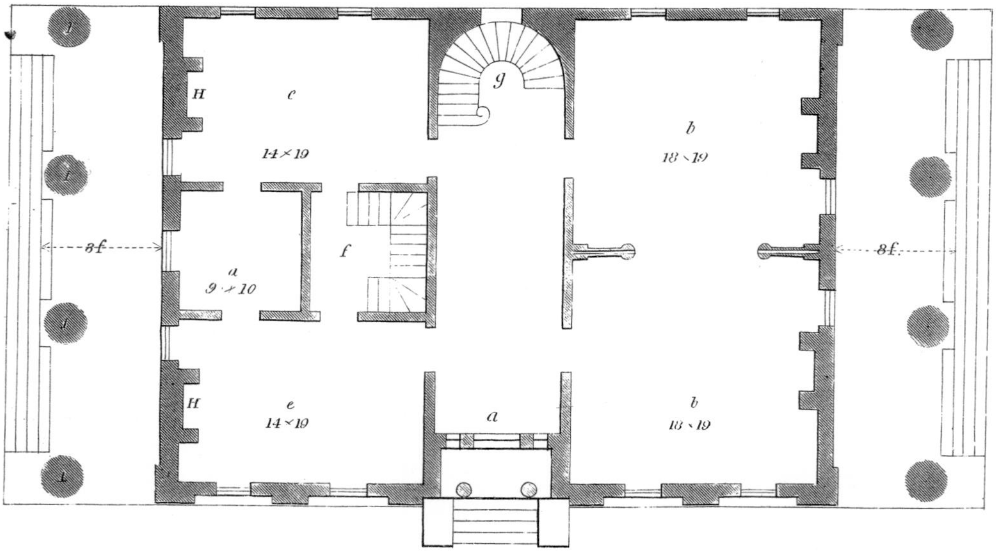

Fig. 2.

W. W. Wilson Sc.

Pl. 10

DORIC

Fig. 1.

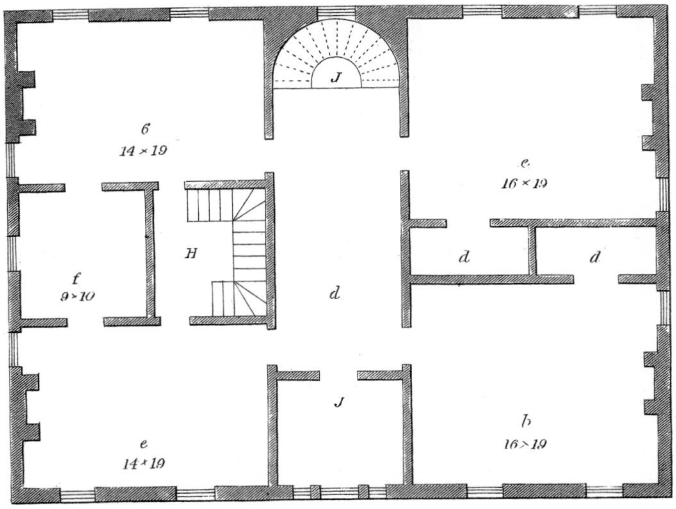

Fig. 2.

W. W. Wilson Sc.

Pl. 11

DORIC

Fig. 1.

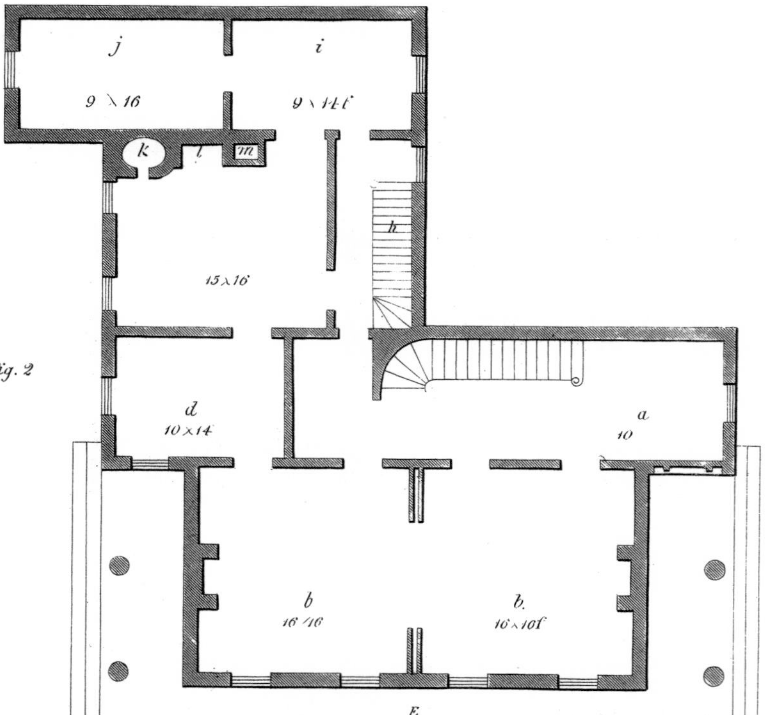

Fig. 2

W. W. Wilson Sc.

DORIC.

Fig. 1.

Fig. 2.

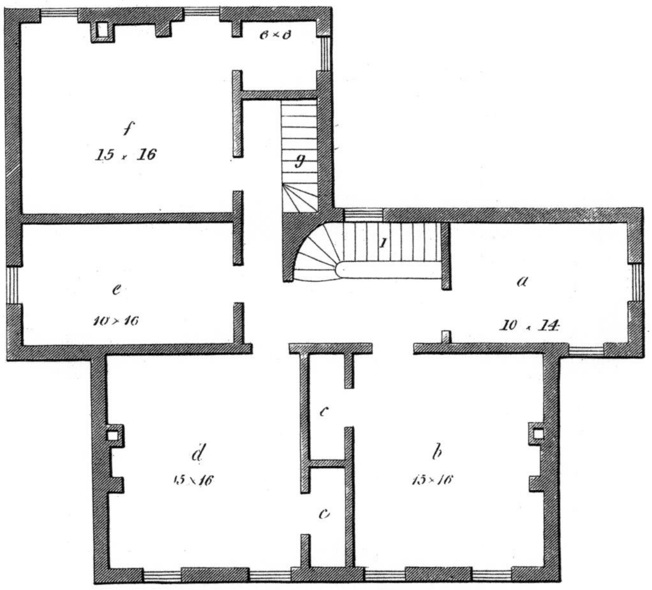

W. W. Wilson Sc.

Pl. 13

DORIC

Fig. 1

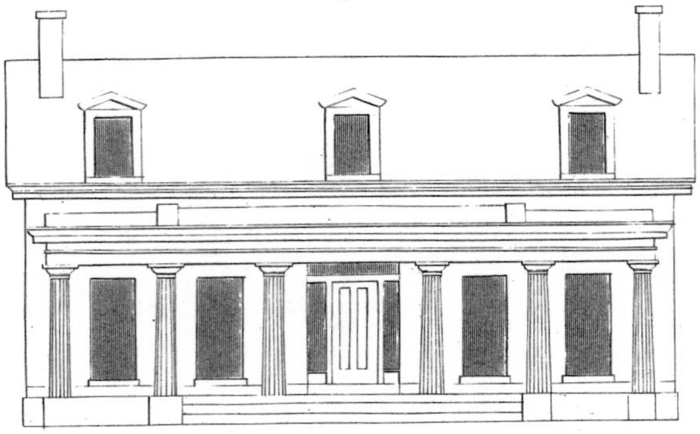

Fig. 2

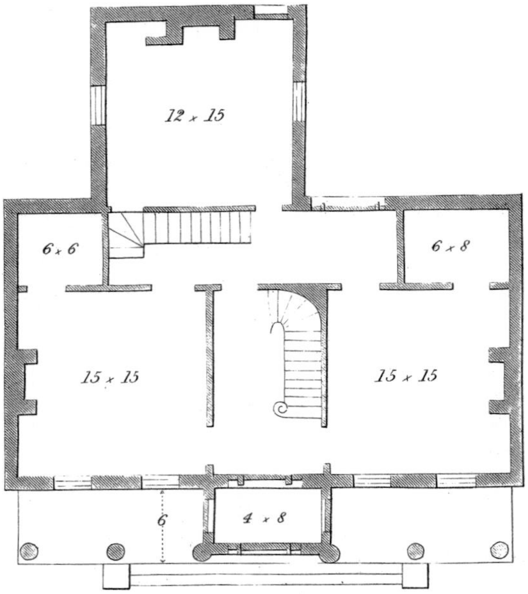

W. W. Wilson Sc.

Pl. 14

DORIC

Fig. 1

Fig. 2

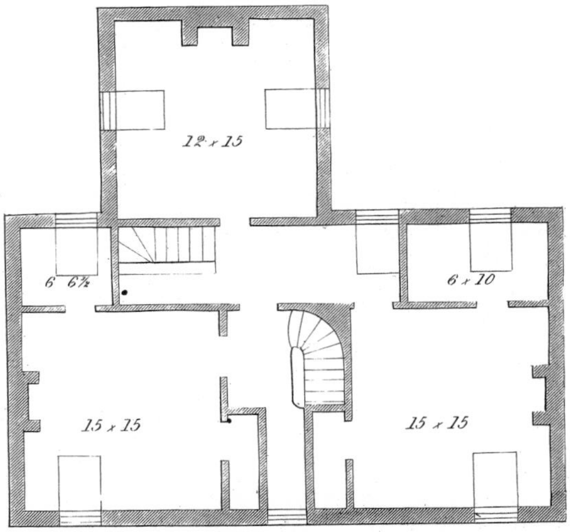

W. W. Wilson Sc.

Pl. 15

GRECIAN IONIC.

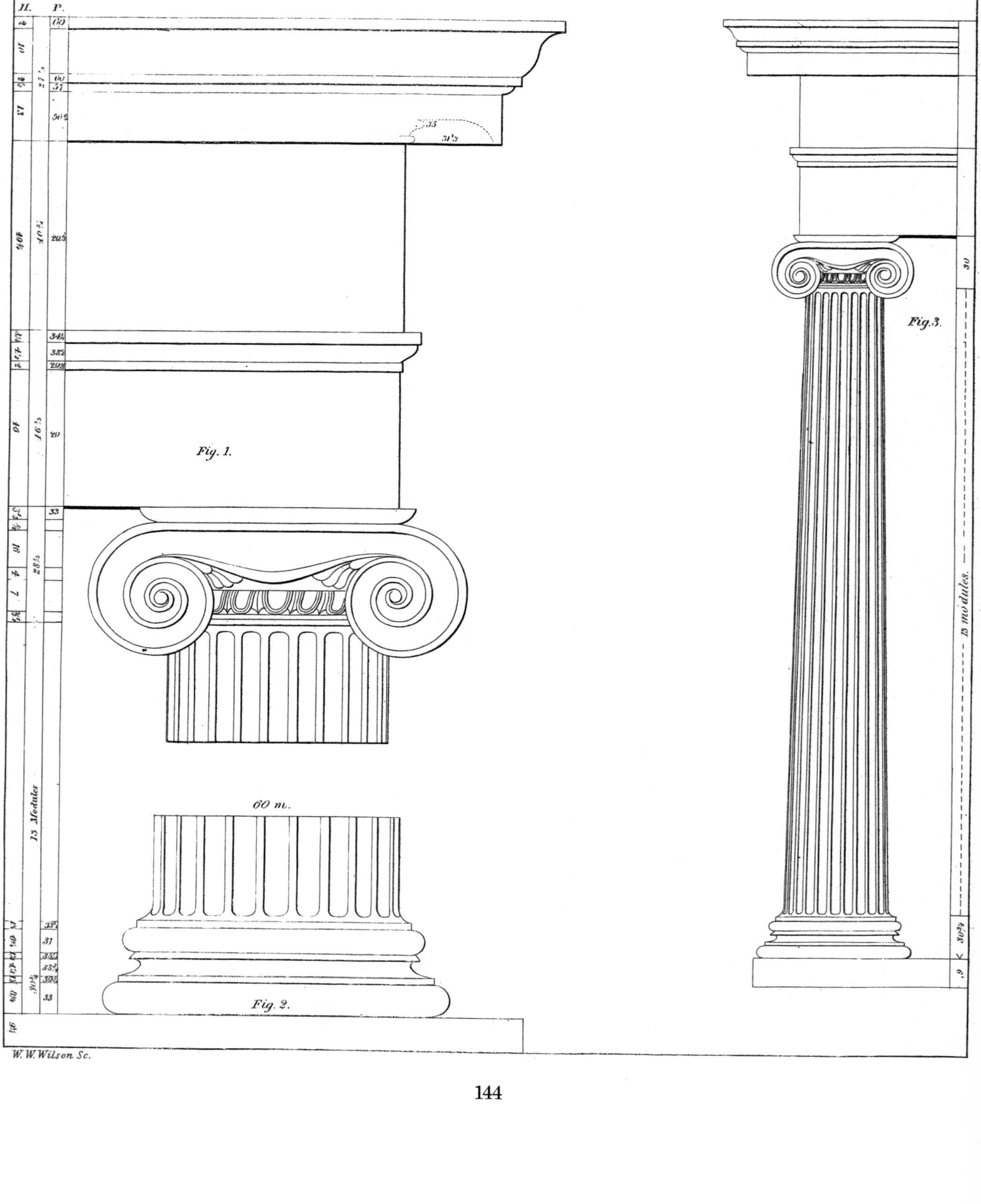

W. W. Wilson Sc.

Fig. 1.

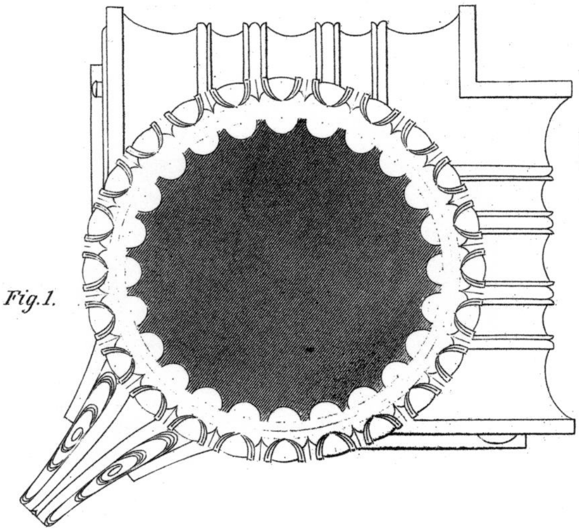

Fig. 2.

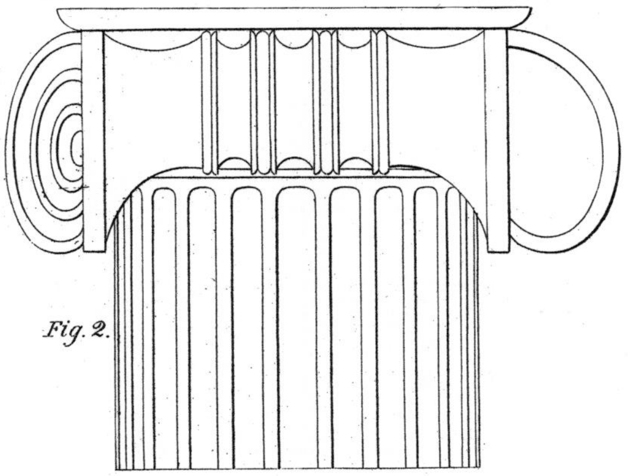

Fig. 3.

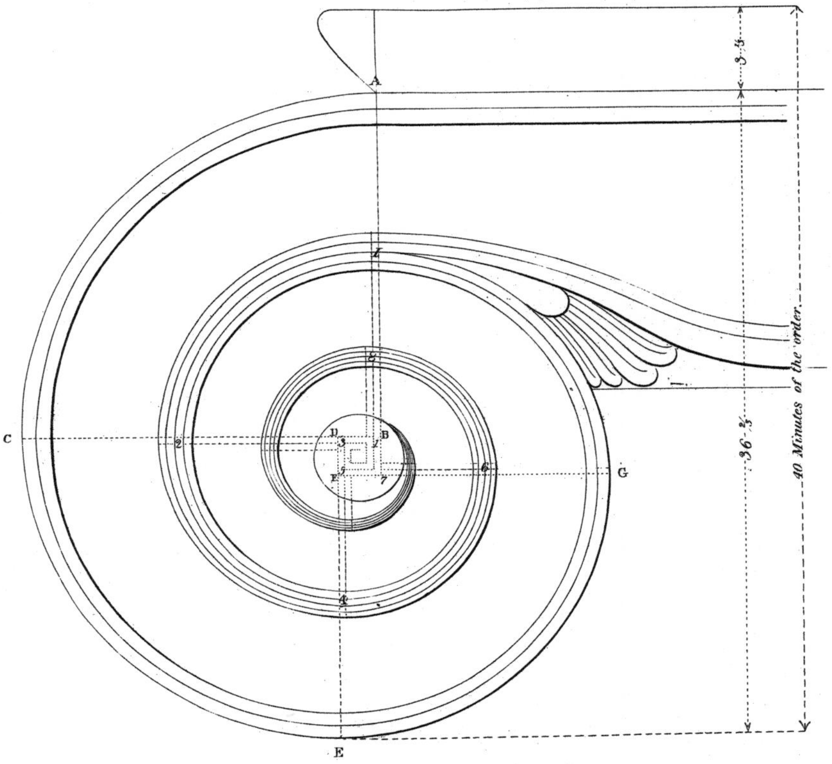

W.W. Wilson Sc.

Pl. 17.

GRECIAN IONIC

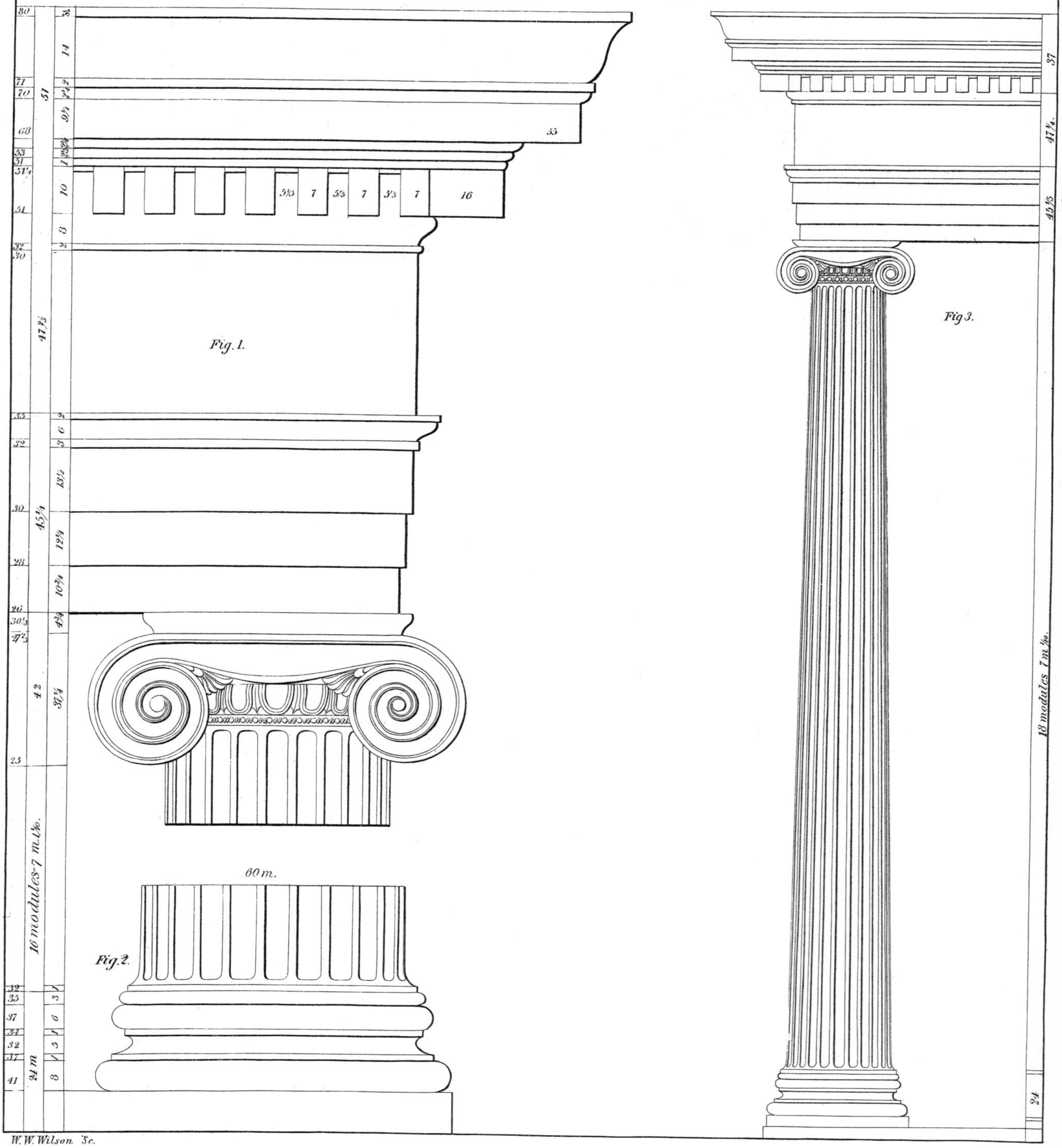

W. W. Wilson Sc.

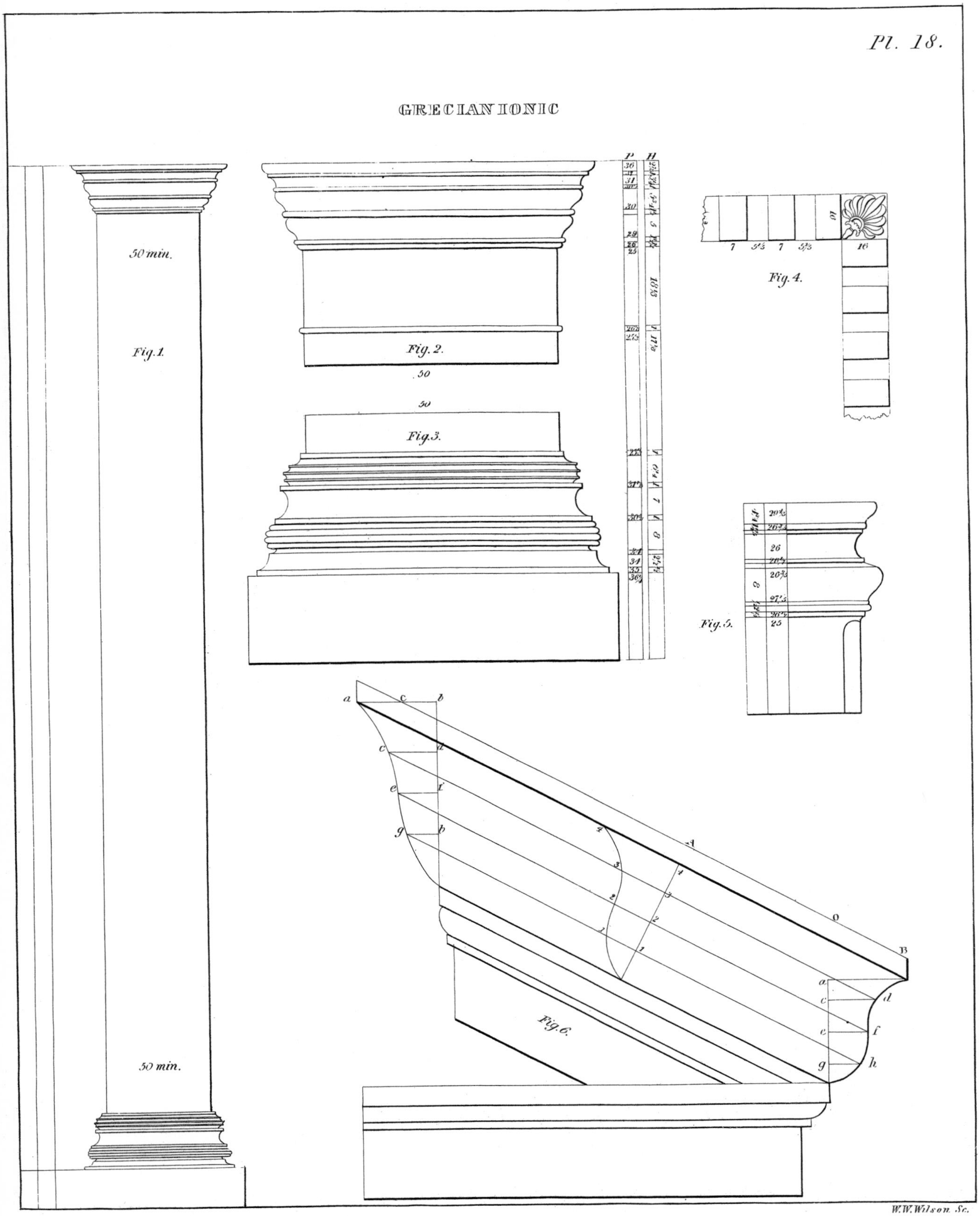
Pl. 18.
GRECIAN IONIC
50 min.
Fig. 1.
50 min.
Fig. 2.
50
50
Fig. 3.
P
H
Fig. 4.
Fig. 5.
Fig. 6.

W. W. Wilson Sc.

Pl. 19. MOULDINGS

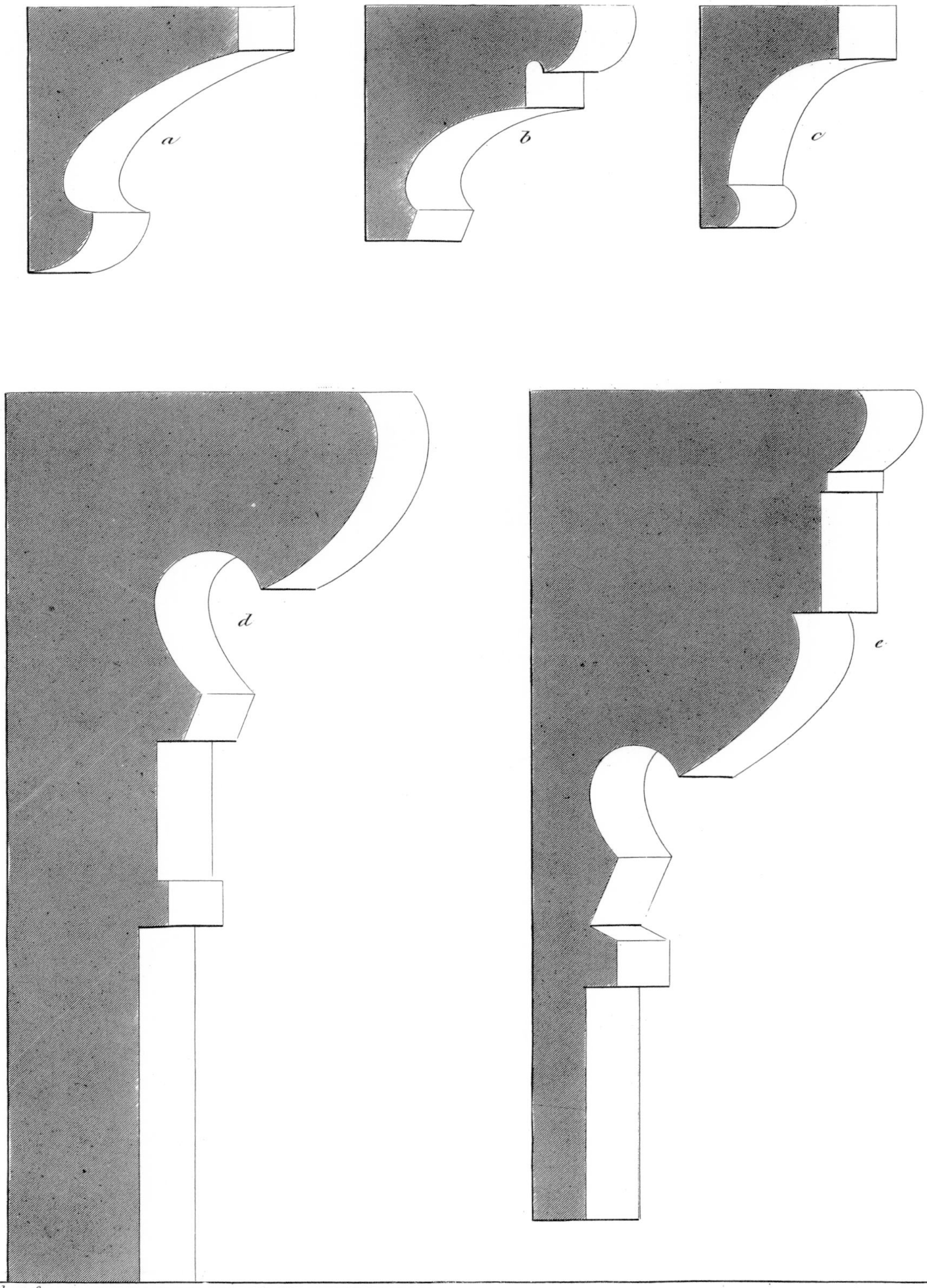

W. W. Wilson Sc.

MOULDINGS

Pl. 20.

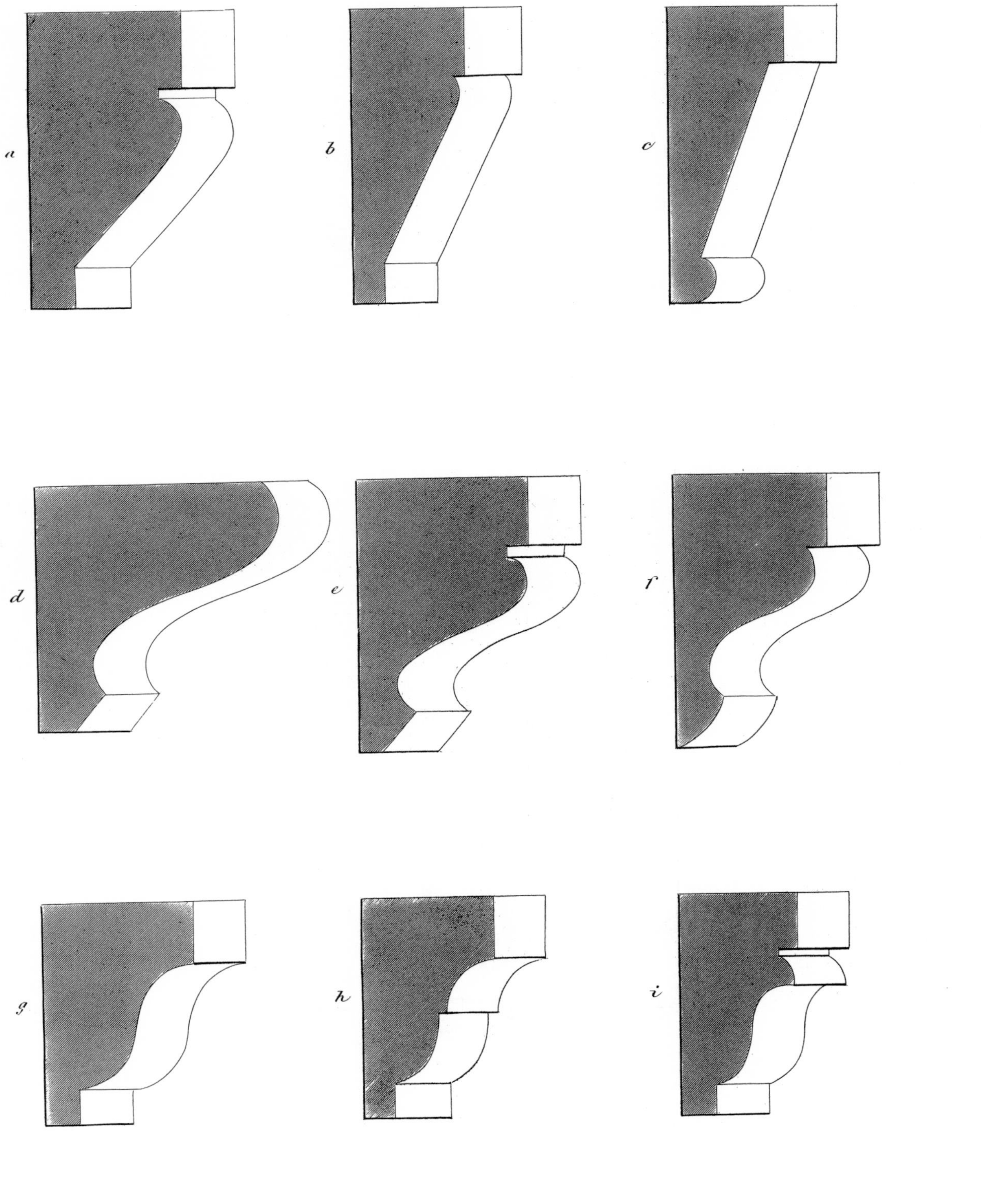

W. W. Wilson Sc.

Pl. 21

IONIC

Fig. 1

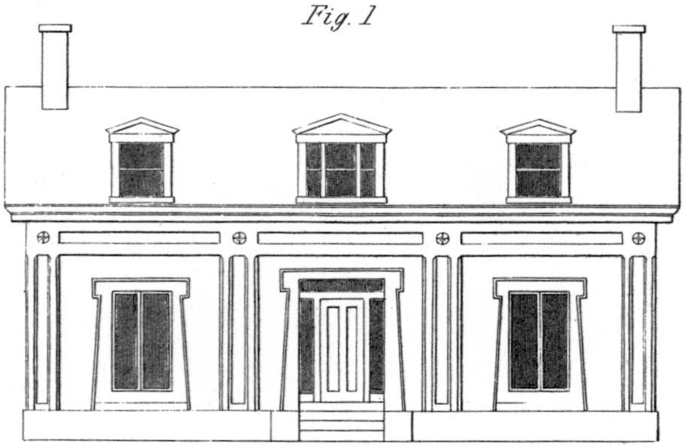

Fig. 2

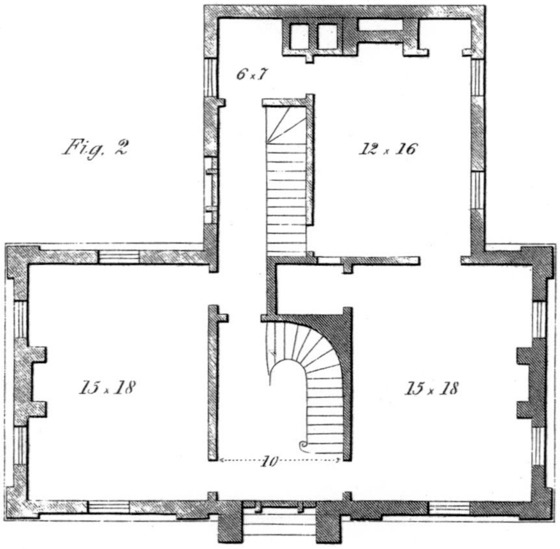

W. W. Wilson. Sc.

IONIC

Pl. 22.

Fig. 1

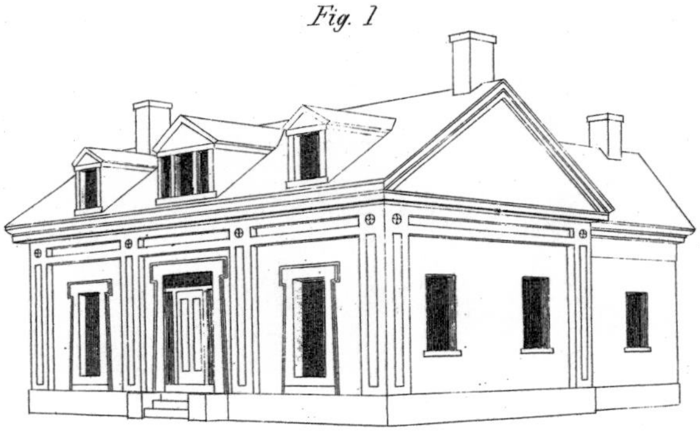

Fig. 2

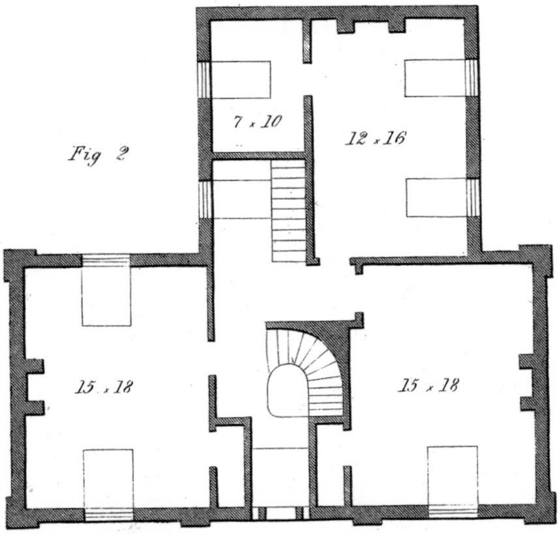

W.W. Wilson Sc.

Pl. 23

IONIC

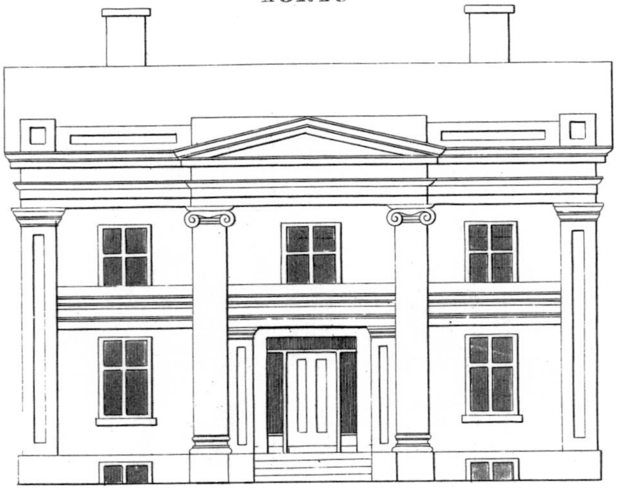

Fig. 1.

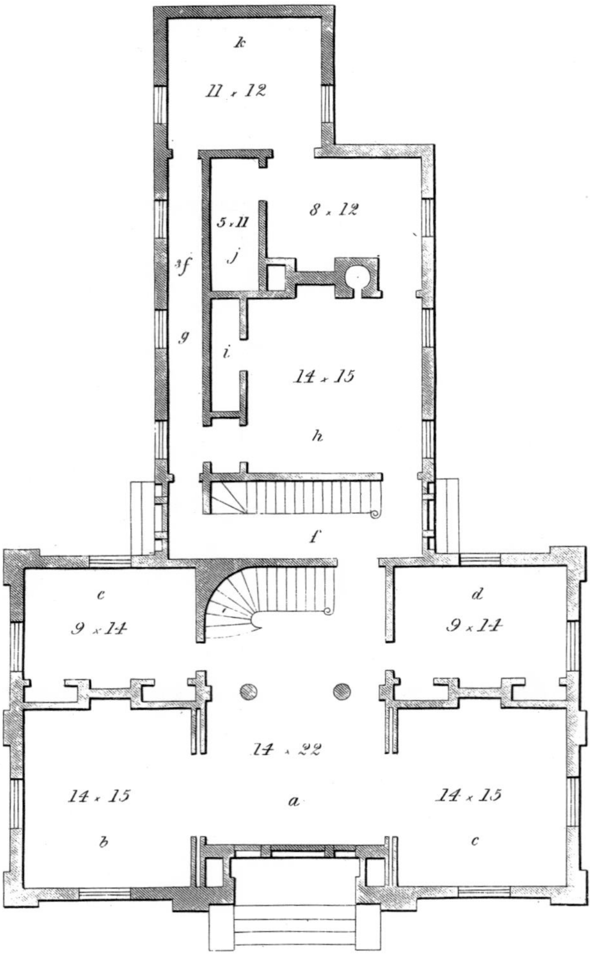

Fig. 2.

W. W. Wilson Sc.

IONIC

Fig. 1.

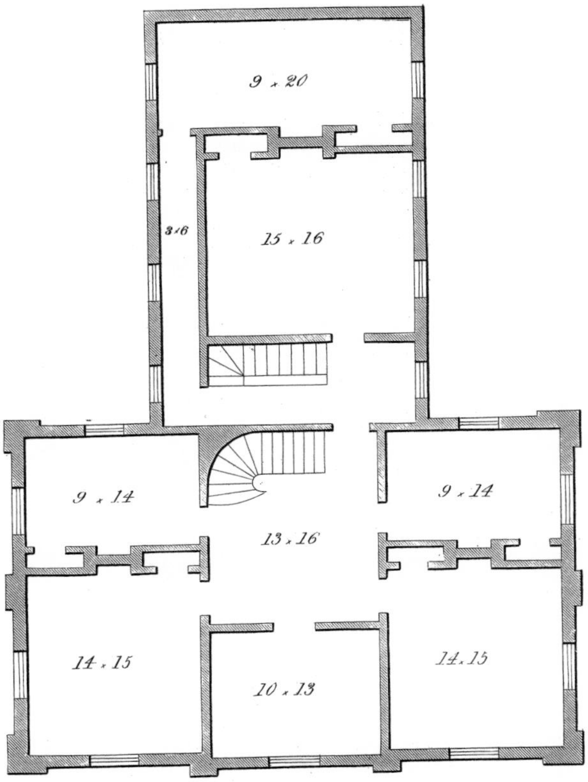

Fig. 2.

W. W. Wilson Sc.

Pl. 25

GRECIAN IONIC

Fig. 1

Fig. 2

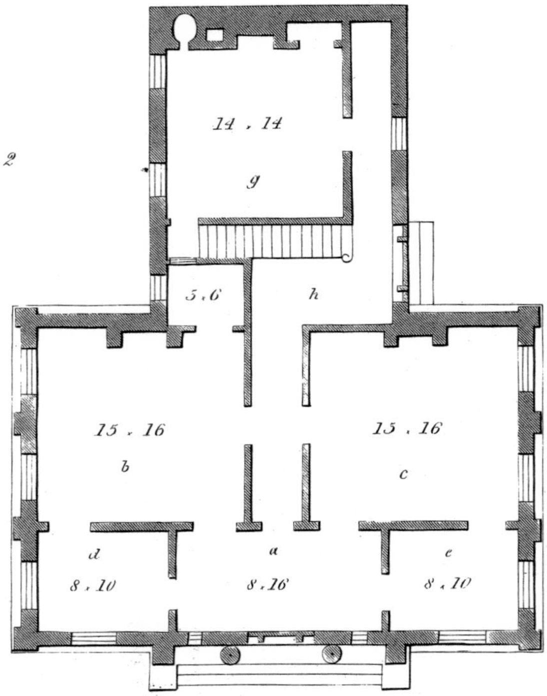

W. W. Wilson Sc.

GRECIAN IONIC

Fig. 1

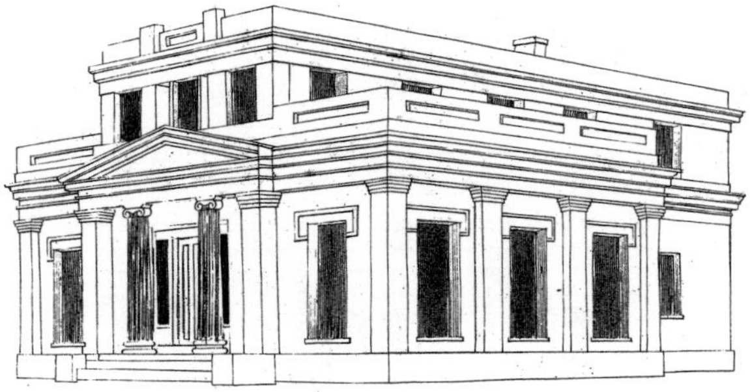

Fig. 2

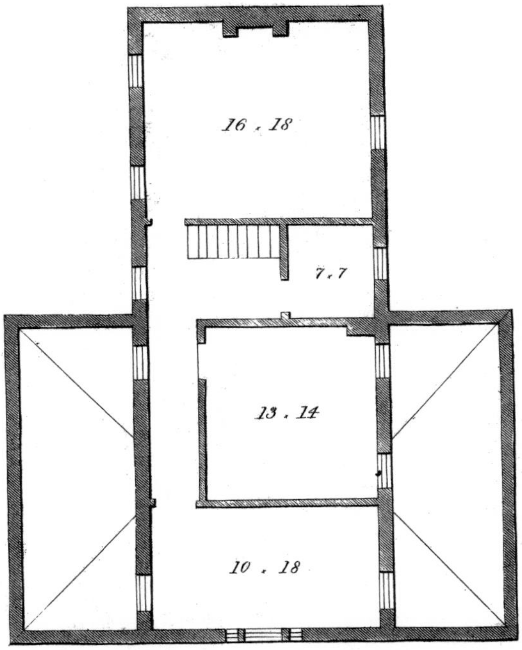

W. W. Wilson. Sc.

Pl. 27.

IONIC

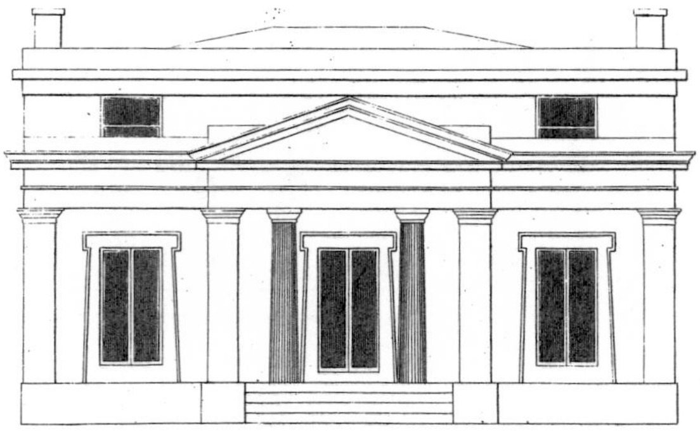

Fig. 1.

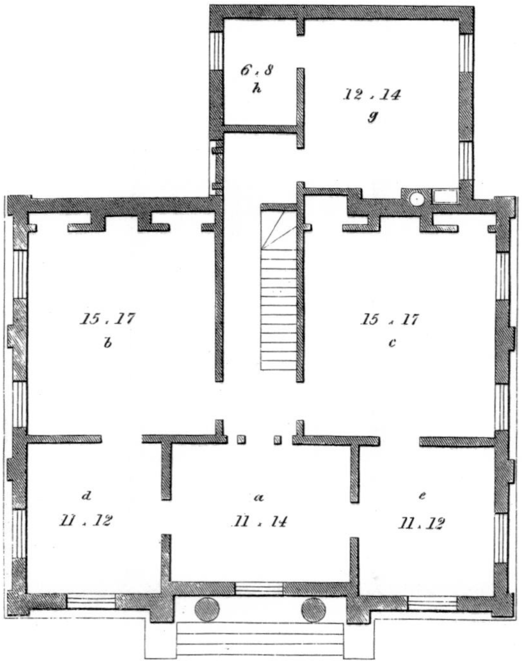

Fig. 2.

W. W. Wilson Sc.

IONIC

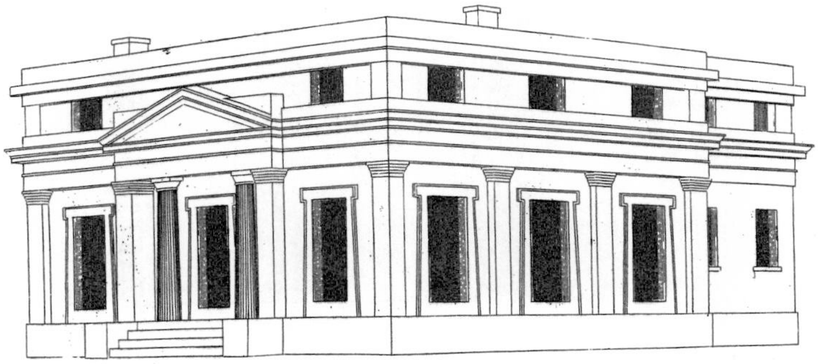

Fig. 1.

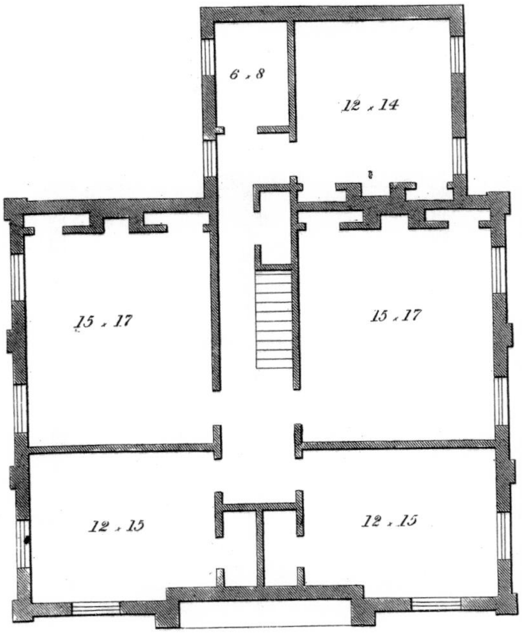

Fig. 2.

W. W. Wilson Sc.

Pl. 29.

IONIC.

Fig. 1

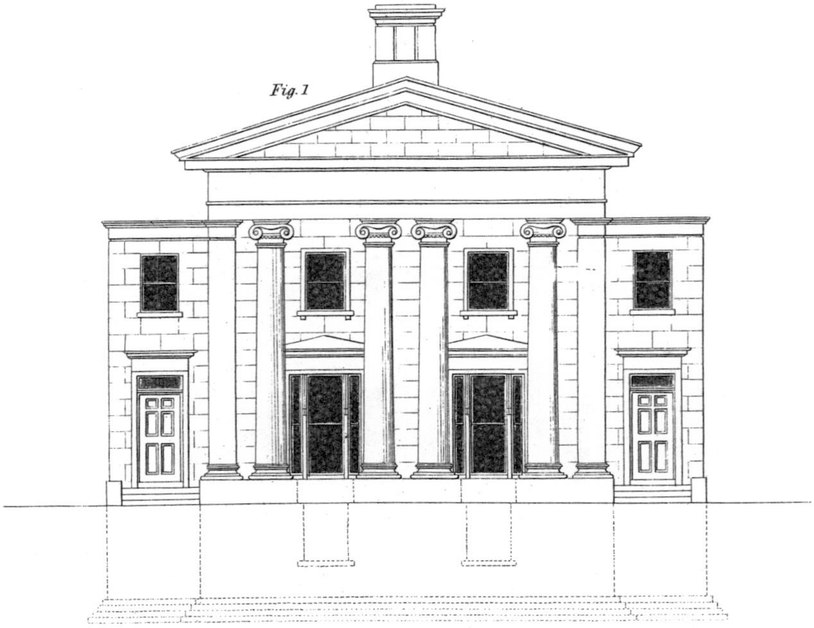

Fig. 2

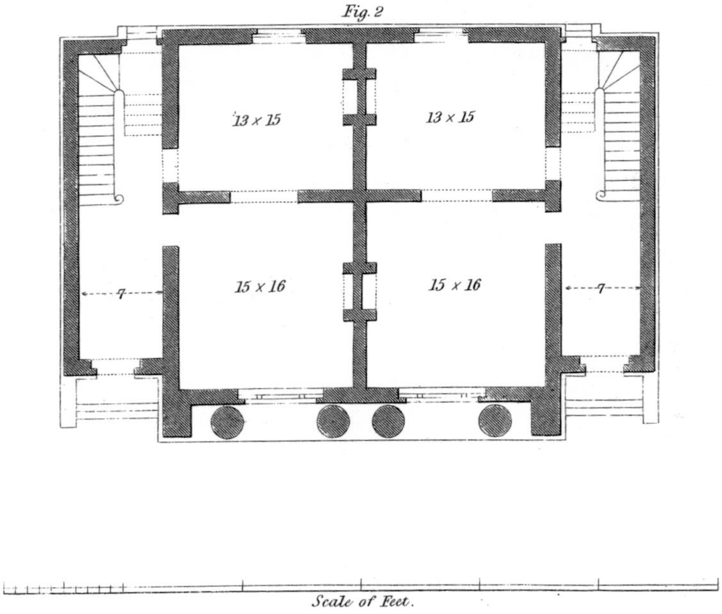

W. W. Wilson. Sc.

IONIC. *Pl. 30.*

Fig. 1

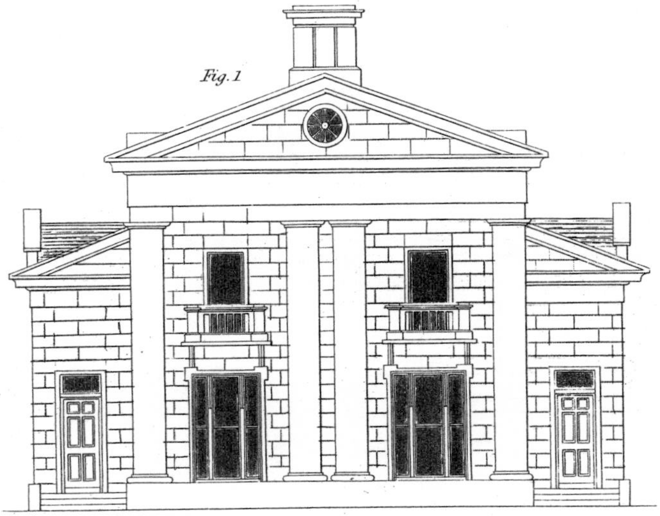

Fig. 2

Scale of Feet.

W. W. Wilson Sc.

Pl. 31.

GRECIAN CORINTHIAN.

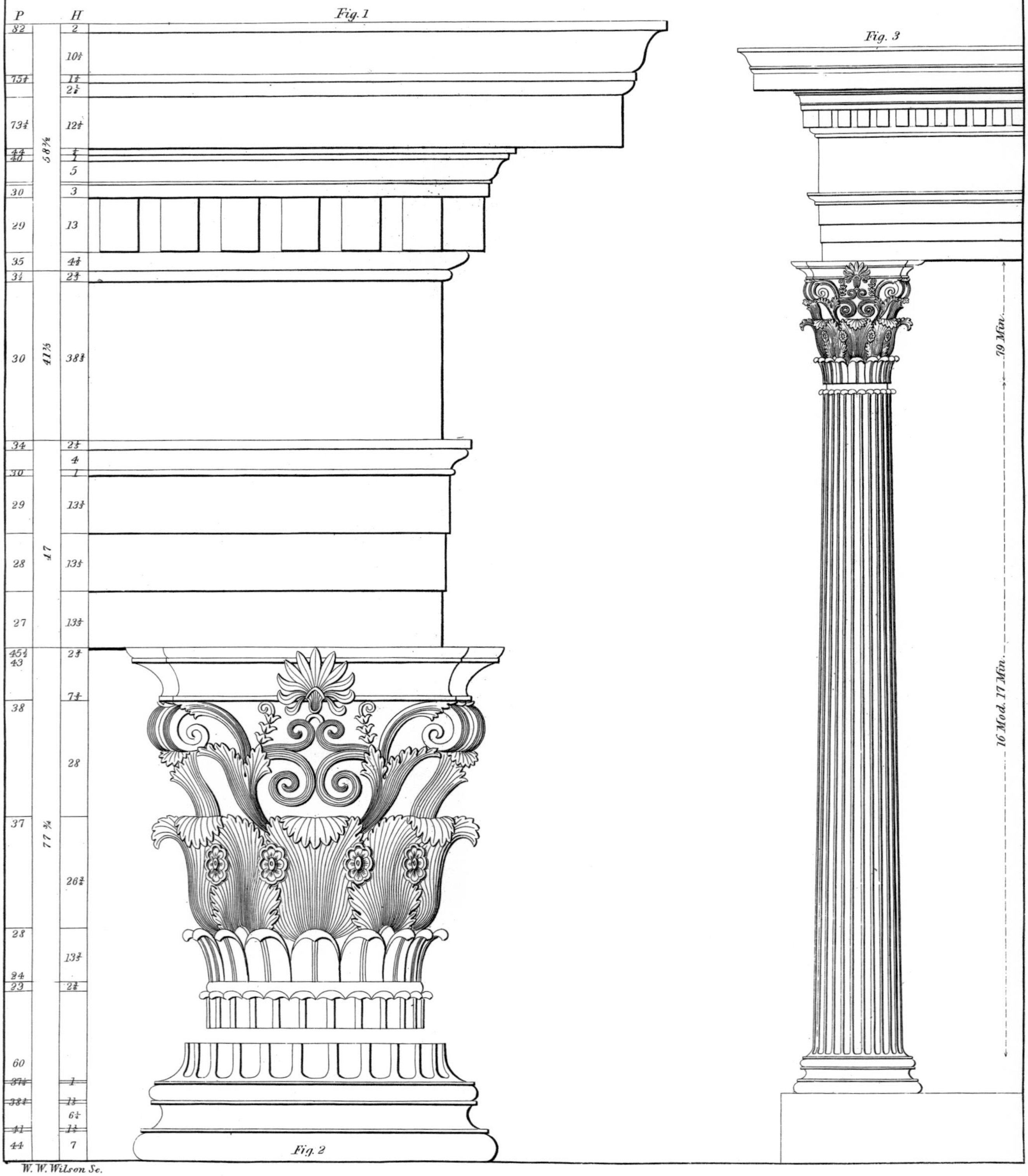

Pl. 32.

GRECIAN CORINTHIAN.

Fig. 1

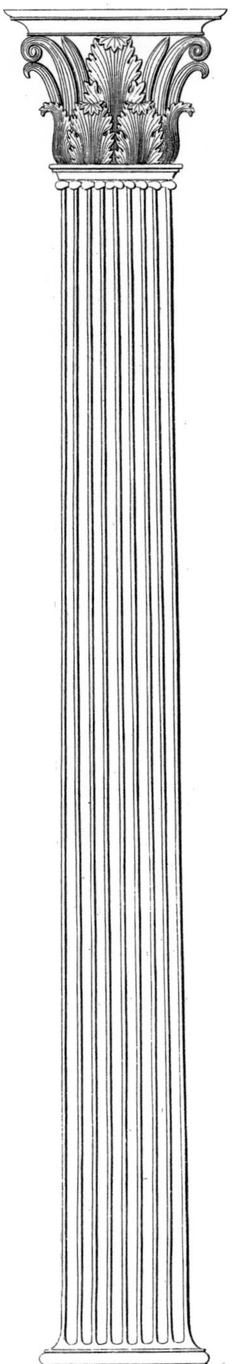

Fig. 2

Fig 3

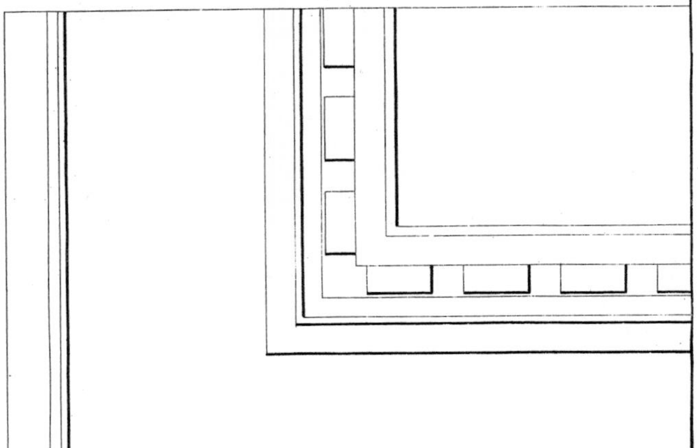

W. W. Wilson Sc.

Pl. 33.

ROMAN CORINTHIAN

W. W. Wilson Sc.

ROMAN CORINTHIAN

Fig. 1.

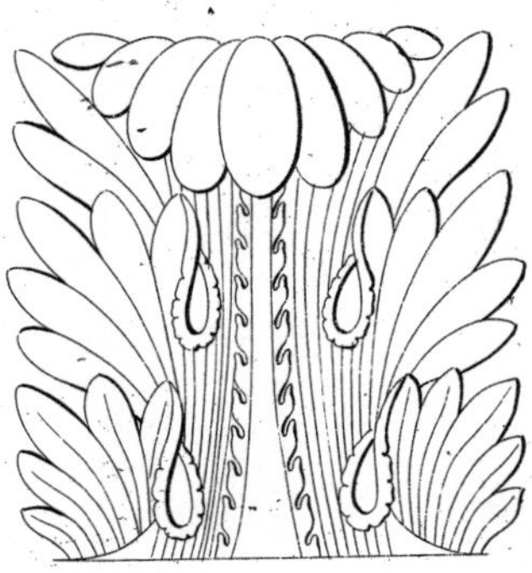

Fig. 3.

Fig. 4.

Fig. 2.

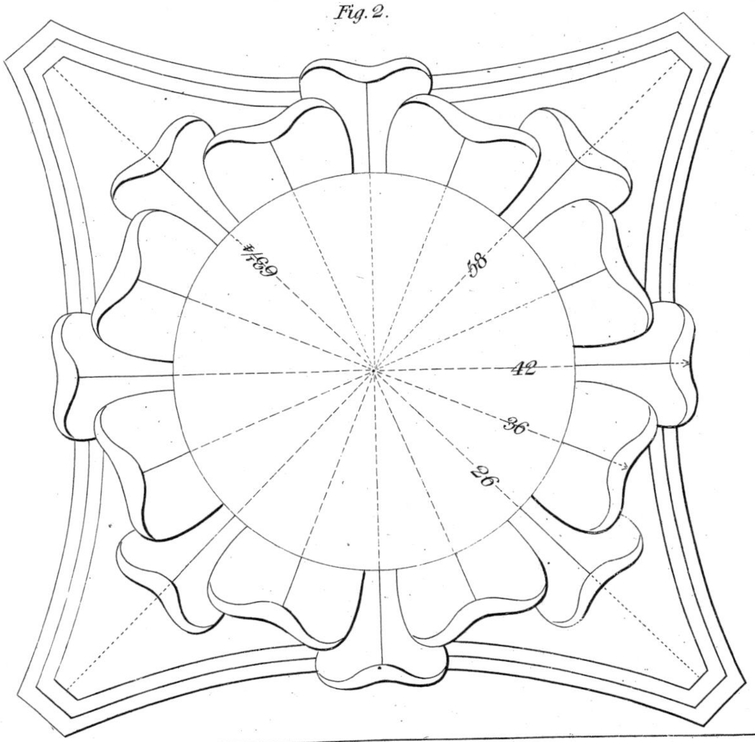

Fig. 5.

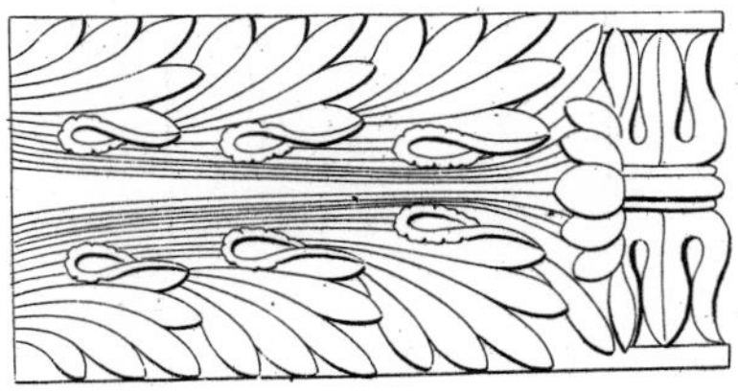

W. W. Wilson Sc.

Pl. 35.

CORINTHIAN

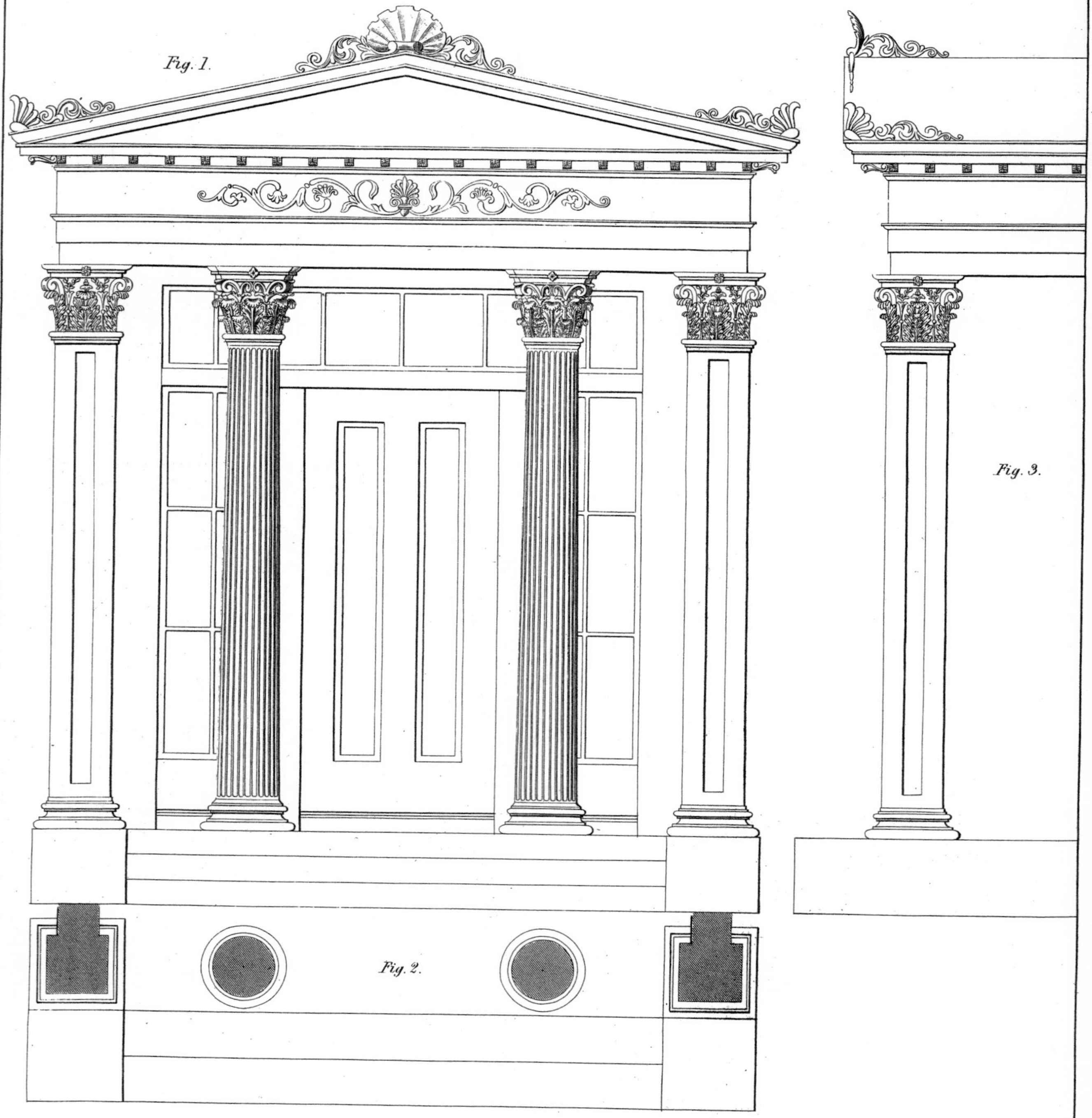

W. W. Wilson Sc.

Pl. 36.

DETAILS

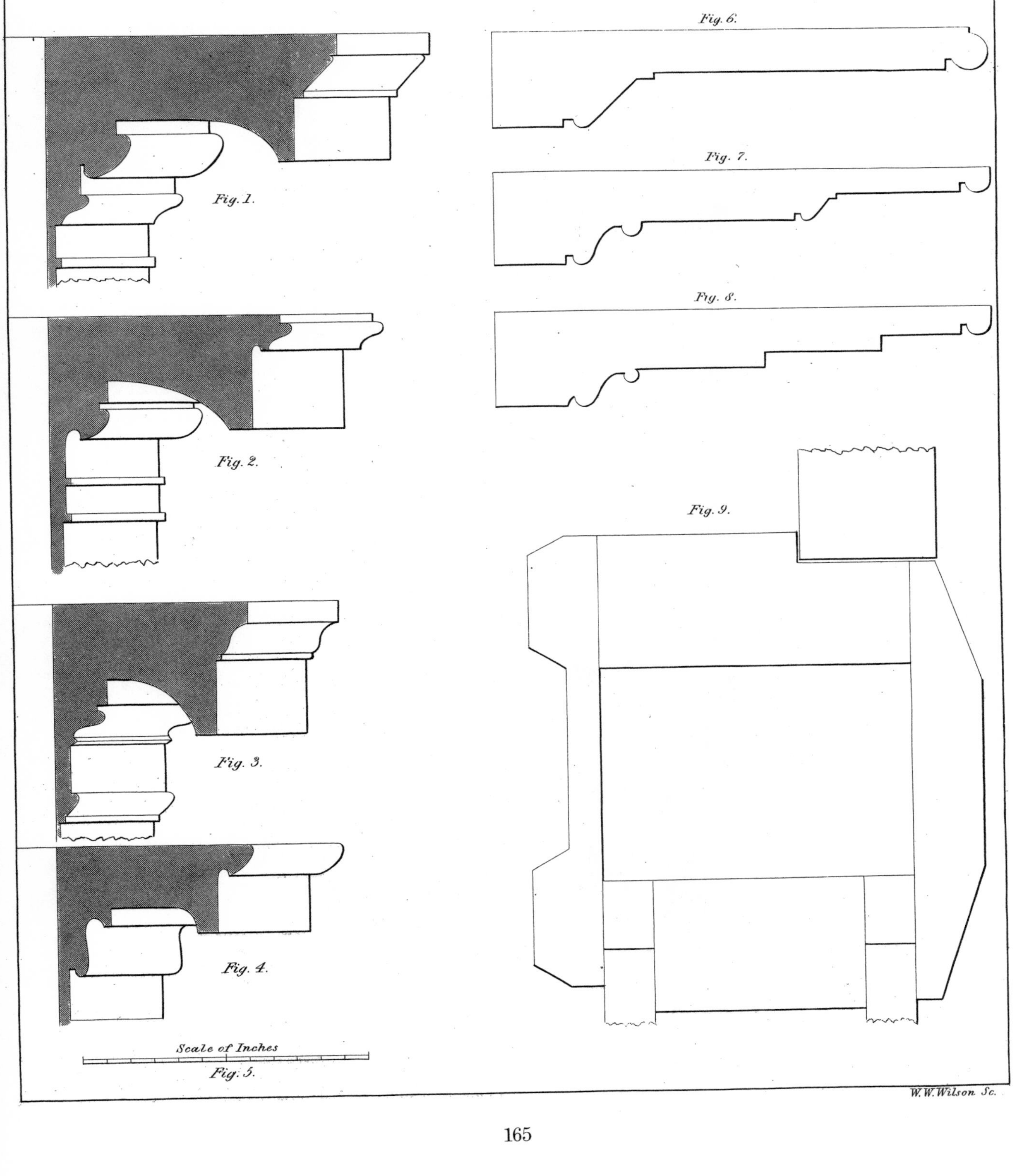

W. W. Wilson Sc.

Pl. 37.

CORINTHIAN

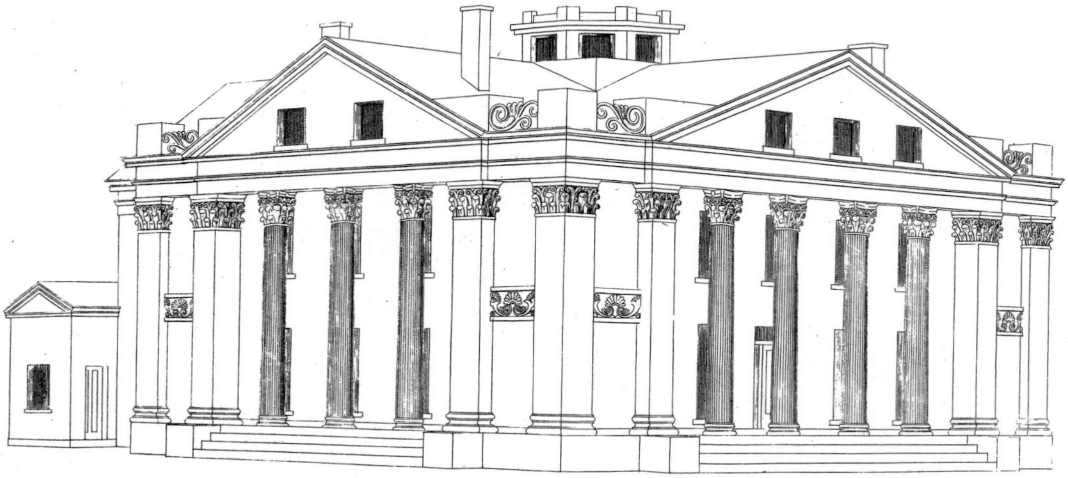

Fig. 1.

Fig. 2.

W. W. Wilson Sc.

CORINTHIAN

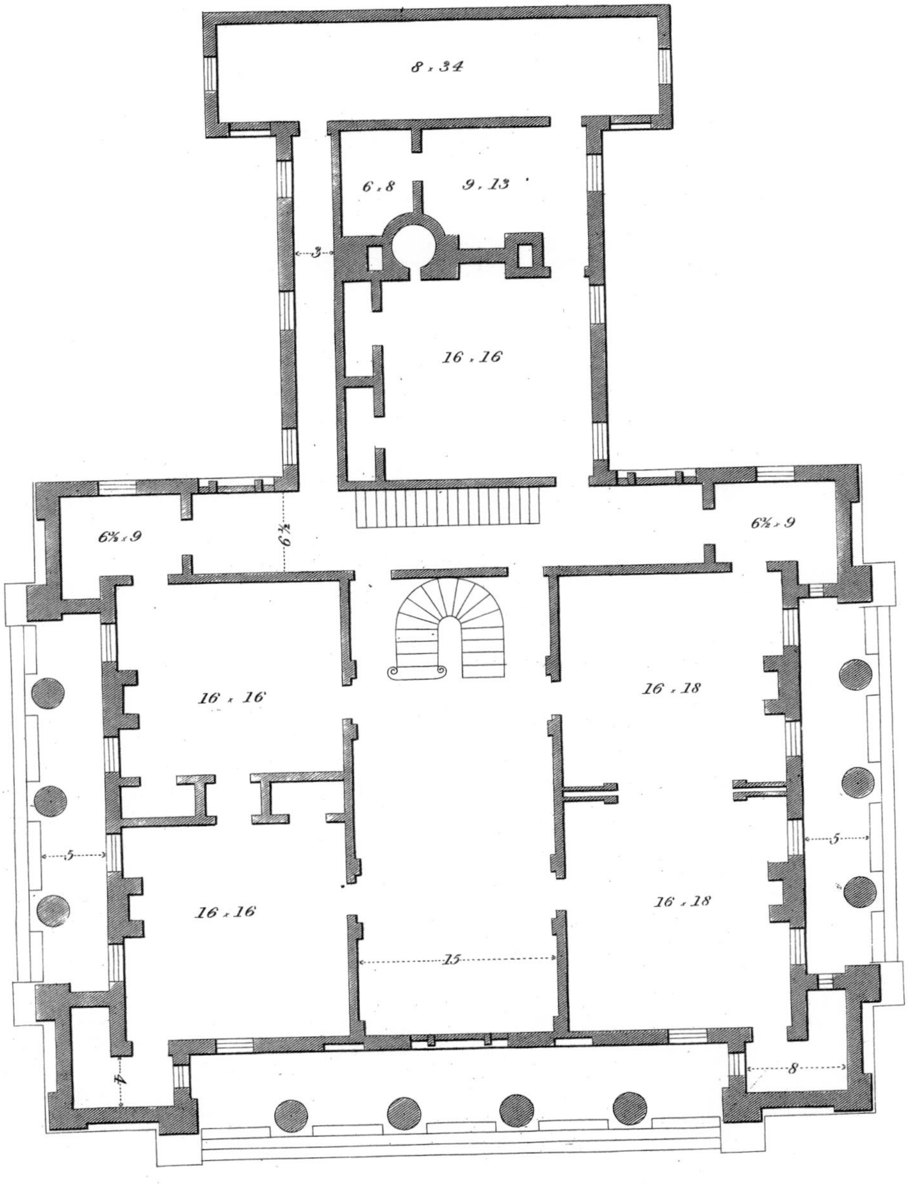

W. W. Wilson. Sc.

Pl. 39.

PLAN OF FIRST FLOOR

Plate 37.

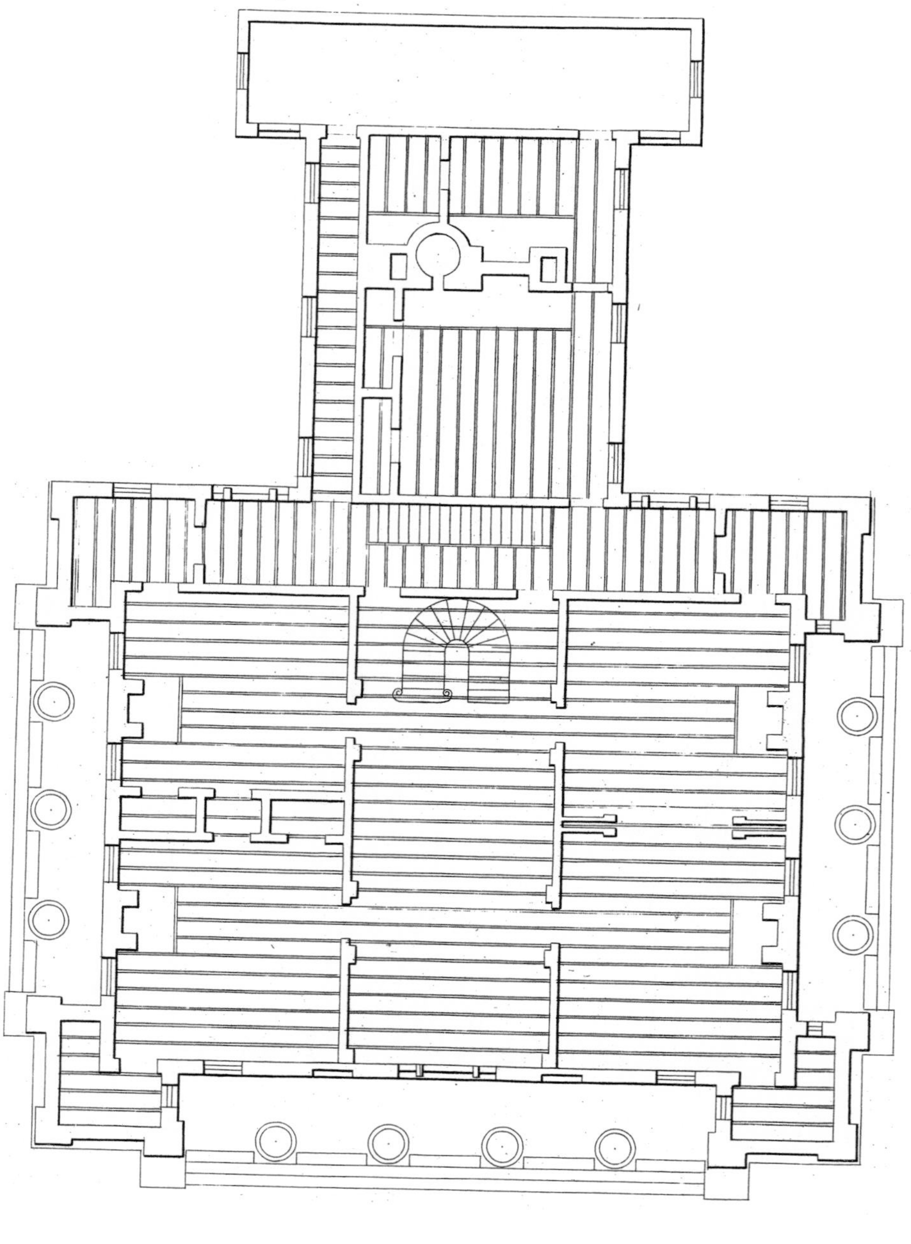

W. W. Wilson Sc.

Pl. 40.

PLAN OF SECOND FLOOR

Plate 37.

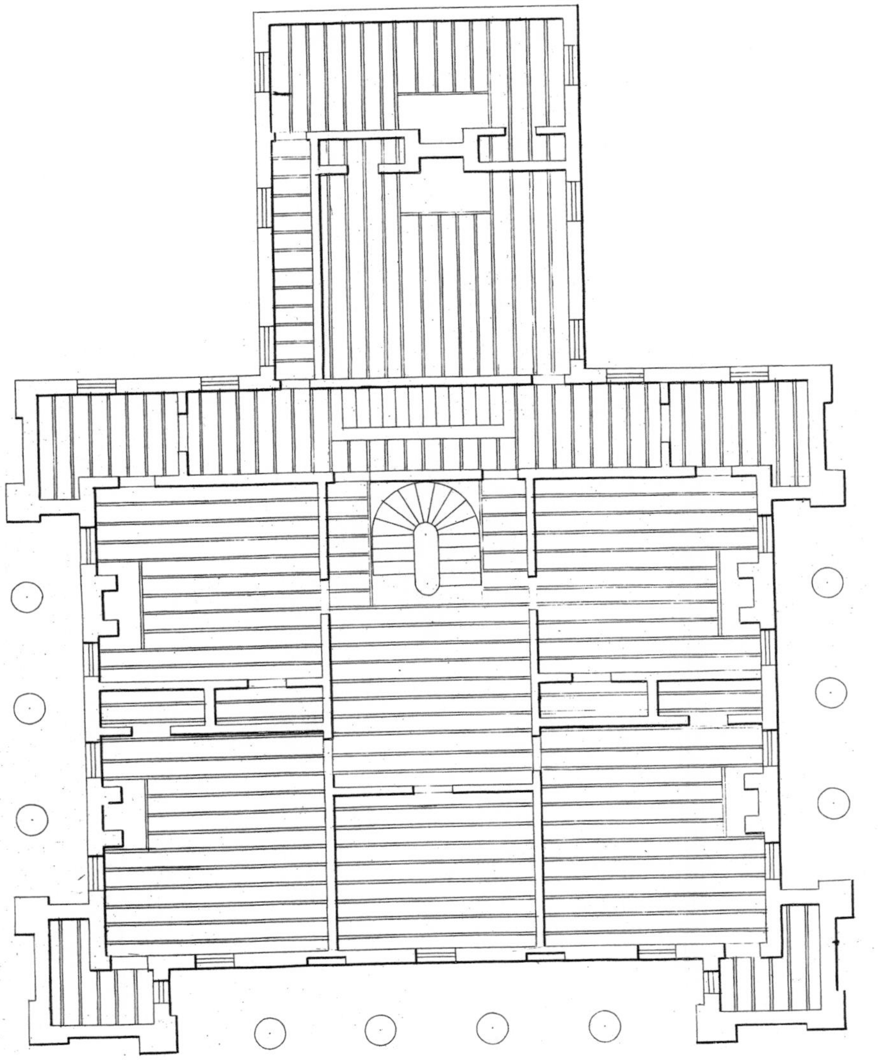

W. W. Wilson Sc.

Pl. 41.

GOTHIC

Fig. 1.

Fig. 4.

Fig. 7.

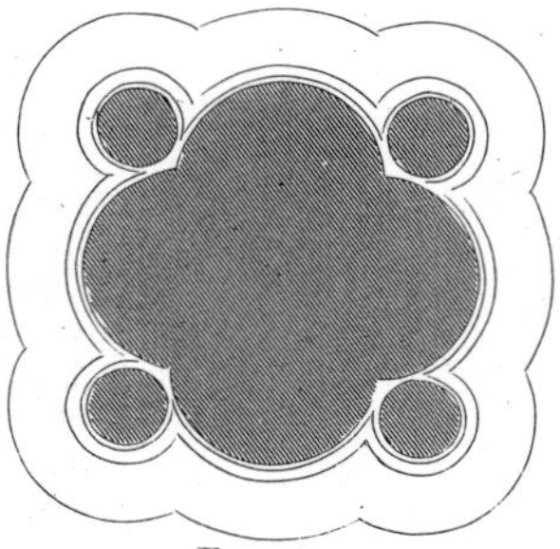

Fig. 2.

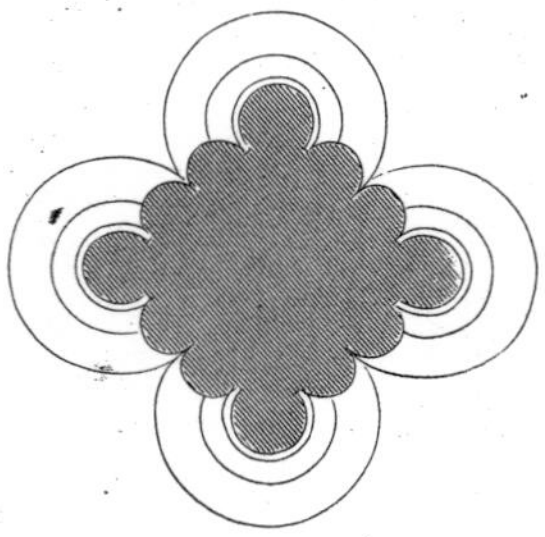

Fig. 5.

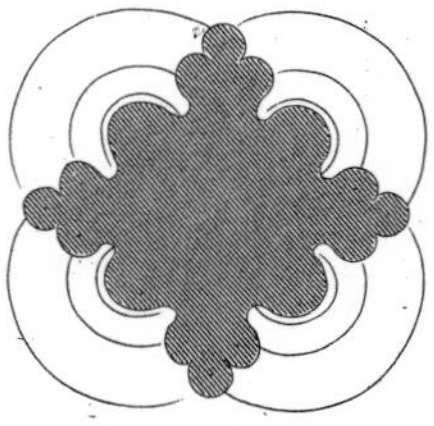

Fig. 8.

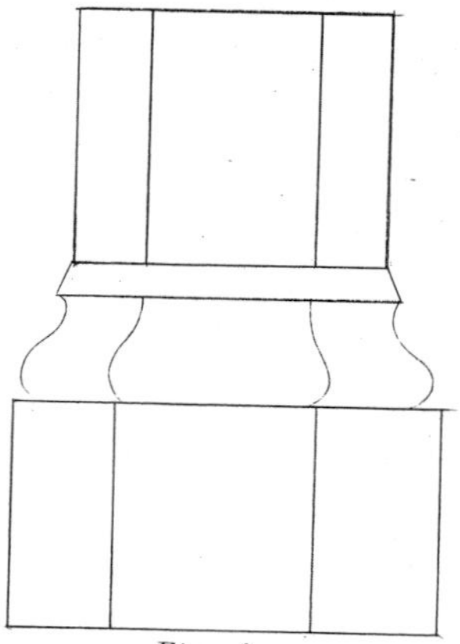

Fig. 3.

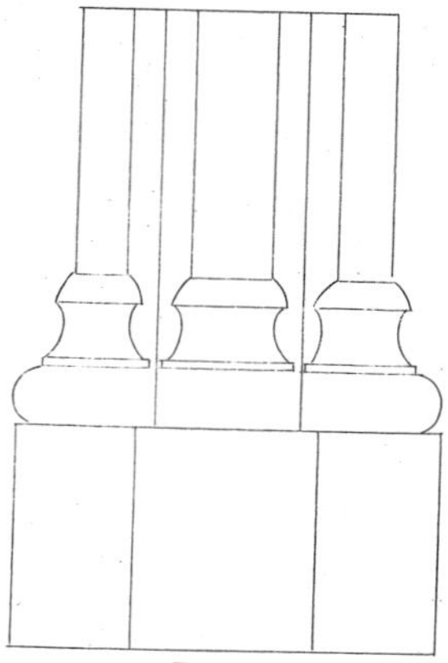

Fig. 6.

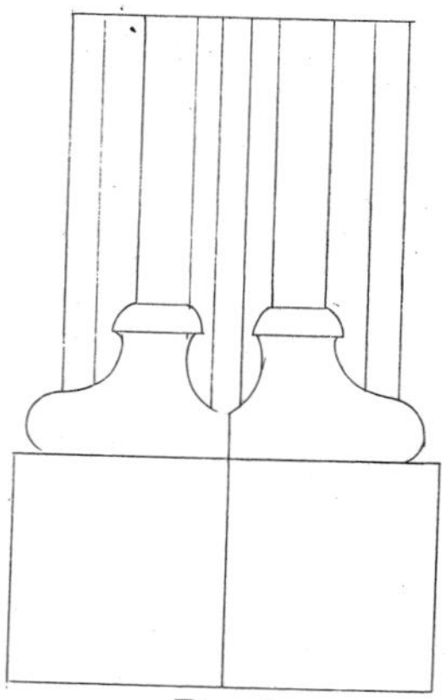

Fig. 9.

W. W. Wilson Sc.

Pl. 42.

GOTHIC

Fig. 1.

Fig. 2.

W. W. Wilson Sc.

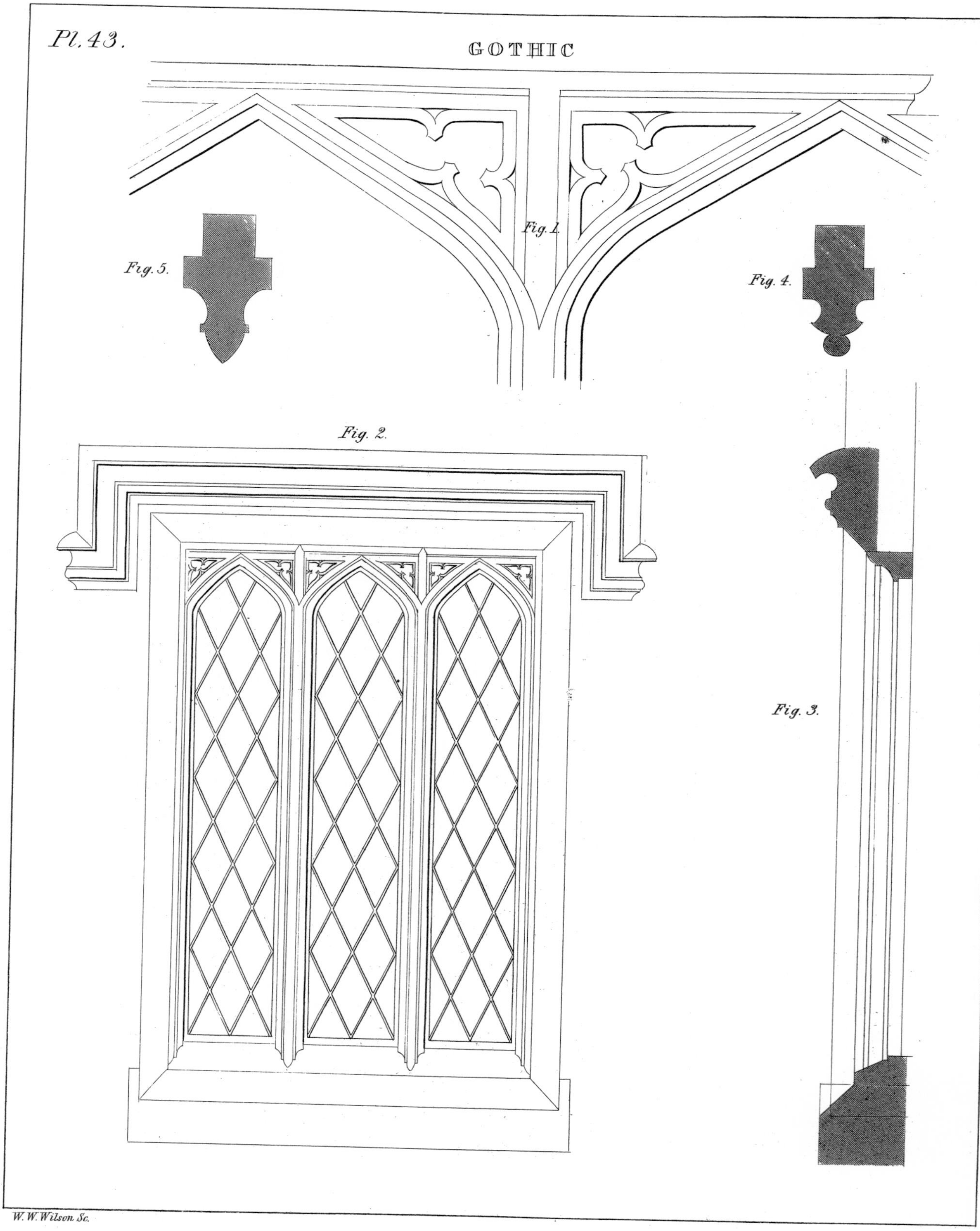
Pl. 43.
GOTHIC
Fig. 1.
Fig. 5.
Fig. 4.
Fig. 2.
Fig. 3.
W. W. Wilson Sc.

GOTHIC

Pl. 44.

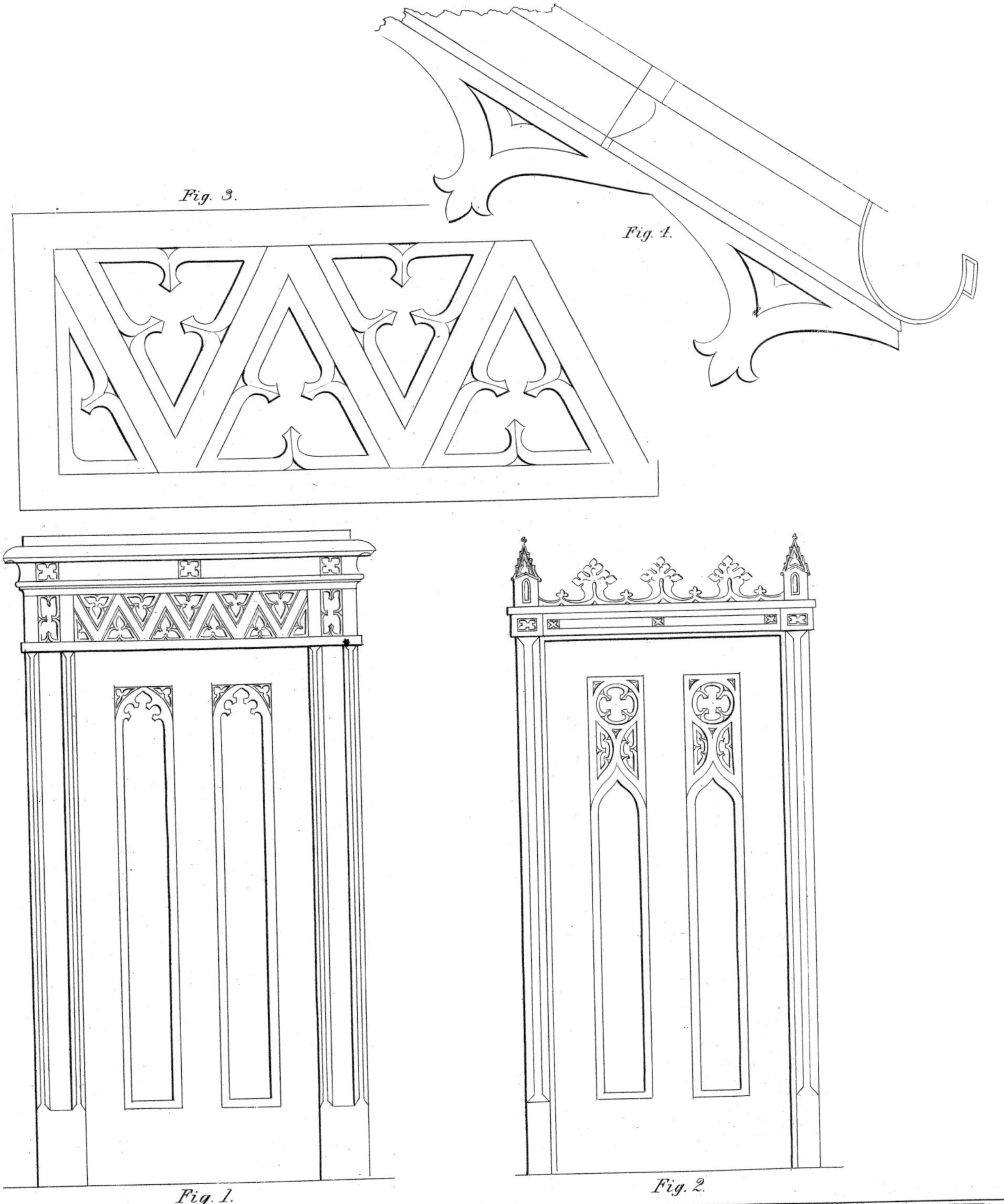

W. W. Wilson Sc.

Pl. 45.

GOTHIC

Fig. 1.

Fig. 2.

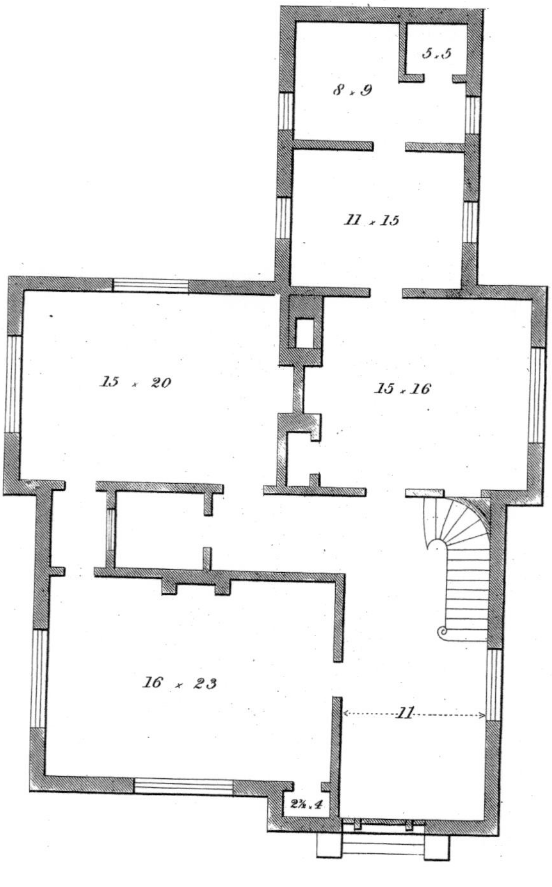

W. W. Wilson Sc.

Pl. 46.

GOTHIC

Fig. 1.

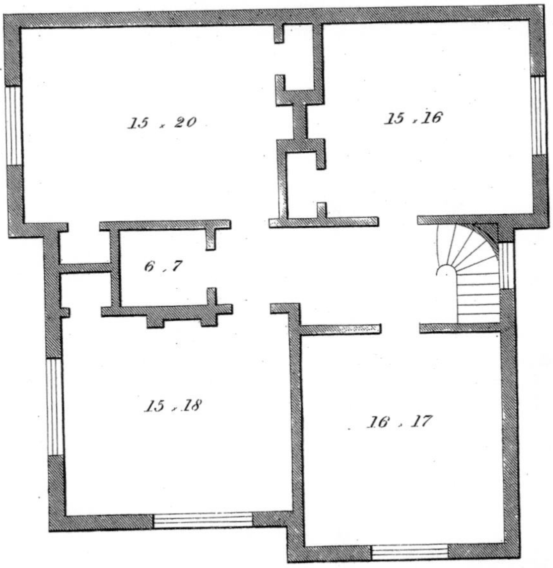

Fig. 2.

W. W. Wilson Sc.

Pl. 47.

GOTHIC

Fig. 1.

Fig. 2.

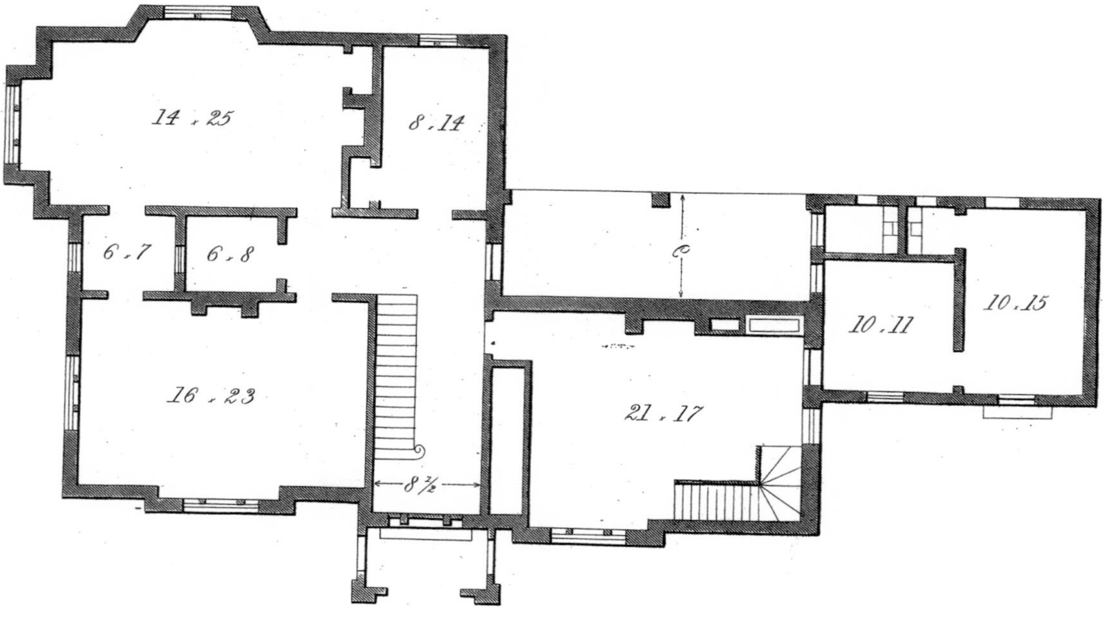

W. W. Wilson Sc.

GOTHIC

Fig. 1.

Fig. 2.

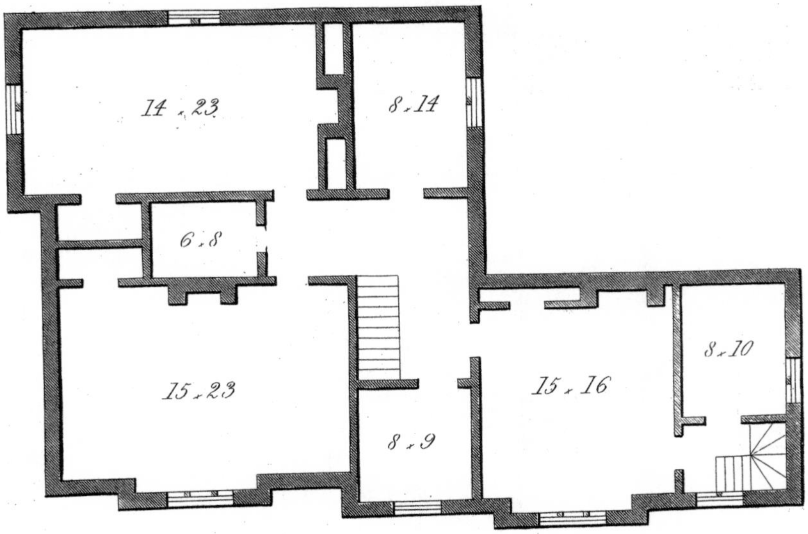

W. W. Wilson Sc.

Pl. 49.

GROIND ARCHES AND VAULTING.

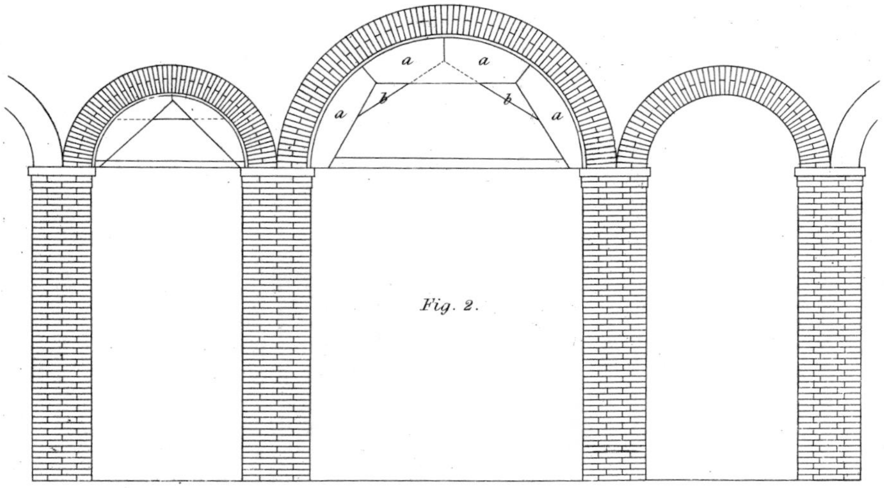

Fig. 2.

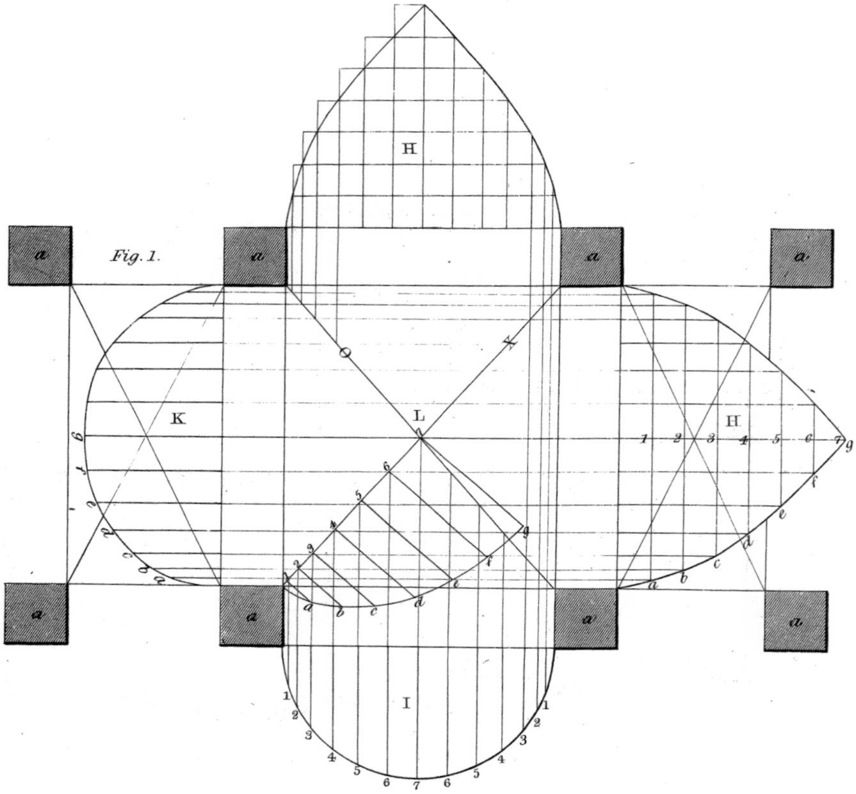

Fig. 1.

W. W. Wilson Sc.

IONIC DETAILS.
Pl. 50.
Fig. 1
Fig. 2
Fig. 3
Fig. 4
Fig. 5
Fig. 6
Fig. 7.
Fig. 8
Fig. 9
Fig. 10
Fig. 11.
Fig. 12
Fig. 13
Fig. 14
Fig. 15
Fig. 16.
GOTHIC
Fig. 17.
Fig. 18
Fig. 19
Fig. 20
Fig. 21
Fig. 22
Fig. 23
Fig. 24
Fig. 25
A
B
C
D
E
F
G
H
W.W. Wilson Sc.

Pl. 51.

GOTHIC CHURCHES

Fig. 1.

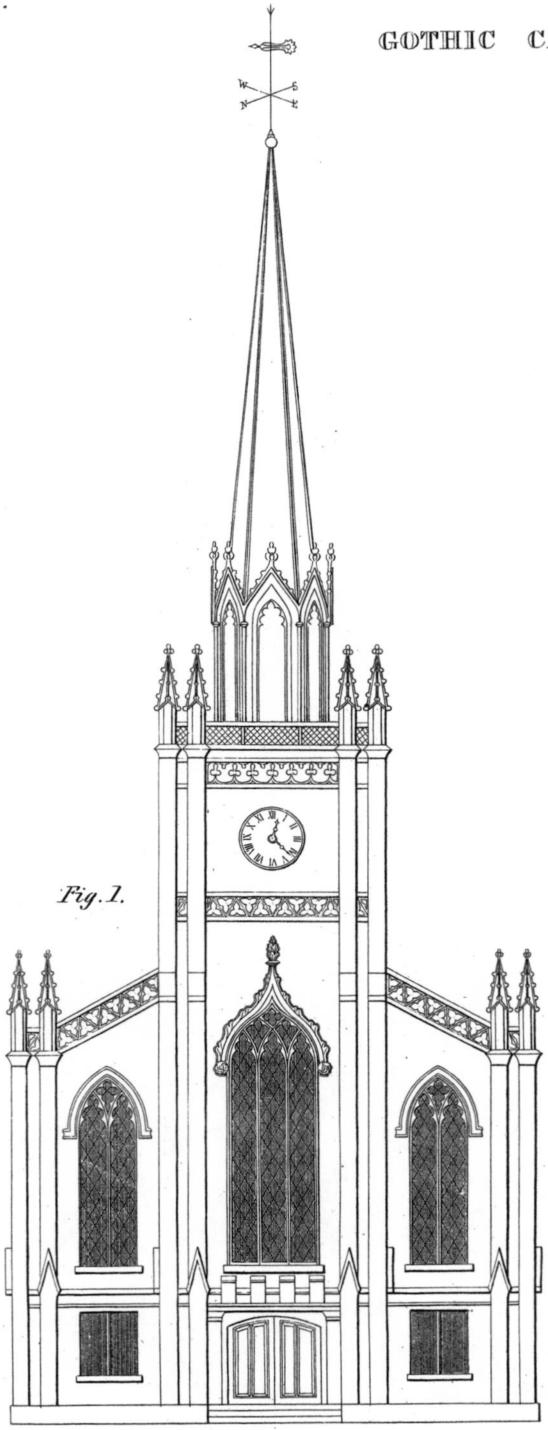

Fig. 2.

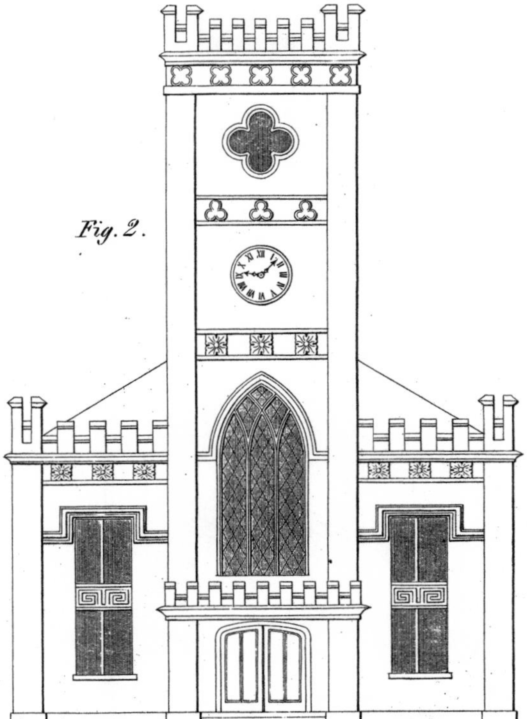

W. W. Wilson Sc.

Pl. 52.

GOTHIC CHURCHES

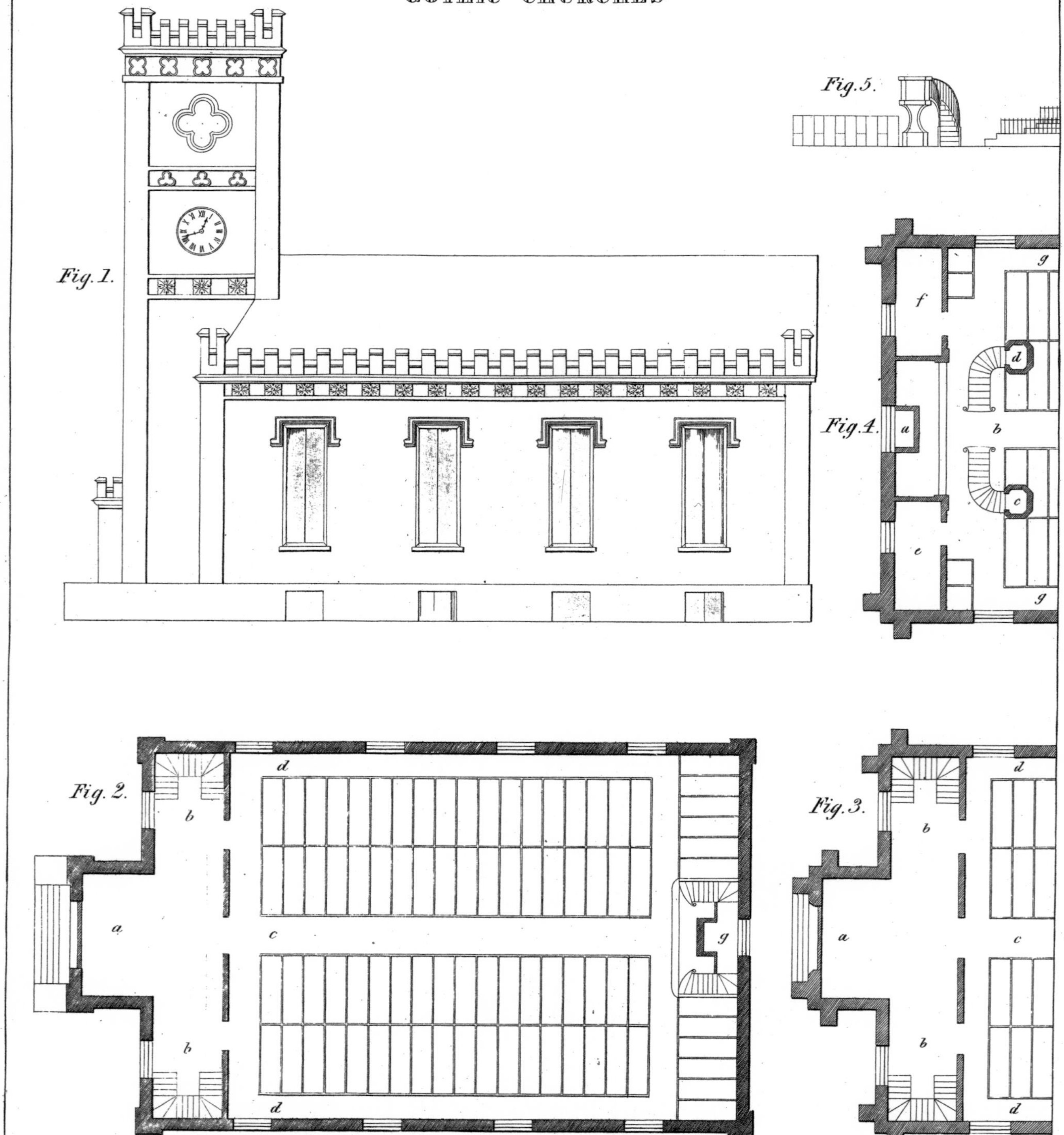

W.W. Wilson Sc.

Pl. 53

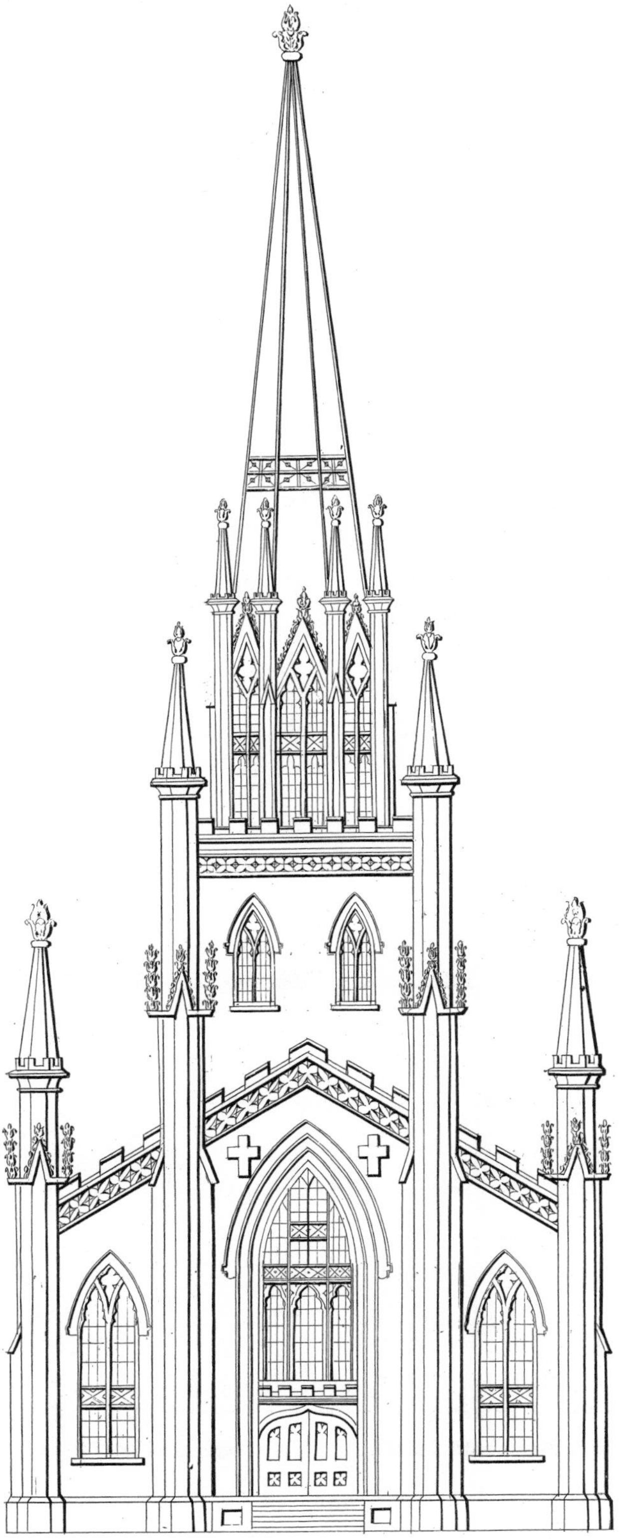

Pl. 54.

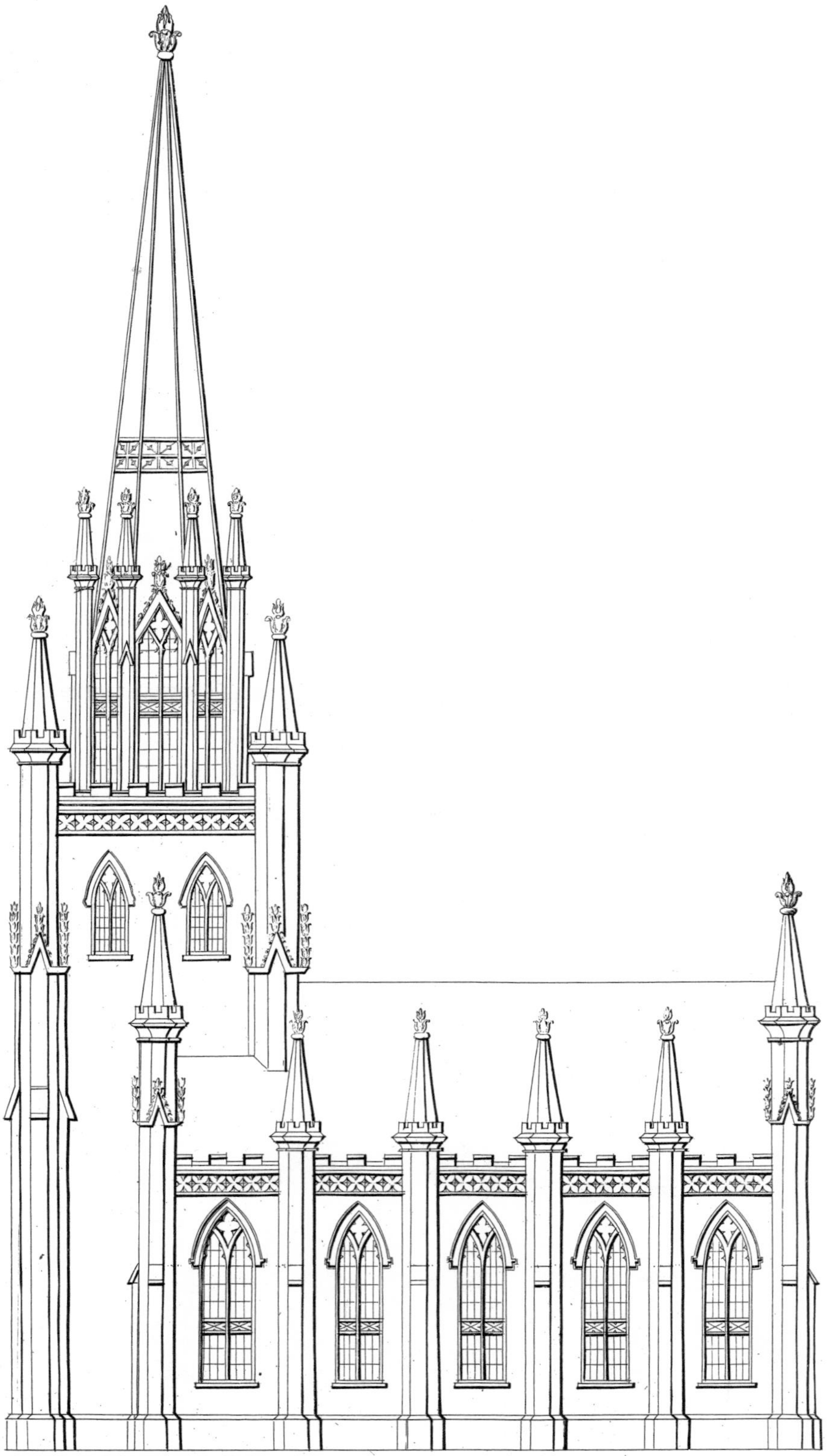

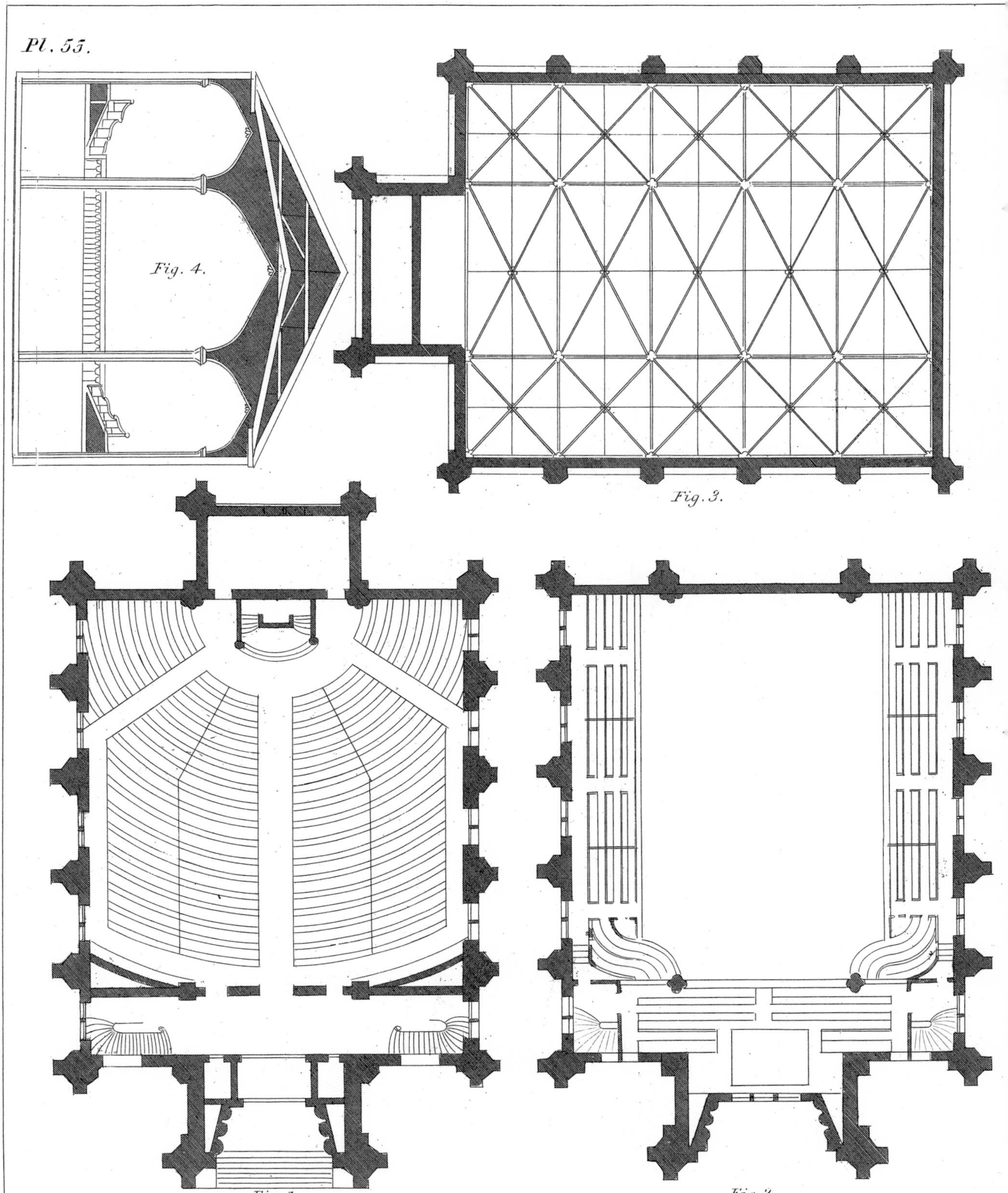
Pl. 55.
Fig. 4.
Fig. 3.
Fig. 1.
Fig. 2.

Pl. 56.

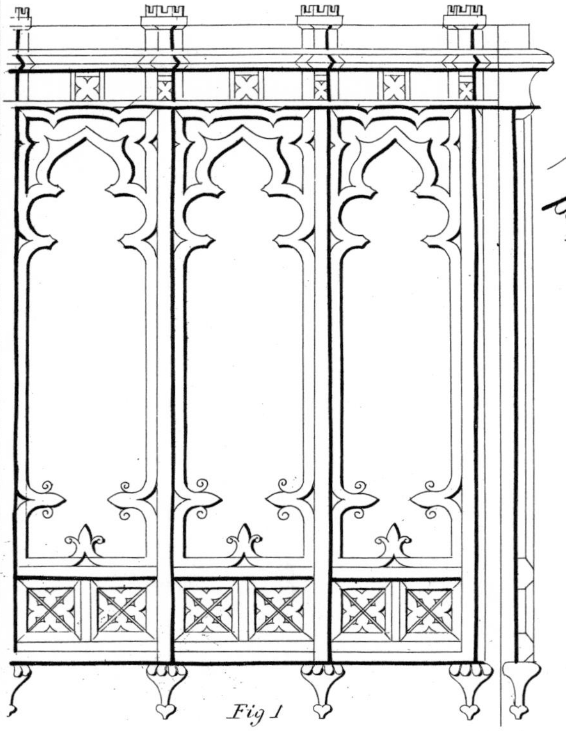

Fig 1

Fig. 3.

Fig. 2

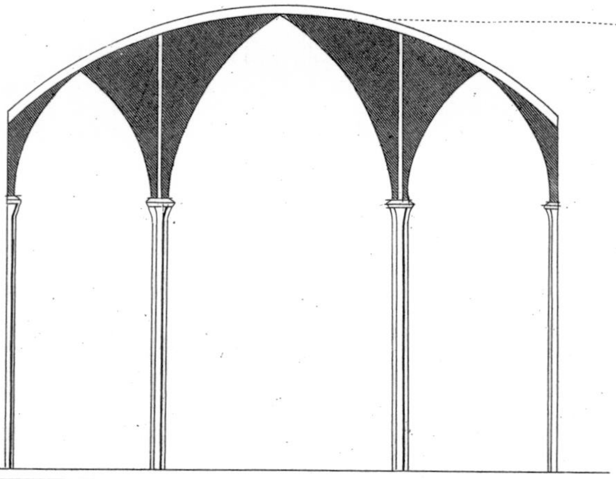

Fig. 5.

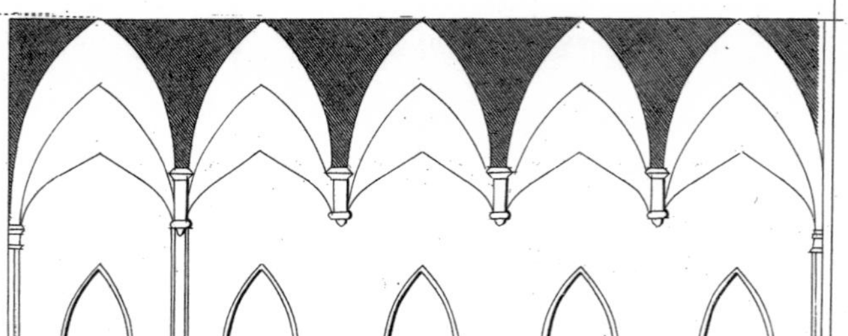

Fig. 4.

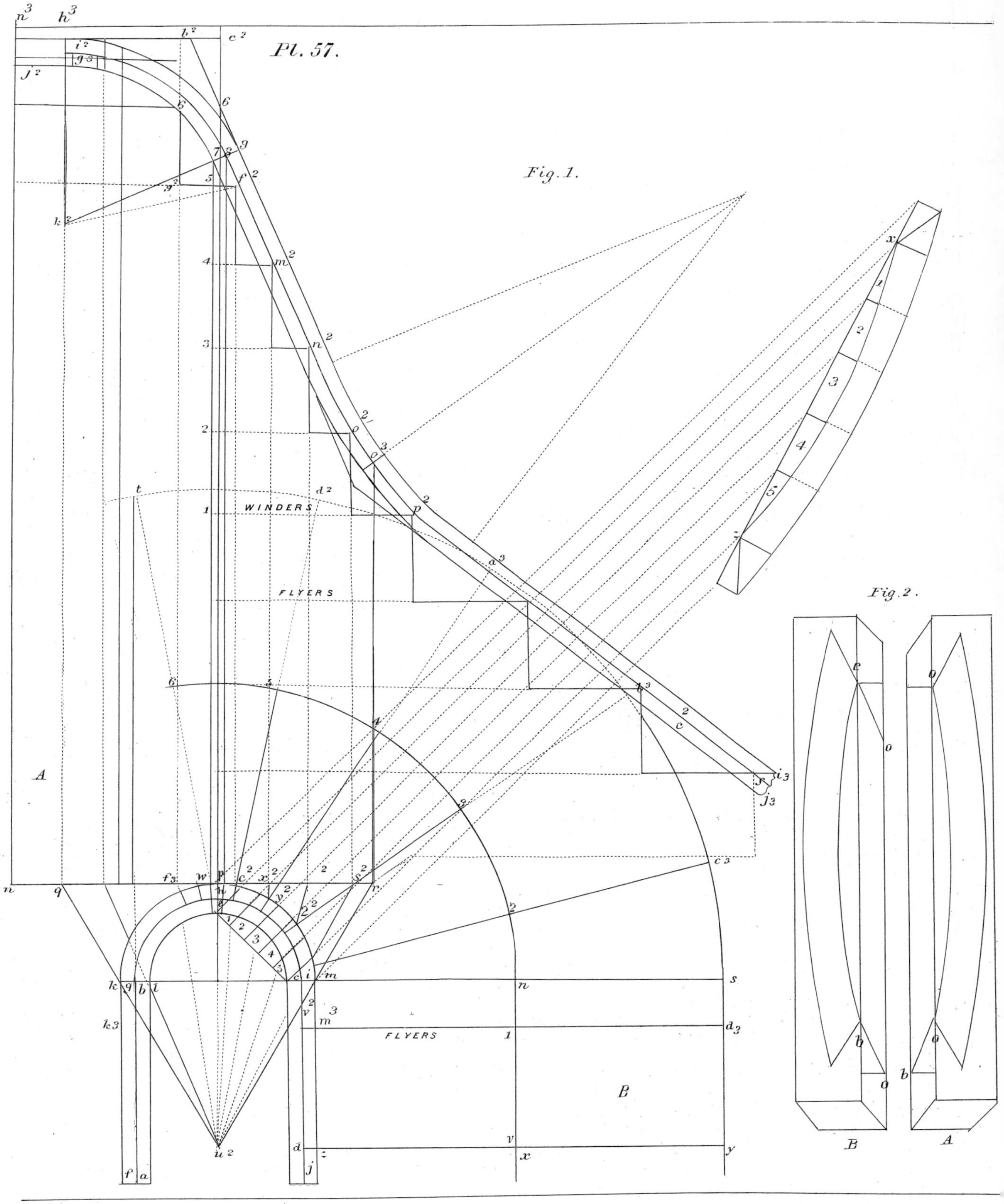
Pl. 57.
Fig. 1.
WINDERS
FLYERS
FLYERS
A
B
Fig. 2.

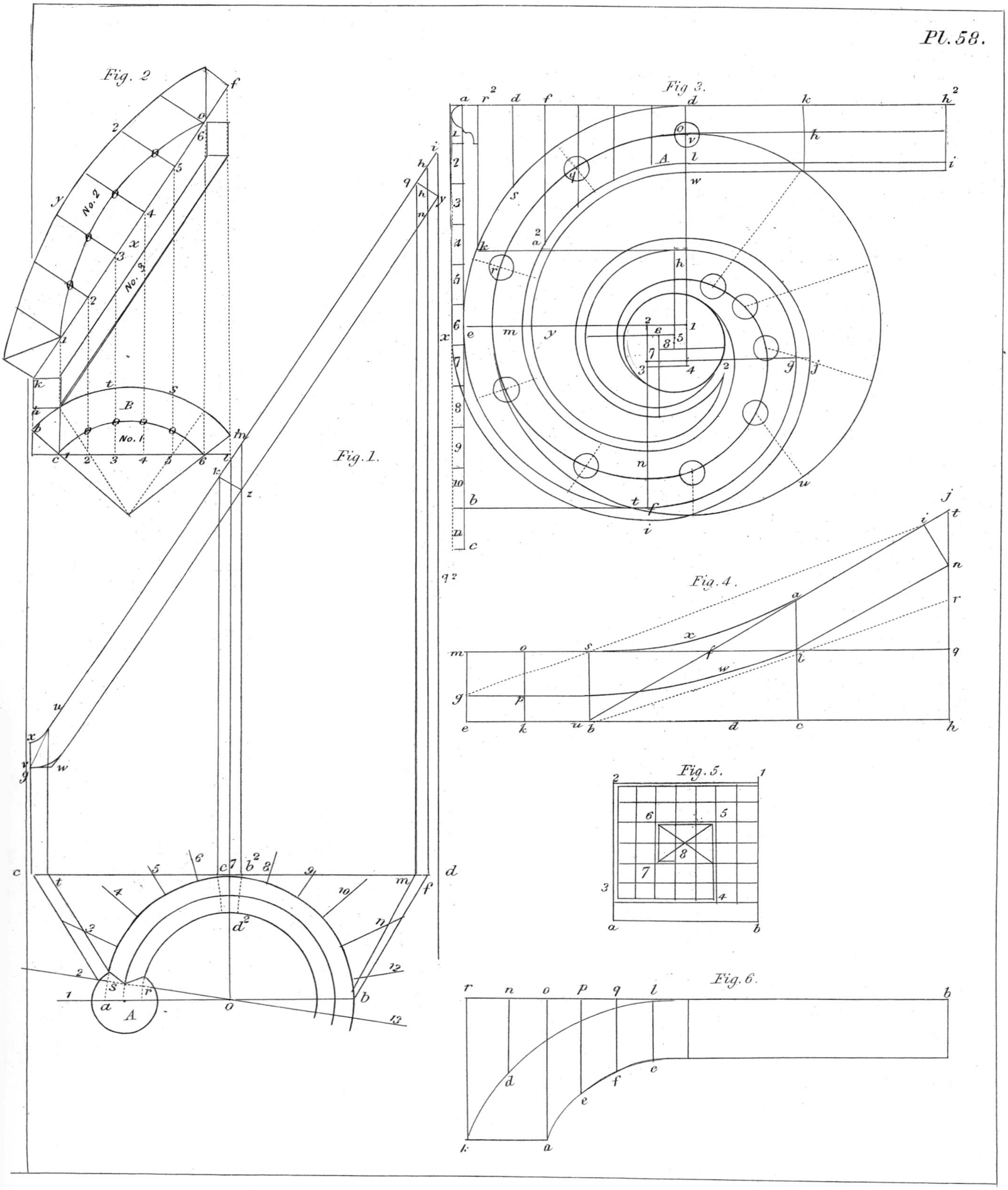
Pl. 58.
Fig. 1.
Fig. 2
Fig 3.
Fig. 4.
Fig. 5.
Fig. 6.
No. 1
No. 2
No. 3

Pl. 59.

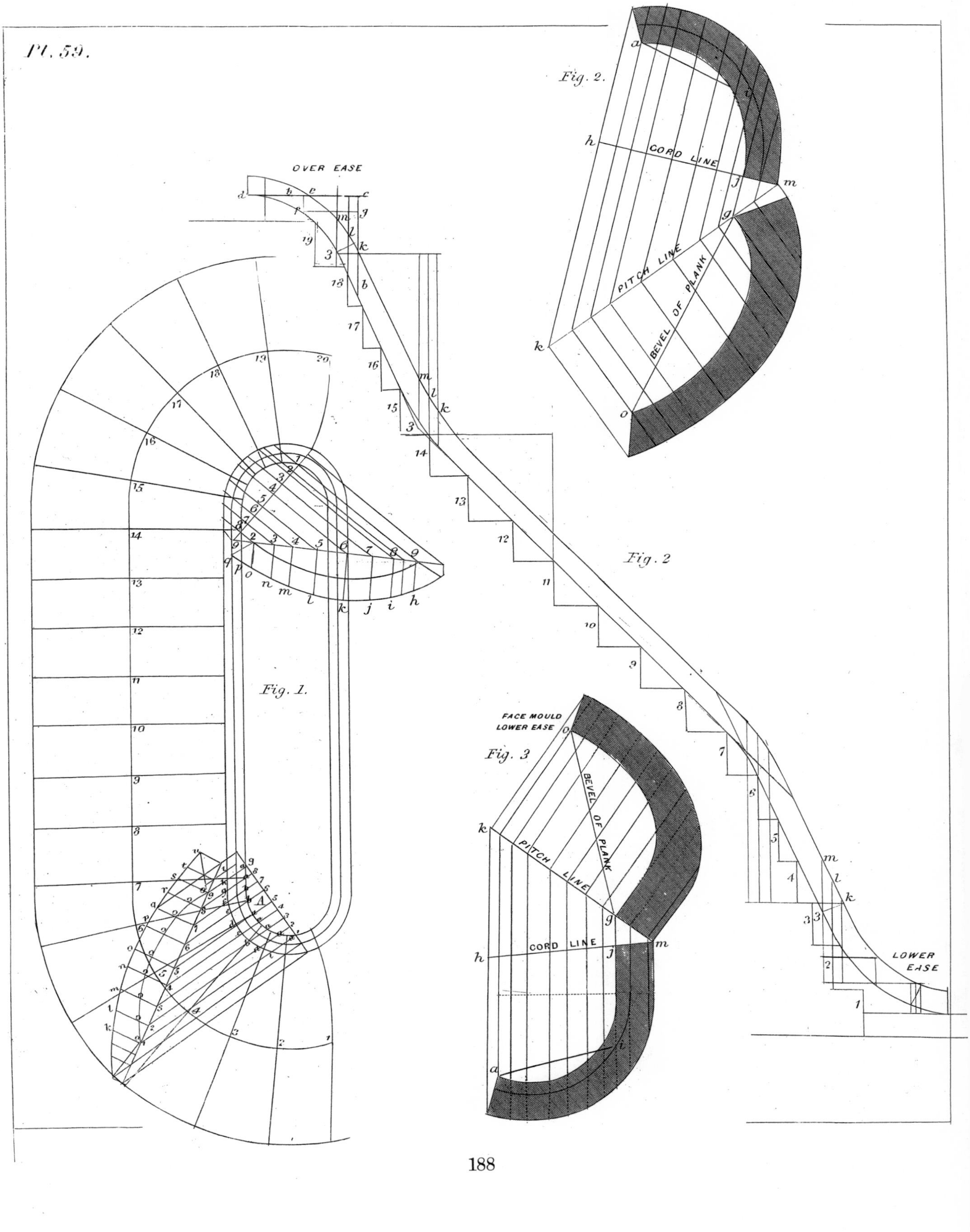

OVER EASE
Fig. 2.
CORD LINE
PITCH LINE
BEVEL OF PLANK
Fig. 1.
Fig. 2
FACE MOULD
LOWER EASE
Fig. 3
BEVEL OF PLANK
PITCH LINE
CORD LINE
LOWER
EASE